HENRY JAMES: MAN & AUTHOR

Henry James
from the painting by John S. Sargent
in the National Portrait Gallery, London.

HENRY JAMES
MAN AND AUTHOR

BY

PELHAM EDGAR

NEW YORK / RUSSELL & RUSSELL

FIRST PUBLISHED IN 1927
REISSUED, 1964, BY RUSSELL & RUSSELL
A DIVISION OF ATHENEUM PUBLISHERS, INC.
L. C. CATALOG CARD NO: 64-12141
PRINTED IN THE UNITED STATES OF AMERICA

CONTENTS

7

PREFATORY

WHEN George Withermore was asked by Ashton Doyne's widow to undertake the biography of her husband, the young man accepted with zest the flattering commission. Working night by night in the room itself where so many masterpieces had been conceived and executed he grew sensible of the inflowing of the dead man's spirit, and his own pages became miracles of divination. In them the master lived again, his every tone and gesture recaptured, and every lovable idiosyncrasy revived with an intimacy from which there was no escape. So the flowing work continues until one evening the menacing figure of the great man stands on the threshold of the library, and Withermore accepts the portent as an indication that the world had already been vouchsafed in the master's written record the only revelation it was entitled to receive. Whatever the application that James intended by his apologue of *The Real Right Thing*, it is true that no writer of our modern day has succeeded better than the subject of this study in sheltering his privacy in life and providing for it after his death. For the legitimate curiosity of posterity he felt that he had made sufficient provision in the volumes in which, with tantalising complexity it must be confessed, he traced the pattern of his early years; and when the circle that claimed his friendship shall have disappeared these biographical

9

PREFATORY

records and the letters must be the only material from which the future may reconstruct his merely human identity. For the reconstruction of his mind he has, like Ashton Doyne, bequeathed the world his books.

Mindful then of the menacing figure on the threshold, my concern in the pages that follow will not be to re-establish Henry James in his habit as he lived; gossip and anecdote will not be invoked for aid; and such stray wisps of biographical fact as drift into the record will serve only to indicate the conditions under which his work was produced.

EARLY YEARS

HENRY JAMES was born at 2 Washington Place,
New York, on 15th April 1843. An Irish and Scottish
strain predominated in his blood, but he was eager
to emphasize the admixture through his paternal
grandmother of a mild English tincture. The
founder of the family in America, William James,
had come out from Ireland shortly after the Revolutionary War, and had organised in Albany a
prosperous business which established his numerous
descendants in permanent comfort. His son Henry,
the second by a third marriage, was born in Albany
in 1811. At the age of thirty he married Mary
Walsh, of New York. Their eldest son was William,
the philosopher, born in 1842, and after Henry
three children were born, Wilkinson (" Wilky "),
Robertson (" Bob "), and Alice.

" Wilky " and " Bob " never counted for much in
their brother's life. But to Alice, in spite of the frequent divergence of their opinions, he was devoted,
and to William he gave such love and admiration
as few brothers can have received. From the years
of their earliest boyhood the spell was upon him.
One of his first impressions was of his brother's
" occupying a place in the world to which I couldn't
at all aspire . . . as if he had gained such an
advance of me in his sixteen months' experience

of the world before mine began that I never for all
the time of childhood and youth in the least caught
up with him or overtook him. He was always
round the corner and out of sight, coming back into
view but at his hours of extremest ease. We were
never in the same schoolroom, in the same game,
scarce even in step together, or in the same phase
at the same time : when our phases overlapped,
that is, it was only for a moment—he was clean out
before I had got well in. How far he had really at
any moment dashed forward it is not for me now to
attempt to say ; what comes to me is that I at least
hung inveterately and woefully back, and that this
relation alike to our interests and to each other
seemed proper and preappointed. . . ."

Until his twelfth year Henry and his brother
were submitted to an unsystematic course of casual
schools and random tutors in New York, when the
educational adventure was transferred to a foreign
scene, with Geneva, Paris and London as shifting
centres. The desultory character of the training
was often irksome to the nascent professorial mind
of the elder brother, but Henry's reminiscences
breathe no hostile criticism of the weird educational
experiment devised by his philosophic parent. Ineffective though his official studies were, the boy's
imagination was actively enough at work, and
yielded itself without protest to the colour and
character of the European scene. After an interval
of a year at Newport the boys returned to Geneva
for the winter of 1859-1860, and in the autumn of
1860, his age being then seventeen, young James
was again established with his family at Newport.

EARLY YEARS

Nothing is accessible of Henry James's creative attempts before the year 1865. In the *Notes of a Son and Brother* we find no reference to any incipient literary ambitions he may have thus early cherished, but a friend of that time, Mr Thomas Sergeant Perry, assures us of their existence. " After his return to America in 1860, the question of what he should do with his life became more urgent. Of course it was in literature that he took the greatest interest. One task that he set himself was translating Alfred de Musset's *Lorenzaccio*, and into this version he introduced some scenes of his own. Exactly what they were I do not recall, though I read them with an even intenser interest than I did the original text. He was continually writing stories, mainly of a romantic kind. The heroes were for the most part villains, but they were white lambs by the side of the sophisticated heroines, who seem to have read all Balzac in the cradle, and to be positively dripping with lurid crimes. He began with these extravagant pictures of course in adoration of the great master whom he always so warmly admired." [1]

The Civil War interrupted the idyllic Newport life, and it is not likely that during its progress James could have had much inclination for literary work. An accident, which from his own obscure account seems to have been a wrench to his sacro-iliac joint, precluded his participation in the struggle, and his consequent distress of mind no less than the large looming of national issues is sufficient to account for his inactivity in production. One may suspect also that his critical instincts were already

[1] Quoted by Mr Percy Lubbock in *The Letters of Henry James*.

riper than his creative powers, and that conscious of the slender merit of his juvenile scribbling he was contented to await the corrective which a fuller experience of life would bring.

His brother William, abandoning art for science, had established himself at Harvard in 1861, and thither with dimmed intentions of legal studies Henry followed him in the ensuing year. The rest of the family migrated to Boston in 1864, and two years later his parents made their final settlement in Cambridge.

Friendship with Professor Norton and W. D. Howells now gave James access to *The Nation* and *The Atlantic Monthly*. In the former periodical he copiously employed his critical faculty, and from 1865 onwards the latter magazine and *The Galaxy* gave hospitable refuge to his creative ventures.

The number of our author's short stories and *nouvelles*—that is, of productions between five thousand and seventy thousand words—being well in excess of a hundred, it seems advisable to group them in the distinctive categories into which they naturally fall. A large proportion of these are stories dealing with American characters and conditions, and they frequently involve the "international question," for the treatment of which James considered himself to possess quite special qualifications. A smaller but highly characteristic group explores the subtleties of the artistic conscience. Another leads us into the region of the supernatural, and still another concerns itself with various aspects of the social problem in England or on the continent of Europe.

II

THE AMERICAN SHORT STORIES AND THE AMERICAN SCENE

EXAMINING the American group of brief narratives in successive decades we can afford to pass lightly by his merely clever first attempts. If the young author could achieve a romantic effect he was content to let reflection and representation take care of themselves. As a matter of fact, prior to 1870, though his bent is definitely romantic his sense of romance is relatively weak, and of the dozen stories contributed in half that term of years to *The Galaxy* and *The Atlantic Monthly* none reveals qualities over which retrospective prophecy would care to linger. *A Landscape Painter* is the diary of a wealthy young artist who eases the pangs of despised love by retiring to a fishing village where he hopes to achieve happiness by a simulated poverty. He finds lodgment with an old sailor, who of course has a pretty daughter to captivate him. When he marries her he learns that she had read his diary whilst he was ill, and that her arts of fascination had not been free from the element of design. The weakest and most wildly romantic of this early group is *De Grey*, and the most readable *The Romance of Certain Old Clothes*, a story of sisterly jealousy with a supernatural conclusion.

With the turn of the next decade came a marked

accession of power. The localisation of his previous stories had been shadowy, and the characterisation had been so vague that the question of nationality scarcely emerged. Now to be an American begins to imply for James the assertion of distinctive character, and if he does not achieve a wide range of differentiation in his figures, his types have still a recognisable identity.

In 1869 James crossed again to Europe, varying his stay of a year by a first visit to Italy, which thrilled him as no country yet had done. He writes to his brother from Rome in October : " From mid-day to dusk I have been roaming the streets. Que vous en dirai-je ? At last—for the first time—I live ! It beats everything : it leaves the Rome of your fancy—your education—nowhere. . . . I went reeling and moaning through the streets in a fever of enjoyment."

Two years of diligent literary work on his return to Cambridge produced only one piece that he thought worthy of preservation — to wit, *A Passionate Pilgrim*. It was preceded by a short romance of 1870—*Travelling Companions*—written for the pleasure of talking about Milan, Padua and Venice. The narrator meets an attractive American girl with her father in the first-named place, and as the young people are both enthusiastic sightseers they seize their opportunity to fall in love while the old man dozes in convenient chairs. Alone in Padua they miss their train in their excitement, but, like true Americans, they refuse to feel themselves com-promised, and eventually marry because they wish to and not because they must.

A PASSIONATE PILGRIM

A Passionate Pilgrim (1871) is his first production of power. It still smacks somewhat of the
guide-book, but the descriptions are after all the
real story, and hence inevitable. The narrator puts
up at the Red Lion hostelry, with its savour of
eighteenth-century England: " I had seen the
coffee-room of the Red Lion years ago at home—at
Saragossa, Illinois—in books, in visions, in dreams,
in Dickens, in Smollett, in Boswell." We are evidently in presence of a case of atavistic home-
sickness, but it is a mild one beside that which we
encounter when the Passionate Pilgrim enters. He
is positively crazed with his enthusiasms, and the
story that follows is the account that is given us
by his new-found friend of a consuming passion for
forms of beauty that speak with the authority of
the slow-maturing centuries. Clement Searle had
been lured to Europe by a legal adviser who assured
him that he had a valid claim to the ancestral family
estate. His hopes prove illusory, and after some
agitating experiences at the old house he retires
to Oxford to die in the happy belief that he had
mystically renewed the associations of a former life.

The story is vividly conceived, and one feels it
to be an ideal projection of the author's private
enthusiasms. Its immaturity is betrayed less by
the overwrought nature of the descriptions, which
as I have said are virtually the story, than by the
bookish tone of the dialogue. Clement, for example,
is chatting one day with his friend in St John's
College garden: " Mightn't one fancy this the very
central point of the world's heart, where all the
echoes of the general life arrive but to falter and die ?

Doesn't one feel the air just thick with arrested
voices? It's well there should be such places,
shaped in the interest of factitious needs, invented
to minister to the book-begotten longing for a
medium in which one may dream unwaked and
believe unconfuted : to foster the sweet illusion
that all's well in a world where so much is damn-
able, all right and rounded, smooth and fair, in
this sphere of the rough and ragged, the pitiful un-
achieved especially, and the dreadful uncommenced.
The world's made—work's over. Now for leisure!
England's safe—now for Theocritus and Horace, for
lawn and sky. . . . My diminished dignity reverts
in any case at moments to the naked background
of our own education, the deadly dry air in which
we gasp for impressions and comparisons. I assent
to it all with a sort of desperate calmness ; I accept
it with a dogged pride. We're nursed at the
opposite pole. Naked come we into a naked world.
There's a certain grandeur in the lack of decorations,
a certain heroic strain in that young imagination of
ours which finds nothing made to its hands, which
has to invent its own traditions and raise high into
our morning air, with a ringing hammer and nails,
the castles in which we dwell."

We might search far to find a better example of
fine rhetoric misapplied.

Watch and Ward, of the same period, has length
enough to be considered his earliest novel, but its
author held it in such disesteem that he chose to
give that distinctive title to *Roderick Hudson*. Genius
is supposed to set its mark in some corner of the
most unregarded work, but the skill of arrangement

and the characterisation in this unambitious tale
are within the reach of many a forgotten writer.
At a later time he would have given his theme more
substance and more poetry : as it is we find his
story curiously unlocalised and with no compensating beauty to redeem its abstract quality. The tale
relates the very mild love-passion of a guardian for
his ward, and the secret of its failure we may ascribe
to the diminished interest its author had begun to
feel in the ordinary habit of American life.

In 1872 James again crossed the Atlantic, with a
commission from *The Nation* to write a series of
travel sketches which may still be read with enjoyment in *Transatlantic Sketches, Foreign Parts* and
English Hours. He visited Germany for the first
time, and a letter to his parents betrays his relative
disrelish of Northern Europe. Of München he says :
" It is a singular place, and one difficult to write of
with a serious countenance. It has a fine lot of old
pictures, but otherwise it is a nightmare of preten-
tious vacuity : a city of chalky stucco—a Florence
and Athens in canvas and planks. To have come
thither from Venice is a sensation ! We found
reality at last at Nüremberg . . . but I would give
a thousand N.'s for one ray of Verona ! . . . To
me this hasty and most partial glimpse of Germany
has been most satisfactory : it has cleared from my
mind the last mists of uncertainty and assured me
that I can never hope to become an unworthiest
adoptive grandchild of the fatherland. It is well to
listen to the voice of the spirit, to cease hair-splitting
and treat oneself to a good square antipathy—when
it is so very sympathetic ! I may ' cultivate '

mine away, but it has given me a week's wholesome nourishment."

He was in Florence during the winter and spring of 1874 elaborating his first important novel, *Roderick Hudson*. His letters betray as usual his contentment with his physical surroundings, but he was beginning to long for more settled and more fruitful social contacts: "I have been meaning, as you know, for some time past to return in the autumn, and I see as yet no sufficient reason for changing my plans. I shall go with the full prevision that I shall not find life at home *simpatico*, but rather painfully, and as regards literary work obstructively, the reverse, and not even with the expectation that time will make it easier; but simply on sternly practical grounds—*i.e.* because I can find more abundant literary occupation by being on the premises and relieve you and father of your burdensome financial interposition. But I shrink from Willy's apparent assumption that going now is to pledge myself to stay for ever. I feel as if my three years in Europe (with much of them so *maladif*) were a very moderate allowance for one who gets so much out of it as I do; and I don't think I could really hold up my head if I didn't hope to eat a bigger slice of the pudding (with a few more social plums in it, especially) at some future time. If at the end of a period at home I don't feel an overwhelming desire to come back, it will be so much gained; but I should prepare myself for great deceptions if I didn't take the possibility of such desire into account. One oughtn't, I suppose, to bother too much about the future, but arrange as best one can with the present ; and the present bids me go home and try and get more things published. What makes the question particularly difficult to decide is that though I should make more money at home, American prices would devour it twice as fast ; but even allowing for this, I should keep ahead of my expenses better than here. I know that when the time comes it will be unutterably hard to leave, and I shall be wondering whether, if I were to stay another year, I shouldn't propitiate the Minotaur and return more resignedly. But to this I shall answer that a year wouldn't be a tenth part enough and that besides, as things stand, I should be perplexed where to spend it. Florence, fond as I have grown of it, is worth far too little to me, socially, for me to think complacently of another winter here. Here have I been living (in these rooms) for five weeks—and not a creature, save Gryzanowski, has crossed my threshold—counting out my little Italian, who comes twice a week, and whom I have to *pay* for his conversation ! If I knew anyone in England I should be tempted to go there for a year, for there I could work to advantage —*i.e.* get hold of new books to review. But I can't face, as it is, a year of British solitude.''

He faced instead a formidable year of American life, which was followed by a year spent chiefly in Paris, before his final election of London in 1876 as his centre of abode. The French experiment was on the whole unsatisfying. He managed to get *The American* written, but he realised that Paris did not furnish a milieu in which his genius could flourish. He confesses to Howells : '' I have seen almost

nothing of the literary fraternity, and there are
fifty reasons why I should not become intimate
with them. I don't like their wares, and they don't
like any others ; and besides they are not *accueilants*.
Turgenev is worth the whole heap of them, and yet
he himself swallows them down in a manner that
excites my extreme wonder." And in a letter to his
brother the same note of dissatisfaction is sounded :
" Your remarks on my French tricks in my letters
are doubtless most just, and shall be heeded. But
it's an odd thing that such tricks should grow at a
time when my last layers of resistance to a long-
encroaching weariness and satiety with the French
mind and its utterance have fallen from me like
a garment. I have done with 'em, for ever, and am
turning English all over. I desire only to feed on
English life, and the contact of English minds—I
wish greatly I knew some. Easy and smooth-
flowing as life is in Paris, I would throw it over
to-morrow for an even very small chance to plant
myself for a while in England. If I had but a single
good friend in London I would go thither. I have
got nothing important out of Paris nor am likely to.
My life there makes a much more succulent figure in
your letters, my mention of its thin ingredients as
it comes back to me, than in my own consciousness.
A good deal of Boulevard and third-rate Americanism : few retributive relations otherwise. I know
the Théâtre Français by heart ! "
No sign of this lack of enthusiasm for Paris peeps
through the novels, and James's general critical
tone with reference to French literature is also more
cordial than the references just quoted would

indicate. However, he obeyed his instinct and rapidly acclimatised himself in London, where the first months of 1877 found him happily settled. From now onward there was no stint of social intercourse, and with easy opportunity of access to his favourite Continental haunts, and with the menace of American experience correspondingly removed, he was prepared to enjoy life at last on his own terms. His brother repeatedly counselled him to guard his growing reputation at home. His replies indicate the completeness of his initiation into English life. "It would be great folly for me, à *peine* established in London and getting a footing here, to break it all off for the sake of going to spend four or five months in Washington. I expect to spend many a year in London—I have submitted myself without reserve to that Londonising process of which the effect is to convince you that, having lived here, you may, if need be, abjure civilisation, and bury yourself in the country, but may not in pursuit of civilisation, live in any smaller town. I am still completely an outsider here, and my only chance for becoming a little of an insider (in that limited sense in which an American can ever do so) is to remain here for the present. After that—a couple of years hence—I shall go home for a year, embrace you all, and see everything of the country I can, including Washington. Meanwhile, if one will take what comes, one is by no means cut off from getting impressions here. . . . I know what I am about, and I have always my eyes on my native land."

In several of the stories of this decade the American

quality is so faintly pronounced that their inclusion in the American group is a mere matter of convenience. Such for example is *The Last of the Valerii* (1874), where the young wife and the narrator happen to be Americans, but where the interest wholly centres in the development of the latent pagan strain in the Count Valerio. He falls in love with a disinterred Juno, and his wife does not succeed in regaining his affection until the goddess is again returned to the earth. *Madame de Mauves*, of the same year, presents us again with the case of an American girl married, though this time less congenially, to a foreigner. Euphemia Cleve as a young girl had the same romantic respect for tradition that we discover in a later heroine, Maggie Verver. In both cases this high sense of historic values might be wrongly defined as snobbishness. Like Maggie, then, Euphemia dreamed of marrying " a man of hierarchical rank—not for the pleasure of having herself called Madame la Vicontesse, for which it seemed to her she should never greatly care, but because she had a romantic belief that the enjoyment of inherited and transmitted consideration, consideration attached to the fact of birth, would be the direct guarantee of an ideal delicacy of feeling." Her disillusionment is sudden and severe. Richard de Mauves, the brother of a friend of her convent girlhood, is a dissipated specimen of his class, who having made her his wife to extricate himself from debt neglects her forthwith, and expects her to find her own distractions and consolation. The narrator of the story, a young American named Longmore, is moved by her beauty and evident unhappiness to interest himself in her more than is consonant with the safety of either. He finds it after a struggle possible to come to terms with his Puritan conscience, but Madame de Mauves is of sterner mould, and insists upon his return to America. The husband somewhat inconsequently seeks his wife's favour and forgiveness. With him, too, she is obdurate, and he blows out his brains. The story does not hint that Longmore takes advantage of this circumstance to renew his suit.

Four Meetings (1877) has comedy and pathos admirably blended. The heroine is Miss Caroline Spencer, a spinster school teacher of thirty, who has been saving her dollars for years to get to Europe. She is relieved of these savings by an importunate cousin at Le Havre, and returns after precisely thirteen hours spent on the dull margin of her paradise. She gets a nauseating draught of Europe when her cousin's widow, a *soi-disant* countess, comes to live with her in North Vermont.

Daisy Miller (1878) almost succeeded in making Henry James a popular story-teller. She is a pretty girl from Schenectady, New York, who, when the story opens, is stopping at a Vevey hotel with her mother and her extremely national young brother. To the same hotel, Winterbourne, an American of more sophisticated type, comes from Geneva on a brief visit to his aunt, Mrs Costello. One morning he encounters Daisy in the garden, and finds to his surprise, delight and amusement that all barriers between them are very quickly broken down. *Mauvaise honte* and decorum are not words that are

in the girl's vocabulary. It is quickly arranged that
he shall conduct her personally to the Castle of
Chillon, a proposal which gratifies the mother, but
shocks the handsome courier Eugenio. His aunt
is stiffly displeased with the whole proceeding, and
refuses to meet such vulgar people.

Winterbourne meets the Miller family again in
Rome during the winter season. Daisy has succeeded
in getting herself much talked about by reason of
her easy promiscuity, and more especially for her
indiscreet appearances with a handsome third-rate
Italian, Signor Giovanelli. Winterbourne maintains
his interest in the girl—an interest that is clearly
shading to love—but the respectable American
colony gives her the cold shoulder. Daisy's final
indiscretion is a visit by moonlight to the Colosseum
under the escort of the ineffable Giovanelli. She is
seized with malarial fever and dies.

Indefiniteness of outline has yielded in this narrative to a crispness of characterisation of which
James had begun to learn the secret in the process
of elaborating such full-length pictures as *Roderick
Hudson* and *The American*. Daisy herself is of course
a minor triumph of delineation to which the spirit of
satire and pity have contributed in equal measure,
but even the lesser figures, the boy and his mother,
are vividly portrayed. The youngster is represented
as a typical specimen of the American *enfant terrible*.
An extract from the mother's conversation will give
us sufficiently her measure. Winterbourne, who is
annoyed at Daisy's reckless behaviour with Giovanelli, has gone to her mother to expostulate and
to warn :

" She was at home, but she apologised for receiving him in Daisy's absence.

" 'She's gone out somewhere with Mr Giovanelli. She's always going round with Mr Giovanelli.'

" 'I've noticed they're intimate indeed,' Winterbourne concurred.

" 'Oh, it seems as if they couldn't live without each other!' said Mrs Miller. 'Well, he's a real gentleman, anyhow. I guess I have the joke on Daisy—that she *must* be engaged!'

" 'And how does your daughter take the joke?'

" 'Oh, she just says she ain't. But she might as *well* be,' this philosophic parent resumed. 'She goes on as if she was. But I've made Mr Giovanelli promise to tell me if Daisy don't. I'd want to write to Mr Miller about it—wouldn't you?'

"Winterbourne replied that he certainly should, and the state of mind of Daisy's mamma struck him as so unprecedented in the annals of parental vigilance that he recoiled before the attempt to educate at a single interview either her conscience or her wit."

Daisy, despite her alert intelligence, is as serenely unconscious as her mother of the formal obligations of life. In this age of emancipation her aberrations would not so deeply shock the Pincian; but what James wished at the time to emphasise in her was the intriguing combination of charm and innocence with the most flaunting vulgarity, and the most compromising frankness. He succeeded almost against his intention in producing a genuinely poetic figure.

An International Episode (1878-1879) concerns itself with the impressions produced on two young Englishmen who, in 1874, visit New York and

Newport, and with the experiences and impressions a year later of a young woman from Boston who sees England for the first time. The Englishmen are Percy Beaumont and his cousin, Lord Lambeth, heir of the Duke of Bayswater. Mr Westgate, an office-haunting New Yorker, hands them on to his wife in Newport, where Lambeth becomes interested in Miss Alden of Boston, a sister of his hostess. Beaumont contrives to get Lambeth summoned home, and the risk is for the time averted. The following year Lord Lambeth heaps attentions on Mrs Westgate and Miss Alden, and we momentarily expect the announcement of an engagement. Miss Alden, however, does not find that Lambeth takes his hereditary responsibilities seriously enough, and the inference is that she rejects his advances. In any event she returns to America, and we are afforded no hint of an engagement.

James uses here, as frequently elsewhere, the device of contrast for securing his effect. The characteristic appearances of the New York and Newport of 1874 could not have been reproduced through the medium of an American observer, for the features would have lost all their saliency. The "rumness" and interest of things resides for Lambeth and Beaumont in their deviation from the British convention, and the amused attention of the two islanders permits even the initiated reader to savour the large promiscuities and genial vulgarities of American life. An hotel dining-room, the heat, Mr Westgate's office, his wife's Newport house, and shopping in the pony-cart are trifling items that are invested with a kind of excited interest merely because they are seen through the retina of two pairs of foreign eyes.   Bessie Alden provides the same resource when her fresh vision rests upon the English scene, and it is one of the humours of this mild romance that the maid from Boston rejects her lordly lover because he appears to face with too little seriousness the high responsibilities of his station.

The Pension Beaurepas and *A Bundle of Letters*, both of the year 1879, are impressions of manners rather than stories, and abound in amusing strokes of characterisation.   *The Europeans* (1878), *Confidence* (1879) and *Washington Square* (1880) are the three long stories or short novels that close a busy decade.

Confidence is in quality the least satisfactory of the three.   There is virtue in a book which one is compelled to read again in order to confirm an original strong impression.   But when one re-reads to revive a fading memory the inference is permitted that even the first perusal was superfluous.   In the best of James, though adventures do not abound, the element of intensity is never absent.   When I have said, therefore, that in *Confidence* we discover a very pallid reflection of reality, I have absolved myself from the necessity of dealing with the book on the basis of positive merits which are far to seek.

The story in itself is not so bad as to have defied successful treatment, but for some unaccountable reason it is weakly handled precisely in those particulars where James usually shows his strength. For example, the characters successively inhabit Siena, Baden-Baden, Paris, London, New York, and a Normandy seaside village, but these places speak no more to our senses than names on a map. His people are American, yet their racial qualities are so superficially explored as to leave the reader quite indifferent to their origin. *Confidence* does not differ from the ordinary Jamesian novel in its circumscribed range of ideas, and resembles them also in referring every development in the situation to the experience of a central character. In the successful books this concentration of interest in the theme itself provides so much entertainment that the reader has no occasion to regret the meagreness of the general reflections upon life, and the central figures are always competently aware of the circumstances in which they are involved. The fine consequence of this is that from every situation as it arises the maximum of possible effect is produced, and every event is governed by its ideal logic. In this story the stage is set for similar fine effects, the situations hold within themselves the promise of development, but the results are curiously futile. Among many possible explanations of James's failure to arouse our interest I would suggest his choice of so insipid a figure as Bernard Longueville as his centre of reference.

The Europeans and *Washington Square* resemble one another in their surface characteristics. They are both light, ironic, brilliant improvisations, but the irony of the latter has an acerbity that is quite unusual in our author. It seems born of the essentially youthful theory that the truth is necessarily cruel, and the resultant harshness of tone is, if not repellent, at least perplexing in an author who ordinarily translates something of his own capacity for enjoyment into the mood and mind of his characters.

Dr Sloper, an eminent medical practitioner of New York in the forties and fifties of the past century, is presented to us as a wealthy widower in the decline of his middle life, with a dull daughter on his hands whom he considers a very inadequate compensation for the wife and son he has lost. He has recently moved to the uptown region of Washington Square, and from considerations of pity that rarely inspire him he has made his brainless widowed sister, Mrs Penniman, a member of his household. When his daughter Catharine is about twenty years of age, a handsome young man, Morris Townsend, of no ostensible means, pays assiduous court to her. The father, suspecting mercenary designs upon a girl so utterly devoid of charm, looks up his record, finds it unfavourable, and has his suspicions of the young man's unsatisfactory character confirmed by an interview with Townsend's sister, Mrs Montgomery. Catharine is desperately afraid of her stern sarcastic parent, and the suspense of the book derives from our doubt as to whether her fear of her father and filial duty or her infatuation for Morris Townsend will prevail. The silly aunt is perpetually trying to engineer a runaway match, but Catharine is not romantic and Morris Townsend wishes to assure himself that as a compensation for so much dullness he will gain control of her father's fortune. When it is made clear to him that Catharine, marrying him, will have only her mother's portion, his ardour cools. Dr Sloper takes his daughter to Europe less in the hope that she will forget her lover, for he has reconciled himself to her stupid obstinacy, than with the expectation that Morris will relinquish his interested pursuit of a girl so essentially unattractive. Thus indeed it falls out, for Dr Sloper is an infallible judge of human nature, and a very complacent admirer of his own infallibility. He is robbed, however, of the satisfaction of knowing precisely what has occurred, for his daughter, dully resenting his sarcastic attitude, revenges herself by withholding her confidence. But the reader is allowed to share her inarticulate tragedy, and we are present at the interviews where Morris seeks to free himself from his engagement. The girl, however, is too dull and too much in love to fathom his intentions, until she receives a letter in which Morris refuses, on the ground of magnanimity, to stand between her and her father. Years pass, Dr Sloper dies, and Catharine, a confirmed old maid, still lives on with her aunt in the house in Washington Square. Mrs Penniman makes a final effort in the interests of romance by introducing the now fat and bald adventurer to the house, but Catharine dismisses him with a spirit engendered by long years of bitterness.

It would be a mistake to deal too seriously with a book that was not planned for greatness. Suffice it to say that the theme, slight as it would appear to be from the above sketch, is adequately carried out. Given a clever and sarcastic father, a dull daughter, a romantic meddling aunt, and a designing worthless lover, the resultant story is as satisfactory as the author planned to make it. The characters fit neatly but somewhat too tightly into the mould already prepared for them. Dr Sloper has to be sarcastic, his daughter stupid, the aunt silly and romantic, and the lover wholly self-interested.

The Europeans is equally light, but there is much more frivolity and fun in the lightness, and the shafts of irony are not so cruelly barbed. James here, as so frequently elsewhere, finds solid footing and support in the contrasted manners of the new and the old worlds. There is not much fable. Felix Young and his sister, the Baroness Münster, come to America to look up some distant Boston cousins. That is about the whole story. Felix falls in love with his cousin, Gertrude Wentworth, and the Baroness would, on her part, willingly let her princely husband cancel their morganatic marriage if she could bring Robert Acton to the point of proposing to her. She does not succeed, but Felix gains his prize, and the Baroness leaves for ever a country whose low standard of civilisation and narrow standard of morality she alike despises.

The formula of this little book is sufficiently simple, but was found by James to be elastic enough to stand a lot of stretching. The aspect of New England life that he emphasises here is its joylessness, as later in *The Ambassadors* he was to emphasise the joylessness of Woollett, Massachusetts. The Wentworths, like the Newsomes and the Pococks, are a sad family, and like them they possess at least one member who yearns for emancipation. Chad and his cousin Mamie find it at its source in Paris. To Gertrude Wentworth it is communicated by the infectious gaiety of her cousin Felix.

The characters and intention of the story will

33

be clear from the two passages I quote. Madame Münster is interrogating her brother on his return from his first visit to the Wentworth house :

" ' And the daughters ? ' Madame Münster demanded. ' How many are there ? '

" ' There are two, Charlotte and Gertrude.'

" ' Are they pretty ? '

" ' One of them,' said Felix.

" ' Which is that ? '

" The young man was silent, looking at his sister. ' Charlotte,' he said at last.

" She looked at him in return. ' I see. You are in love with Gertrude. They must be Puritans to their finger-tips ; anything but gay ! '

" ' No, they are not gay,' Felix admitted. ' They are sober ; they are even severe. They are of a pensive cast ; they take things hard. I think there is something the matter with them ; they have some melancholy memory or some depressing expectation. It's not the Epicurean temperament. My uncle, Mr Wentworth, is a tremendously high-toned old fellow ; he looks as if he were undergoing martyrdom, not by fire, but by freezing. We shall cheer them up ; we shall do them good. They will take a good deal of stirring up ; but they are wonderfully kind and gentle. And they are appreciative. They think one clever ; they think one remarkable.' "

The Wentworths offer their visitors a small house on the estate. The author informs us that this liberality was wholly prompted by a sense of duty, and that the advent of the brilliant strangers was not considered in the light of an exhilarating occurrence.

34

" This was not Mr Wentworth's way of treating any human occurrence. The sudden irruption into the well-ordered consciousness of the Wentworths of an element not allowed for in its scheme of usual obligations, required a readjustment of that sense of responsibility which constituted its principal furniture. To consider an event, crudely and baldly, in the light of the pleasure it might bring them was an intellectual exercise with which Felix Young's American cousins were almost wholly unacquainted, and which they scarcely supposed to be largely pursued in any section of human society. The arrival of Felix and his sister was a satisfaction, but it was a singularly joyless and inelastic satisfaction. It was an extension of duty, of the exercise of the more recondite virtues ; but neither Mr Wentworth, nor Charlotte, nor Mr Brand, who, among these excellent people, was a great promoter of reflection and aspiration, frankly adverted to it as an extension of enjoyment. This function was ultimately assumed by Gertrude Wentworth, who was a peculiar girl, but the full compass of whose peculiarities had not been exhibited before they very ingeniously found their pretext in the presence of these possibly too agreeable foreigners. Gertrude, however, had to struggle with a great accumulation of obstructions, both of the subjective, as the metaphysicians say, and of the objective, order ; and indeed it is no small part of the purpose of this little history to set forth her struggle. What seemed paramount in this abrupt enlargement of Mr Wentworth's sympathies and those of his daughters was an extension of the field of possible mistakes ; and the doctrine, as it may almost be called, of the oppressive gravity of mistakes was one of the most cherished traditions of the Wentworth family."

I have elsewhere noted James's admission of the designed lightness of the theme of this unimportant but entertaining story. The idea behind it is not more profound than the above quotations indicate, and he gets what amusement he can out of the contrast of New England seriousness and Continental insouciance. The moral implications involved in the contrast he reserved for treatment until his confidence in his own powers had strengthened. He had an obscure premonition that one day he would write *The Wings of the Dove* and *The Golden Bowl*.

The years 1880-1890 that we now approach were sufficiently prolific, as we shall see, in short stories, but not to the neglect of larger themes. It was the period of *The Portrait of a Lady*, *The Bostonians*, *The Princess Casamassima* and *The Tragic Muse*, after which book his disconcerting dramatic experiments supervened. Of these larger books the first two are predominantly American in character, and virtually all the short stories of the period are of the same complexion.

James had come now to consider himself in everything but name an Englishman. To his friend Norton he writes in 1880 : " I am at least now a thoroughly naturalised Londoner—a Cockney *convaincu*. I am attached to London in spite of the long list of reasons why I should not be. I think it on the whole the best point of view in the world. There are times when the fog, the smoke, the universal uncleanness, the combined unwieldiness and flatness of much of the social life—these and many other matters—overwhelm the spirit and fill it with a yearning for other climes ; but nevertheless one reverts, one sticks, one abides, one even cherishes ! Considering that I lose all patience with the English about fifteen times a day, and vow that I renounce them for ever, I get on with them beautifully and love them well. Our dear Vasari, I fear, couldn't have made much of them, and they would have been improved by a slight infusion of the Florentine spirit, but for all that they are, for me, the great race—even at this hour of their possible decline. Taking them altogether they are more complete than other folk, more largely nourished, deeper, denser, stronger. I think it takes more to make an Englishman, on the whole, than to make anyone else—and I say that with a consciousness of all that often seems to me to have been left out of their composition." On the whole his enthusiasm for the country and the race was maintained to the end, but to the same friend he shortly afterwards makes admission of certain doubts that he entertains of the persistence of these virtues in the " damaged " upper class. " The condition of that body seems to me to be in many ways very much the same rotten and *collapsible* one as that of the French aristocracy before the Revolution—minus cleverness and conversation—at all events, much of English life is grossly materialistic and wants blood-letting."

In 1881-1882 James spent a winter in the United States, and in the February of that year his mother died. He sailed for England in May, armed with a commission from *Harper's Magazine* to do a series of articles on Southern France. The illness of his father summoned him back to America in December, but his death had occurred before his arrival. His brother William having been detained in Europe he had the unwonted and unwelcome task of settling the family affairs, and returned to London only in August of 1883. He was not in America again for over twenty years.

Of further episodes during the period we are considering there is, save of the usual visits to the Continent, little record preserved. His sister Alice came to live with him in 1884, and at about the same time at Bournemouth his warm friendship with Robert Louis Stevenson was established.

In 1886 he moved from his somewhat cheerless lodgings in Bolton Street to a flat in Kensington at 34 De Vere Gardens. From here he writes rather amusingly to Miss Grace Norton of his ineffectual efforts to escape from society. One remembers his earlier longing to effect his entrance. " My small house," he writes, " seems most pleasant and peculiar (in the sense of being my own), and my servants are as punctual as they are prim—which is saying much. But I enjoyed my absence " (he had been as usual in Italy), " and I shall endeavour to repeat it every year, for the future, on a smaller scale ; that is, to leave London, not at the beginning of the winter but at the end, by the mid-April, and take the period of the insufferable Season regularly in Italy. It was a great satisfaction to me to find that I am as fond of that dear country as I ever was, and that its infinite charm and interest are one of the things in life to be most relied upon. I was afraid that the dryness of age—which drains us of so many sentiments—had reduced my old *tendresse* to a mere memory. But no—it is really so much in my pocket, as it were, to feel that Italy is always there. . . . I shall be here for the rest of the summer—save for little blotches of absence—and I look forward to some quiet months of work. I am trying, not without success, to get out of society—as hard as some people try to get in. I want to be dropped and cut and consummately ignored. This only demands a little patience, and I hope eventually to elbow my way down to the bottom of the wave—to achieve an obscurity. This would sound fatuous if I didn't add that success is easily within my grasp."

The popularity of *Daisy Miller* had proved a false dawn, and this withdrawal of public favour both troubled and perplexed him. He makes his friend Howells his confidant. " I am troubled about many things, about many of which you could give me, I think (or rather I am sure), advice and direction. I have entered upon evil days—but this is for your most private ear. It sounds portentous, but it only means that I am still staggering a good deal under the mysterious and (to me) inexplicable injury wrought—apparently—upon my situation by my last two novels, *The Bostonians* and *The Princess*, from which I expected so much and derived so little. They have reduced the desire, and the demand, for my productions to zero—as I judge from the fact that though I have for a good while past been writing a number of good short things, I remain irremediably unpublished. Editors keep them back, for months and years, as if they were ashamed of them, and I am condemned apparently to eternal silence. You must be so widely versed in all the reasons of things (of this sort, to-day) in the United States that if I could discourse with you awhile by the fireside I should endeavour to draw from you some secret to break the spell. However, I don't despair, for I think I am now (1888) in better form than I have ever been in my life, and I propose yet to do many things. Very likely too, some day, all my buried prose will kick off its various tombstones at once. Therefore don't betray me till I myself have given up. That won't be for a long time yet."

If he had had this fireside conversation with Howells he would have learned that his diminishing appeal to his own countrymen was not due to any defect of virtue in his compositions. He was still eminently clear and readable, and his art had not yet advanced to the stage when it required a special initiation—a literary sixth sense—for its appreciation. What Howells would have told him was that he had neglected to flatter his fellow-citizens, and that they cherished the opinion that he had deserted them because he could not tolerate their manners, their opinions, or their institutions. If you must criticise us, and the obligation does not seem inevitable, at least stay at home and do it. Some hint of this solution is delicately conveyed in the letters of both Howells and his brother, but what neither of them could understand was that the fastidiousness which they deemed rather a vice than a virtue had its source no less in his intellect than in his temperament. Civilisation at its highest pitch was the master passion of his mind, and his preoccupation with the international aspects of character and custom issued from the conviction that the rawness and rudeness of a young country were not incapable of cure by contact with more developed forms, and that the process of assimilation was already under way. " For myself, at any rate, I am deadly weary of the whole ' international ' state of mind—so that I *ache*, at times, with fatigue at the way it is constantly forced upon me as a sort of virtue or obligation. I can't look at the English-American world, or feel about them, any more, save as a big Anglo-Saxon total, destined to such an amount of melting together that an insistence on their differences becomes more and more idle and pedantic ; and that melting together will come the faster the more one takes it for granted and treats the life of the two countries as continuous or more or less convertible, or at any rate as simply different chapters of the same general subject. Literature, fiction in particular, affords a magnificent arm for such taking for granted, and one may so do an excellent work with it. I have not the least hesitation in saying that I aspire to write in such a way that it would be impossible to an outsider to say whether I am at a given moment an American writing about England or an Englishman writing about America (dealing as I do with both countries), and so far from being ashamed of such an ambiguity I should be exceedingly proud of it, for it would be highly civilised."

The Point of View, which first appeared in *The Century Magazine* of December 1882, was possibly one of the delayed ventures of which James speaks, for it is a virtual continuation of the *Pension Beaurepas* of several years before. *The Siege of London* of the following year is the first story of the decade that need detain us. Its heroine, Mrs Headway, aged thirty-seven, but still devastatingly pretty, is a new type. She is a much divorced Westerner who has recently been left a legitimate widow with ample means. For this we have her own unsupported statement to Littlemore, a chance friend of earlier San Pablo days, who, one evening, accompanied by his friend Rupert Waterville, of the American embassy of London, encounters her in the Théâtre Français. Her protector of the evening is a fatuous young English baronet, Sir Arthur Demesne, who had fallen in love with her recently in Homburg, and whose fascination by her charms is rendered more intense from the puzzled bewilderment in which he stands with reference to her past. Mrs Headway after her notorious Western career had sought to establish herself respectably in New York, but had there been ignominiously snubbed for her pains. It is her ambition of course to snub New York in her turn, and to this end she cultivates the innocuous Sir Arthur, to whose mother she hopes to present, Littlemore aiding, a certificate of respectability. His refusal to endorse her occurs shortly before her marriage—but the new Lady Demesne has still to achieve the conquest of her dowager mother-in-law, of the American embassy, and of Littlemore's careful sister, Mrs Dolphin. Her satisfaction is that New York people were beginning to inquire " who in the world Lady Demesne had been."

LADY BARBARINA

In *Lady Barbarina* (1884) James breaks new ground. He endeavours to represent the difficult acclimatisation of an English girl of good birth in even the most civilised American milieu, New York. The transmission of wives had ordinarily been in the opposed direction, and the accompanying millions tended to make the fusing process work with smoothness. It is unnecessary for me to indicate here how Jackson Lemon, a young American doctor of great inherited wealth, came into contact with the daughter of the impoverished but splendid Marquis of Canterville. Wooing her he finds a somewhat complicated matter, as this has to be performed under the sanction of authority, and the preliminary and advanced stages alike are beset with difficulties. Indeed it looks as if the affair would never ripen to a conclusion, for Lemon does not prove an accommodating person, and balks at the idea of marriage settlements. He might have continued in this independent spirit had he not been piqued by the freely uttered doubts—the prognostications of disaster even—concerning the marriage expressed by his old American friends the Dexter-Freers. He waives his point, and having subscribed to all forms and formalities he takes his bride and her sister, Lady Agatha, to New York. This latter young lady fully acclimatises herself, and yields with alarming facility to the fascination exercised by the cheerful vulgarity of a Californian adventurer, Herman Longstraw. But Lady Barbarina Lemon is stubbornly incapable of adaptation, and makes no faintest disguise of her contempt, expressed though it is by mere lassitude, for the social usages of New York. Her sister's runaway match with Longstraw affords the pretext for a return to England, and there the story indefinitely leaves the ill-assorted pair.

Working out his material James appears to have discovered more interest in Jackson's problem, which has a certain frustrate intensity, than in that of Lady Barb, which exhibits only an obstinate lassitude that produces results of mere negative activity. But after all the results *are* produced, and it will be time when Jackson and his wife return to live in America to say that as a means to an end beautiful languor is not a more effective instrument than square-jawed determination.

A New England Winter (1884) is by James's own admission an ineffective picture of Bostonian conditions. We may pass on accordingly to *Pandora* (1885), in which brief narrative the recording medium is Count Otto Vogelstein, who has recently been appointed to the German embassy at Washington. With Teutonic thoroughness he begins his observations of American character on shipboard, and is particularly interested in the pretty Miss Pandora Day of Utica, whom he judges to be the typical American girl. He is warned by Mrs Dangerfield, an American lady of fashion, that Pandora is very bad style, and that his diplomatic position demands, especially at the outset, a prudent consideration as to the people whom it is proper to know. Pandora is encumbered with vulgar parents and a younger brother and sister who will not facilitate the social career on which her ambition is fixed. Otto gathers too from Pandora's frank lips that she is engaged to a young Utican of the shopkeeping class.

At the end of a year and a half of Washington life Otto attends an evening reception at the exclusive Bonnycastles'. The President is among the invited guests, and Mrs Steuben of New York is to bring a Miss Day who has been the success of the metropolitan season. This is our Pandora, who, on her arrival, gathers all the dignitaries in a throng about her. Otto hears the President make her a laughing promise, the tenor of which he divines when a few days later Mr Bellamy, the shopkeeper of Utica, flourishes before his fiancée's eyes the document appointing him as Minister to Holland.

What James is here studying for the first time is the " self-made girl," and I may borrow from him his own reflections on the type : " She was not fast, nor emancipated, nor crude, nor loud, and there wasn't in her, of necessity at least, a grain of the stuff of which the adventuress is made. She was simply very successful, and her success was entirely personal. She hadn't been born with the silver spoon of social opportunity ; she had grasped it by honest exertion. You knew her by many different signs, but chiefly, infallibly, by the appearance of her parents. It was her parents who told her story ; you always saw how little her parents could have made her. Her attitude with regard to them might vary in different ways. As the great fact on her own side was that she had lifted herself from a lower social plane, done it all herself, and done it by the simple lever of her personality, it was naturally to be expected that she would leave the authors of her mere material being in the shade. Sometimes she had them in her wake, lost in the bubbles and the foam that showed where she had passed; sometimes, as Alfred Bonnycastle said, she let them slide altogether; sometimes she kept them in close confinement, resorting to them under cover of night, and with every precaution; sometimes she exhibited them to the public in discreet glimpses, in prearranged attitudes. But the general characteristic of the self-made girl was that, though it was frequently understood that she was privately devoted to her kindred, she never attempted to impose them on society, and it was striking that, though in some of her manifestations a bore, she was at her worst less of a bore than they. They were almost always solemn and portentous, and they w. re for the most part of a deathly respectability. She wasn't necessarily snobbish, unless it was snobbish to want the best. She didn't cringe, she didn't make herself smaller than she was; she took on the contrary a stand of her own and attracted things to herself. Naturally she was possible only in America—only in a country where whole ranges of competition and comparison were absent."

Georgina's Reasons, also of the year 1885, has more contrivances of episode than James usually permitted himself in his briefer compositions. Georgina, whose caprice approaches madness, compels her husband to conceal their marriage. Benyon is rather awkwardly kept away from her for years by naval duties in foreign waters, and by an equally inept contrivance he discovers that his wife has contracted another marriage. Falling in love with Kate Theory, he hastens home to denounce Mrs Georgina Roy, but she carries matters with so high a hand that he fails of his purpose.

Mrs Temperly (1887) and *Louisa Pallant* (1888) are two colourless romances scarcely worthy of James's maturity, and they contribute nothing of importance to the general problem of manners. *The Reverberator* (1888), on the other hand, is an excellent comedy that abounds in local reference. The Dosson family of Boston, U.S.A., the father, a wealthy retired business man, and his two daughters, Delia and Francie, are established when the story opens in a Paris hotel. George Flack, the Paris correspondent of *The Reverberator*, an American society journal, comes to see them as soon as they are installed, for the obvious purpose of paying his court to Miss Francie, the beautiful younger daughter. He had crossed with them on a previous trip, and having been established in Paris during the interval he feels that he will be a useful guide to the attractions of the town. He does in fact make himself persistently useful, but without apparently much furthering his suit. One of his arrangements (announced in *The Reverberator*) is that Miss Francie shall sit for her portrait to a young impressionist artist, a fellow-countryman named Waterlow, who was making a reputation in Paris. He takes the young ladies to the studio to settle the matter, and Waterlow and Gaston Probert, a Gallicised American, are vastly delighted with Miss Francie's beauty. So deeply is Gaston affected that he calls twice at the hotel, joins them at dinner on the second occasion, and a week later accompanies them on an excursion to Saint-Germain. Delia meanwhile has been operating on her pliable sister to induce her to be cold to Flack's advances, for she imagines that a more distinguished future awaits her if she consents to Probert's suit, who evidently is a man of the last refinement and brilliant social connections. The advice is not lost on Francie, who takes the opportunity at Saint-Germain of amiably refusing the offer of Flack's hand.

In the autumn we find them all in Paris again, except Flack, whom the interests of his paper have called to America. The painting is proceeding famously, and Probert, more in love than ever, is deterred from committing himself to an engagement only by the dread of his family's disapproval. He ultimately, with the aid of his sister, Madame de Brécourt, induces his father and his other sisters to recognise and pay attention to the Dossons. The engagement becomes formal, but while Gaston is in America attending to some business for his prospective father-in-law a scandalous thing happens. Flack, who has returned to Paris, again connects himself with the Dosson family, in the expectation or hope that something may interfere with Francie's unnatural engagement. Cultivating her society assiduously he gathers from her many details which had been communicated to her by Gaston concerning the intimate history of his family. These private matters are an irresistible " scoop " for an enterprising journalist. The number of *The Reverberator* containing the intimate information comes under the notice of the fastidious Probert family, and Francie, confronted with the facts in their scandalised presence, refuses to deny her complicity. Even though she had been aware that something was going to be " written up " about them, she had had no suspicion that they could be so deeply concerned. Like her innocent parent she had an idea that they would even be secretly flattered.

This is the confusing state of affairs that awaits Gaston's return. After much hesitation and distress of mind he solves his dilemma and Francie's distress by marrying her, despite his family's bitter opposition.

The fathers Dosson and Probert could scarcely be imagined of the same race, and no less emphatic is the discrepancy between the two rival claimants for Francie's hand. Mr Probert is simply a man who has elected Europe for domicile, and in seeking to shed his inherited Americanism has become more French than the French. His son, Gaston, has therefore nothing to shed, and on his colourless surface Francie will be able to stamp what pattern she desires. He resembles rather the inanimate Rosier, Pansy's suitor in *The Portrait of a Lady*, but he has the merit of being electrified into action in the end. Mr Dosson we shall meet under other names in other books. Retired from business with a fortune, he is pathetically astray in Europe, and knows no other use for his money than to inhabit expensive suites, and buy frocks and furbelows for his daughters. He cannot fathom their strange passion for foreign parts, but follows dutifully where they lead. Flack is energetic young America incarnate. He feels that there is nothing he does not know about Paris, but loyal to his own national standards he passes judgment without reserve on the aberrations of Parisian taste and custom. He is our most fruitful document on the relative virtues of publicity and reserve, and since the book sweeps a large circle round this question, a conversation of his with Francie will place us in the centre. He has been making her his confidant about *The Reverberator*.

" ' Still, I'm going to capture the blamed thing, and I want you to help me,' the young man went on ; ' that's just what I wanted to speak to you about. It's a big proposition as it stands, but I mean to make it bigger : the most universal society paper the world has seen. That's where the future lies, and the man who sees it first is the man who will make his pile. It's a field for enlightened enterprise that hasn't yet begun to be worked.' He continued, glowing as if on a sudden with his idea, and one of his knowing eyes half closed itself for an emphasis habitual with him when he talked consecutively. The effect of this would have been droll to a listener, the note of the prospectus mingling with the question of his more intimate hope. But it was not droll to Francie ; she only thought it, or supposed it, a proof of the way Mr Flack said everything on a stupendous scale. ' There are ten thousand things to do that haven't been done, and I'm going to do them. The society news of every quarter of the globe, furnished by the prominent members themselves—oh, *they* can be fixed, you'll see !—from day to day and from hour to hour and served up hot at every breakfast-table in the United States : that's what the American people want, and that's what the American

people are going to have. I wouldn't say it to everyone, but I don't mind telling you, that I consider my
guess as good as the next man's on what's going to
be required in future over there. I'm going for the
inside view, the choice bits, the *chronique intime*, as
they say here; what the people want's just what
ain't told, and I'm going to tell it. Oh, they're
bound to have the plums! That's about played out
anyway, the idea of sticking up a sign of " private "
and " hands off," and " no thoroughfare," and thinking you can keep the place to yourself. You ain't
going to be able any longer to monopolise any fact
of general interest, and it ain't going to be right yóu
should; it ain't going to continue to be possible to
keep out anywhere the Light of the Press. Now
what I'm going to do is to set up the biggest lamp
yet made, and make it shine all over the place.
We'll see who's private then, and whose hands are
off, and who'll frustrate the People—the People *that
wants to know*. That's a sign of the American
people that they *do* want to know, and it's the
sign of George P. Flack,' the young man pursued
with a rising spirit, 'that he's going to help them.
But I'll make the touchy folks crowd in *themselves*
with their information, and, as I tell you, Miss
Francie, it's a job in which you can give me a
lovely lift.'
    " ' Well, I don't see how,' said Francie candidly.
' I haven't got any choice bits or any facts of general
interest.' She spoke gaily because she was relieved;
she thought she had in truth a glimpse of what he
wanted of her."
    Francie unfortunately did possess some " choice

bits," which *The Reverberator* ultimately publishes, with embellishment and amplification. Her candour and courage in the family crisis that follows attest her high spirit and inherent truthfulness, but these are precisely the qualities that are so quaintly consistent with deficient sensibilities where " fine shades and nice feelings " are concerned, and are also the qualities which we found to co-exist in Daisy Miller with the same disrelish for forms and conventions. The difference is perhaps to be noted that Daisy defies them from disdain even more than from ignorance, whereas Francie's deviations derive from her lack of initiation. She will prove amenable to the mild discipline of manners in the end.

The Modern Warning, published in 1888 under the title of *The Two Countries*, was with good judgment excluded by the author from his collected works. The characters are four in number—Mrs Grice, her son Macarthy, her daughter Agatha, and an English politician, Sir Rufus Chasemore, who has fallen in love with the girl at Cadenabbia. The son arrives and his resolute Americanism revolts at the prospect of an alliance. When the mother dies a few years later the marriage occurs, and Sir Rufus presently takes his wife to her own country, his purpose being to make investigations for a book. When Agatha reads the proofs of *The Modern Warning* she is shocked at the hostility of its comment on her beloved country, and is alarmed at the effect it will have on her brother. She induces her husband to refrain from publication, but relents when she sees that her embargo on the book had insensibly affected his regard for her. The book proceeds again with her consent, but unable to face her brother on his arrival from America this easily distracted woman ends her life with poison.

A London Life and *The Patagonia*, both of the same year as the above story, complete the American group of the decade. They are of fine quality, but have nothing in their theme or treatment to justify elaborate comment. Laura Wing of the former story is in much the same predicament as the child Maisie who was soon to follow her. Maisie is so young, however, that she accepts quite naturally the distressing conditions of her environment, until her awakened moral sense discovers the reality to her. The problem here, on the contrary, is to exhibit how a thoroughly matured moral sense reacts in the presence of irregularity, and it is as I have said thoroughly well worked out, though there is nothing to necessitate the American reference.

There is between the years 1890-1900 a marked decrease in the volume of our author's American material. For this several reasons adequately account. The Western world was beginning to be remote to him even in imagination, and he writes to his friend Howells : " One thing only is clear, that henceforth I must do, or half do, England in fiction —as the place I see most to-day and, in a sort of way, know best. I have at last more acquired notions of it, on the whole, than of any other world, and it will serve as well as any other. It has been growing distincter that America fades from me, and as she never trusted me at best, I can trust *her*, for effect, no longer." A further explanation which affected for several years his output of fiction of whatever kind was the sudden awakening of his dramatic ambition. The story of this disastrous interlude falls in another place. Suffice it to mention here that the experiment was not fruitful to him in reputation or money, and was provocative of much unnecessary agitation of mind, that finds full reflection in his letters.

Three brief fictions of the beginning and end of the decade are therefore all that concern us here. These are *The Pupil*, of 1891; *Europe*, of 1899, and *Miss Gunton of Poughkeepsie*, of 1900. In the first of these stories we are introduced to Pemberton, a young and impecunious American, who on graduation from Oxford engages himself for an unspecified fee as tutor to Morgan Moreen, a sickly, precocious youngster of twelve. The story develops out of Pemberton's growing attachment to his pupil, whose penetration has been preternaturally sharpened by the conditions of his life. His parents are shameless adventurers, and the boy's precocious cynicism is the idealistic reaction of a sensitive nature. After two years Pemberton saves himself from complete penury by accepting an engagement to coach an " opulent youth " on his own terms. His somewhat fantastic hope is that he will be able to put by enough money to support himself and young Moreen. A frantic note from Mrs Moreen announcing Morgan's precarious condition brings Pemberton hurriedly back to Paris, and he resumes his old relations with the boy, whose health is obviously shattered. A crisis more than usually severe involves the Moreen family. They give Pemberton full licence to take the boy with him and live

where he pleases, but under the excitement Morgan
collapses and dies.

Europe is an episode narrated in the first person
by a much-travelled New Yorker who is at Brook-
bridge, a suburb of Boston, arranging his sister-in-
law's affairs. With her he pays a visit to the Rimmle
family, consisting of a well-nigh centenarian mother,
and three daughters of her prime: Rebecca, Maria
and Jane. Mrs Rimmle in the dim backward and
abyss of time had visited Europe with her husband,
and her shrinking faculties still kindle at the memory
of the splendours of her trip. Her ageing spinster
daughters, always much encouraged by her, are
perpetually planning the delightful expedition, but
as perpetually the voyage is postponed by alarming
symptoms in the mother. As each plan miscarries
she makes an amazing recovery. Jane eventually
breaks away, and having " tasted blood " refuses to
return. Becky, all hope abandoned, dies—the weird
old witch, Mrs Rimmle, asserting that she has gone
to Europe. Maria is left alone with her mummy
mother.

Miss Gunton of Poughkeepsie is an attractive and
obviously wealthy American girl who has captivated
a Roman prince. The girl has endeared herself in
a puzzling way to Lady Champer, through whose
observation all the incidents of the brief story are
strained. This lady is the confidante in turn of Lily
Gunton and the unnamed Prince. The point of
tension between them is the failure of the Prince's
mother to write to the girl, who does not in the least
appreciate the social *convenances* which prevent
that distinguished lady from making the first

advances. Lily in her impatience sails for America.
The Princess unbends so far as to write the letter,
but it had been crossed by Lily's letter to the Prince
decisively cancelling the whole affair. Lady Champer
tells the Prince that Mr Gunton had died leaving
his daughter a boundless fortune, and that Miss
Gunton had become engaged to Adam P. Bransby,
whom she had met on the voyage home. "*They*,"
she writes, "have beautifully welcomed her."

The Great Condition (1899), which may be loosely
added to the group, is American only by virtue of
Mrs Damerel, the woman in the case. Two Englishmen, Bertram Braddle and Henry Chilver, are in love
with the charming but enigmatic widow whom they
have met on the Atlantic. Braddle having won her
becomes haunted by the obsession that she has had
"a past." His prospective wife seeks to allay his
alarm by promising that she will tell him everything
when they have been six months married, *if he asks*.
He is not content with this, and wanders off to
America and elsewhere in search of the secret he
dreads. Chilver now prosecutes his honourable suit,
marries, and is extremely happy. Braddle returns
from his unavailing quest, and learns from Chilver
that his wife had proposed the same conditions, but
he had given her a year. At the end of this time
Braddle calls on Mrs Chilver, whom he finds alone.
His fixed idea has made havoc of his nerves, and he
cannot control his desire to hear from her lips what
she must now have told her husband. The reply is
smiling and prompt that she had told him just as
much as he had asked—nothing.

These short *résumés* do not suffice to indicate the

growing skill in manipulating his themes which James developed in this period, and of which *The Spoils of Poynton* is the consummate example, but they suffice to confirm his own view that America was now becoming a pallid background for his art. The scene of all these stories is laid in Europe, and in *Miss Gunton* alone is there any whiff of the native air.

This had been an important decade in James's career as an artist. He made two errors of calculation—the first as to his capacity to achieve distinction in the dramatic form, and again with respect to his conviction that he would confine himself henceforward to abbreviated forms of narrative. He is quite precise on this point. *The Tragic Muse*, he tells his brother, "is to be my last long novel, for the rest of my life I hope to do lots of short things with irresponsible spaces between." To Howells and to Stevenson he is equally specific, and indeed the fruit of this decade is evidence of the good faith of his intention. In the list of the six "immortal" short stories he proposed to write I would be willing to include, with a frank recognition of the "mortality" of literary fame, at least four stories of this period : *The Spoils of Poynton*, *What Maisie Knew*, *The Awkward Age* and *In the Cage*; and their effect upon his art was such that when, in the next decade, long stories again came to be written he worked with a quickened consciousness of aim and a more confident reliance on his ability to achieve it.

James's adventures were all intellectual, and there is consequently little to record of incident in the period we have reached. The most exciting episode was his acquisition in 1897 of Lamb House, at Rye; and seldom has a writer been more happily accommodated. His letters exhale an anticipatory rapture which years of possession did nothing to allay. " Two years ago, after I had lost my heart to it—walking over from Point Hill to make sheep's eyes at it (the more so that it is called Lamb House !) —there was no appearance whatever that one could ever have it : either that its fond proprietor would give it up, or that if he did it would come at all within one's means. So I simply sighed and re-nounced, tried to think no more about it ; till at last, out of the blue, a note from the good local ironmonger, to whom I had whispered at the time my hopeless passion, informed me that by the sudden death of the owner and the preference (literal) of his son for Klondyke, it might perhaps drop into my lap. Well, to make a long story short, it *did* immediately drop and, more miraculous still to say, on terms, for a long lease, well within one's means—terms quite deliciously moderate. . . . There are two rooms of complete old oak—one of them a delightful little parlour, opening by one side into the little vista, church-ward, of the small old-world street where not one of the half-dozen wheeled vehicles of Rye ever passes ; and on the other straight into the garden and the approach, from that quarter, to the garden-house aforesaid, which is simply the making of a most commodious and picturesque detached study and workroom." It offered the solution of what he calls " my long-unassuaged desire for a calm retreat between May and November. It is the very calmest and yet cheerfullest that I could have dreamed—in the little old, cobble-stoned, grass-grown, red-roofed town, on the summit of its mildly pyramidal hill and close to its noble old church—the chimes of which will sound sweet in my goodly old red-walled garden. The little place is so rural and tranquil, and yet discreetly animated, that its being within the town is, for convenience and immediate accessibility, purely to the good; and the house itself, though modest and unelaborate, full of a charming little stamp and dignity of its period (about 1705) without as well as within." In short it was one of James's dreams translated into actuality. He had a romantic passion even for other people's houses, and now by lease and subsequent purchase he was to possess a house of his own that had submitted to the touch of the beautifying years. The contentment of his mind is reflected in the serenity of his work, and it deserves to be noted that the change in his literary manner which has so often been remarked synchronises with his establishment at Rye.

For a few years he was so full of his new enthusiasm that he lived on in Lamb House even through the winter season. But he presently modified this plan in favour of alternating periods in Rye and in London with occasional dips into the Continent. In London, his De Vere Gardens apartment not being available, he secured permanent quarters at the Reform Club in Pall Mall, where most of the winter months found him congenially installed. The puzzling exigencies of gardening would usually call him back to Rye in the budding time. It was not the love of flowers, for there was little of the

naturalist in James, but sheer pride in proprietor-
ship that so compelled him. His amused helplessness
clung to any advice, but Miss Muir Mackenzie he
constituted " Hereditary Grand Governess " of the
garden, and hers were the prevailing counsels in all
matters horticultural. " We cling to you ; we will
walk but by your wisdom and live in your light ; we
cherish and inscribe on our precious records every
word that drops from you, and we have begun by
taking up your delightful tobacco-leaves with pious
and reverent hands and consigning them to the lap
of earth (in the big vague blank unimaginative
border with the lupines, etc.), exactly in the manner
you prescribe ; where they have already done
wonders toward peopling its desolation. It is really
most kind and beneficent of you to have taken
this charming trouble for us. We acted, further,
instantaneously on your hint in respect to the poor
formal fuchsias—sitting up in their hot stuffy
drawing-room with never so much as a curtain
to draw over their windows. We haled them forth
on the spot, every one, and we clapped them (in
thoughtful clusters) straight into the same capacious
refuge or omnium gatherum. Then, while the fury
and the frenzy were upon us, we did the same by
the senseless stores of geranium (my poor little
22s.-a-week-gardener's *idée fixe* !)—we enriched the
boundless receptacle with *them* as well—in consequence of which it looks now quite sociable and
civilised. Your touch is magical, in short, and your
influence infinite. . . . Your real place is *here*—
where I would instantly ask your leave to farm
myself out to you. I want to *be* farmed ; I am

utterly unfit to farm myself; and I do it, all round, for (seeing, alas, what it is) not nearly little enough money." And when the famous tobacco-plant had bloomed he writes again to the Hereditary Governess: "I haven't for weeks strolled through my now blighted and stricken *jardinet* without reverting gratefully in thought to you as its titular directress; without wishing, at once, that it were more worthy of you, and recognising, recalling your hand and mind, in most of its least humiliating features. Your kind visit, so scantly honoured, so meagrely recorded (I mean by commemorative tablet, or other permanent demonstration), lives again in some of the faded phenomena of the scene—and the blush revives which the sense of how poor a host I was caused even then to visit my cheek. I want you in particular to know what a joy and pride your great proud and pink tobacco-present has proved. It has overlorded the confused and miscellaneous border in which your masterly eye recognised its imperative —not to say imperial—place, and it has reduced by its mere personal success all the incoherence around it to comparative insignificance. What a bliss, what a daily excitement, all summer, to see it grow by leaps and bounds, and to feel it happy and hearty —as much as it could be in its strange exile and inferior company. It has all prospered—though some a little smothered by more vulgar neighbours; and the tallest of the brotherhood are still as handsome as ever, with a particular shade of watered wine-colour in the flower that I much delight in. And yet—ninny that I am!—I don't know what to do with them for next year. My gardener opines

that we just leave them, as your perennial monument, just as they are. But I have vague glimmerings
of conviction that we cut them down to a mere
small protrusion above ground—and we probably
both are fully wrong. Or do we extract precious
seed and plant afresh ? Forgive my feeble (I repeat)
flounderings. I feel as the dunce of an infant school
trying to babble Greek to Professor Jebb (or such
like). I am none the less hopeful that the garden
will be less dreadful and casual next year. We've
ordered one hundred and five roses—also divers
lilies—and made other vague dashes. Oh, you
should be in controlling permanence! Actually
we are painfully preparing to become bulbous and
parti-coloured. One *must* occupy the gardener.
The grapes have been bad (bless their preposterous
little pretensions!) but the figs unprecedentedly
numerous. And so on, and so on."

Flickerbridge (1902), *Mrs Medwin* (1903) and
Fordham Castle (1904) are the three American
pieces that close the long period of absence from
his native land. The first is a matured version of
A Passionate Pilgrim. Frank Grainger has come
to London from the American colony in Paris to
execute some portrait commissions, and presently
falls a victim to a sharp attack of influenza. A
journalistic-literary friend in Paris, Addie Wenham,
to whom he is not certain whether he is engaged
or not, gives him during his convalescence an
introduction to a newly discovered relative of
hers, likewise Miss Addie Wenham, who lives at
Flickerbridge. Thither Frank Grainger goes, and in
his process of recovery becomes so enamoured of the

uaint dear place and its more quaint and fascinat-
ng mistress, so toned and mellowed by the quiet
·ears, that, on the. report of Addie's threatened
rrival, he packs his belongings and incontinently
lisappears. " He had been floated by the strangest
·f chances out of the rushing stream into a clear
till backwater—a deep and quiet pool in which
bjects were sharply mirrored. He had hitherto
n life known nothing that was old except a few
tatues and pictures ; but here everything was old,
vas immemorial, and nothing so much so as the
·ery freshness itself. Vaguely to have supposed
here were such nooks in the world had done little
nough, he now saw, to temper the glare of their
pposites. It was the fine touches that counted,
nd these had to be seen to be believed."

There is always weakness in flight, but it was
·rainger's only resource if he would keep this
nemory unsullied and unimpaired.

Mamie Cotter, of the second story, is a clever
oung American woman who has succeeded in get-
ing herself taken up by some important people
·hom she has the knack of amusing. She has
lso, for mercenary considerations, introduced enter-
·rising Americans into " society," and when the
.arrative opens she has undertaken the same office,
·ith smaller hope of success, for an Englishwoman,
Irs Medwin. The problem is complicated by the
nopportune arrival of her very American and
npecunious half-brother, Scott Homer, who has
articular need at the moment for ten pounds.
Iamie considers him so disreputable that she fixes
n hour for his return that will not clash with the

arrival of Lady Wantidge, whom she expects. He
design is to float Mrs Medwin through the agenc
of this considerable person, and her queer brothe
would spoil her chance of effecting this. Th
brother arrives ahead of his hour, and Lady War
tidge, encountering him alone, is fascinated precisel
by his queerness. Ultimately he consents to go t
her country house only if Mrs Medwin is among th
invited guests.

Fordham Castle is a clumsily contrived *jeu d'espri*
over-valued by its author, in which a wife compe
her husband to masquerade under another nam
and a daughter submits her mother to the sam
indignity. The relegated pair meet in Geneva, an
each discovers the other's predicament. The wil
and the daughter, we learn, are floating to succes
in Fordham Castle.

James had now reached the age of sixty, and
great longing came over him to revisit the countr
of his birth, which he had last seen with the ey
of forty. As the romantic appeal of Europe ha
originally called him away, so now America spok
to his imagination in the voice of romance, and I
was conscious that he might discover, revisiting h
shores, new shades of beauty and aspects of manne
to which familiarity had formerly blinded hir
Moreover he proposed to take in a much wider scop
of the country than he had ever traversed in th
older time, for his wanderings even then had bee
mainly European, and New York, Boston an
Newport were the only corners of the vast continer
he knew. William James welcomed the propos
visit, but with certain reservations of alarm e

gendered by his foreknowledge of the fastidiousness of his brother's mind. A letter to Henry James of 3rd May 1903 gives expression to both the satisfaction and the fears : " Theodora had already given us your message of an intended visit to these shores ; and your letter made Alice positively overflow with joyous anticipations. On my part they are less unmixed, for I feel more keenly a good many of the désagréments to which you will inevitably be subjected, and imagine the sort of physical loathing with which many features of our national life will inspire you. It takes a long time to notice such things no longer. One thing, for example, which would reconcile *me* most easily to abandoning my native country for ever would be the certainty of immunity, when travelling, from the sight of my fellow-beings at hotels and dining-cars having their boiled eggs brought to them, broken by a negro, two in a cup, and eaten with butter. How irrational this dislike is, is proved both by logic and by the pleasure taken in the custom by the élite of mankind over here. . . . Yet on such irrational sympathies and aversions (quite conventional for the most part) does our pleasure in a country depend, and in your case far more than in that of most men. The *vocalisation* of our countrymen is really, and not conventionally, so ignobly awful, that the process of hardening oneself thereto is very slow, and would in your case be impossible. It is simply incredibly loathsome. I should hate to have you come and, as a result, feel that you had now *done* with America for ever, even in an ideal and imaginative sense, which after a fashion you can still indulge in."

Having received a reassuring reply on the subject of eggs and accent, William abates his fears and writes : " The moment it appears that what you crave is millions of just such shocks, and that a new lease of artistic life, with the lamp of genius fed by the oil of twentieth-century American life, is to be the end and aim of the voyage, all my stingy doubts wither and are replaced by enthusiasm that you are still so young-feeling, receptive and hungry for more raw material and experience. . . . It is pathetic to hear you talk so about your career and its going to seed without the contact of new material; but feeling as you do about the new material, I augur a great revival of energy and internal effervescence from the execution of your project. Drop your English ideas and take America and Americans as they take themselves, and you will certainly experience a rejuvenation."

The book of travels was written in serene neglect of this advice, and it derives its high value in no small measure from the fact that he could bring to bear upon his observations the memories of his youth and early manhood supplemented by a wide experience of life in countries of a more developed civilisation. " I was to return," he said, " with much of the freshness of eye, outward and inward, which, with the further contribution of a state of desire, is commonly held a precious agent of perception. I felt no doubt, I confess, of my great advantage on that score ; since, if I had had time to become almost as ' fresh ' as an inquiring stranger, I had not on the other hand had enough to cease to be, or at least to feel, as acute as an initiated native."

His brother seemed to fear an attitude of superiority, but no snobbishness is to be detected in the narrative, and the unfastidious Dickens showed far more squeamishness in the presence of vulgarity than Henry James ever permitted himself to reveal. I cannot think that a more extended knowledge of scientific and commercial conditions would have made the book better than it is. James proposed to explore the manners and appearances of the country, and he has given us sufficient indications of mechanical developments and commercial backgrounds to fill out his picture. In comparing his achievement with the work of more practical-minded men like Wells and Chesterton, I find his material more abundant, more concrete, more vivid, and infinitely richer in reflective power than their attempts at national portraiture. The matter is organised too with supreme artistic skill, and one is at a loss to understand the limited range of its readers, unless its verbal intricacy may suffice as an explanation.

His brother acclaimed *The American Scene* as in its peculiar way "supremely great," and this in spite of the reservations he is inclined to make with regard to its complexity of style. He proceeds in most amusing and penetrating fashion to elaborate his fraternal and amicable objections to the resolute refusal of his brother to say a thing straightforwardly and have done with it. It is astonishing how one may subscribe to these remarks and yet hold in one's mind a great reserve of admiration for a man who could manipulate language with such originality and often to such admirable effect. There are rhythms in James's later books that no other writer can match, and massive though his mode of utterance is, it is not too encumbered to achieve occasional miracles of subtlety, whether of description or of reflection. Two descriptions in this book particularly linger in my mind, one of them dealing with the teeming life of the New York bay, and the other devoted to the faded glories of Newport. In both value is attained by a fusion of every element that gives dignity and vitality to the descriptive art. We experience the exhilarating sensation of contact with the physical aspects of the scene, each vivid selective phrase performing its work in the process, and stimulating the visual nerve of imagination. This sense of saliency, this feeling for concrete values we may call it, James shares with all other writers of pictorial power, and we may even admit his inferiority to some of them in the range and variety of his observations. What constitutes his superiority to most of them is the play of his mind over the whole surface of the scene. Things must have a meaning for James before they command his interest, and meanings blossom for him in strange and unsuspected places. The American hotel, for example, is an institution that to Mr Chesterton was at once laughter and wonder provoking. It remained for Henry James to give us the philosophical significance of the hotel as a phase of American life. In his description of the Waldorf-Astoria all its zest for publicity, for lavishness and rococo glitter finds its consummate expression. Gorgeousness and promiscuity, too, he finds the note of the country and the city clubs, and everywhere the land over, except in the defeated

South, he observes the same conspiracy of the spirit
of restlessness against repose.   For the genuine
American to be quiet is to be dead, whereas James
cherishes the quite other conviction that the settled
state is relatively blessed, and that only out of
tranquillity can manners and an ordered society
germinate. He might have been more reconciled if
this contagion of unrest had at least bred variety in
the American type, but it has unfortunately oper-
ated in the opposite sense, and has left them the
most undifferentiated people in the modern world.
" The will to grow," he observes, " is everywhere
written large, and to grow at no matter what or
whose expense. I had naturally seen it before—I had
seen it on the other side of the world, in a thousand
places and forms, a thousand hits and misses; these
things are the very screeches of the pipe to which
humanity is actually dancing.   But here, clearly,
it was a question of scale and space and chance,
margin and elbow-room, the quantity of floor and
loudness of the dance-music ; a question of the
ambient air; above all, the permitting medium,
which had at once, for the visitor's personal inhala-
tion, a dry taste in the mouth. Thin and clear and
colourless, what would it ever say ' No ' to ? or
what would it ever paint thick, indeed, with sympathy and sanction ? . . . The great presence that
bristles (for the returning absentee) on the sounding
dock, and that shakes the planks, the loose boards
of its theatric stage, to an inordinate unprecedented
rumble, is the monstrous form of Democracy, which
is thereafter to project its shifting angular shadow,
at one turn and another, across every inch of the

field of his vision. It is the huge democratic broom that has made the clearance and that one seems to see brandished in the empty sky."

The book teems with suggestive items of observation and reflection, and his criticism is free from rancour as it is from illusion. Henry James is a man supremely interested in the social experiment, and if he derives small satisfaction from his survey of the American scene, it is for the reason that the problem of manners has on this continent been most inadequately solved. Since Matthew Arnold, no thinker has been more fully aware of all the implications that are involved in the idea of civilisation, and, as with Matthew Arnold, his fastidiousness has incurred the hostility of precisely those readers whose enlightenment was most to be desired.

Casting a backward glance over the range of types that our author had covered in his American studies prior to his long-delayed return to the country, we recognise amidst all the variety some curious omissions, which are really a tribute to his intellectual honesty. The women are rendered with a greater approach to completeness than the men. The male American he was compelled to study at a second remove, and he cheerfully admitted his inability to cope with him in his most significant aspect in the street and market-place. His specimens are very seldom examined *in situ*, and even in *Washington Square*, *The Europeans* and *The Bostonians*, where the milieu is wholly American, the typical business man is not attempted. He prefers to transfer him overseas and submit him to the acid test of Europe, with the strangest results. He is

THE AMERICAN MAN

almost always retired from business, and is very
rarely compelled to worry about his cab-fare. Our
main interest in him is the degree of emancipation
he is capable of achieving. The theoretical premise
is that the elements of civilisation with difficulty
exist in America, and the men who best succeed
in Europe are those who are conscious of this fact.
Grainger and the Passionate Pilgrim succeed so well
that their country could never contain them again.
The Proberts, too, are completely denationalised,
and Ralph Touchett would never care to be for
long removed from the clatter of Piccadilly. The
robust Americanism of his father is siren-proof, and
old Mr Touchett by exception remains, in spite of
this fidelity to his origin, a most sympathetic figure.
England amuses his critical faculty, and a spirit of
accommodation that extends even to his wife has
no difficulty in embracing a country. Ordinarily
the United Stateser who carries his prejudices abroad
has little to commend him; he is either blatantly
vulgar, like George P. Flack, or tight and dry like
McCarthy Grice. Caspar Goodwood maintains by
a miracle his prejudices and his decency. Felix
Young in *The Europeans* would stand for a type
of the completely emancipated American were it
not for the fact that his native country contributed
nothing to his making. Roderick Hudson might
furnish another example but for the circumstance
of his genius, which of itself constitutes an emancipation. The best specimen of the emergent individual in the early books is Christopher Newman,
who vaguely foreshadows the more contemplative
Strether of a later time.

71

HENRY JAMES : MAN AND AUTHOR

His women are more completely realised, and overflow into new categories. Vivacity is the note of Daisy Miller, Pandora and Mrs Headway, and a brisk and bouncing energy spins old Mrs Touchett on her nervous way. They are in general socially ambitious and endowed with a blundering competence which is half ignorant and therefore only half contemptuous of the prescriptions of form. Of the named group, Mrs Touchett alone would fall within the conventional definition of a lady, but the possibilities of American refinement are much better illustrated in her niece's portrait, Isabel Archer, and best of all perhaps in *Crapy Cornelia* (1910), who reveals to us how even in the New World old associations and memories may be touched with tenderness. James had suffered much distress of mind from the devastating modernity of New York, and in this story he is at little pains to conceal the identification of himself with White-Mason, whom we find tarrying in Central Park until the critical afternoon-tea hour arrives, when he will betake himself to Mrs Worthingham's house and there proffer marriage to the dashing wealthy widow. He is verging on fifty, and is a lover of the old vanished New York. Despite his fixed intention of conquering Mrs Worthingham's assent, he is beset by doubts of whether he can reconcile himself to her accentuated modernity, and is almost relieved when he finds that her drawing-room is occupied by another visitor. His annoyance, at least, at this unexpected presence is but momentary, for after a brief interval he recognises in this silent crêpe-clad figure Cornelia Rasch, an old acquaintance of his youth. She leaves before him, but her intervention has sufficed to check the proposal that was on his lips. In the hall on his departure he sees her card with its pencilled address, and two days later we discover him settled in familiar ease by Cornelia's fireside. Their revival of old memories is sweet music in White-Mason's ears, and we are assured that he will recur repeatedly to the same sweet source of consolation, while the dazzling Mrs Worthingham will pass on to other triumphs.

A Round of Visits (1910) brings us more sharply into contact with the unfeeling restlessness of New York life. Mark Monteith has returned there from Europe in consequence of a notification that his old friend Phil Bloodgood had absconded with most of his fortune. The loss of his money is not his chief worry—it is the breach of fidelity that more concerns him, not unmingled with a certain compassion for the fugitive Bloodgood.

At his resplendent hotel he meets a fellow-sufferer, Mrs Folliott, who pours her woes into his ears, and grants him no opportunity to disburden himself. He joins a rackety lunch she is giving in the hotel, and a pretty girl engages him to see her brother-in-law, Newton Winch—an old acquaintance who had noticed his arrival in New York. Mrs Ash, whom he had always found so stimulating in Paris, has invited him to look in upon her, and Monteith welcomes the opportunity of engaging a sympathetic ear. But he is deluged by all the circumstances of her present separation or divorce proceedings, and obtains no satisfaction where he had most expected it.

With Newton Winch it is another story. He finds

him wonderfully improved, though worn by illness and highly nervous. With him at last he can talk of Bloodgood, and get the proper reactions. As their conversation continues, Winch becomes increasingly nervous, and paces the floor as if trying to determine whether some compromising object was visible to his visitor as he stood on the hearth-rug. Monteith does indeed catch a sinister glimpse of a revolver that Winch had thrust under an arm-chair on his entrance. The confession then follows that Winch is in the same plight as Bloodgood, with the difference only that he has stayed to take his punishment. The electric bell peals from the front door, and Monteith, at Winch's request, goes to answer it. When he is in the vestibule the crack of a discharged pistol is heard, and Monteith rushes into the room with the officers of the law to find Winch on the hearth-rug dead.

Julia Bride (1908) is another New York story, but of less distinction. In its complications of marital irregularities it rivals *What Maisie Knew*, but the development of the idea is so slight as to make comment unnecessary.

On James's return from the United States in August 1905 he resolutely set to work to prepare the collected and selected edition of his works. Consequently, save for his book of American impressions and some scattered short stories, the immediately following years have little creative work to their credit. Yet his editing was in point of fact creative, for it involved the most careful revision of his earlier pieces, and necessitated a critical apparatus of prefaces which, neglected by the casual reader, are invaluable to those who take James seriously and are interested in the constructive principles that underlie all good fiction. " They are, in general," he tells his friend Howells, " a sort of plea for Criticism, for Discrimination, for Appreciation on other than infantile lines—as against the so almost universal Anglo-Saxon absence of these things; which tends so, in our general trade, it seems to me, to break the heart. However, I am afraid I'm too sick of the mere doing of them, and of the general strain of the effort to avoid the deadly danger of repetition, to say much to the purpose about them. They ought, collected together, none the less, to form a sort of comprehensive manual or *vade-mecum* for aspirants in our arduous profession. Still, it will be long before I shall want to collect them together for that purpose and furnish *them* with a final Preface. I've done with prefaces for ever. As for the Edition itself, it has racked me a little that I've had to leave out so many things that would have helped to make for rather a more vivid completeness. I don't at all regret the things, pretty numerous, that I've omitted from deep-seated preference and design; but I do a little those that are crowded out by want of space and by the rigour of the twenty-three volumes, and twenty-three only, which were the condition of my being able to arrange the matter with the Scribners at all. Twenty-three do seem a fairly blatant array, and yet I rather surmise that there may have to be a couple of supplementary volumes for certain too marked omissions; such being, on the whole, detrimental to an all-professedly comprehensive presentation

of one's stuff. Only these, I pray God, without
Prefaces! And I have even, in addition, a dim
vague view of re-introducing, with a good deal of
titivation and cancellation, the too-diffuse but, I
somehow feel, tolerably full and good *Bostonians* of
nearly a quarter of a century ago ; that production
never having, even to my much-disciplined patience,
received any sort of justice. But it will take, doubtless, a great deal of artful re-doing—and I haven't,
now, had the courage or time for anything so formidable as touching and retouching it. I feel at the
same time how the series suffers commercially from
its having been dropped so completely out. *Basta,
pure basta!* " He has been retouching his old
Italian papers, a system which, he continues, " has
succeeded a little with *English Hours*—which have
sold quite vulgarly for wares of mine ; whereas
the previous and original untitivated had long since
dropped almost to nothing. In spite of which I
could really shed salt tears of impatience and yearning to get back, after so prolonged a blocking of
traffic, to too dreadfully postponed and neglected
'creative' work ; an accumulated store of ideas
and reachings-out for which even now clogs my
brain."

The " blocking of traffic " threatened to convert
itself into a complete stoppage by reason of a
nervous illness that kept him prostrate throughout the whole of 1910. His brother and sister-
in-law hastened over to care for him, but it was
William's health after all that was the more gravely
threatened. In June they were all together at Bad
Nauheim, and when his brother's alarming state

necessitated his return home, Henry, himself still severely suffering, could not tolerate the idea of separation. He accordingly accompanied them to America in August, and was with the brother he so devotedly loved when he died at Chocorua before that month had closed. The loss was irreparable— a grief beyond healing. " I sit heavily stricken and in darkness, for from far back in dimmest childhood he had been my ideal Elder Brother, and I still, through all the years, saw in him, even as a small timorous boy yet, my protector, my backer, my authority and my pride. His extinction changes the face of life for me, besides the mere missing of his inexhaustible company and personality, originality, the whole unspeakably vivid and beautiful presence of him. And his noble intellectual vitality was still but at its climax : he had two or three ardent purposes and plans. He had cast them away, however, at the end—I mean that, dreadfully suffering, he wanted only to die. Alice and I had a bitter pilgrimage with him from far off—he sank here, on his threshold ; and then it went horribly fast. I cling for the present to *them*, and so try to stay here through this month. After that I shall be with them in Cambridge for several more—we shall cleave more together."

When he was again settled at Lamb House in September of 1911 he set promptly to work on the reminiscential volumes which, save for some suggestive critical papers—the *Notes on Novelists*, contributed to *The Times Literary Supplement*— monopolised his leisure until the close of 1913.

We have noticed at various times a hesitancy

on our author's part to launch himself into long compositions. This disinclination had happily been relaxed at the turn of the century, and between 1902 and 1904 three major novels of the highest distinction had been produced. These were *The Wings of the Dove, The Ambassadors* and *The Golden Bowl.* There followed the American interlude with its consequent book and, as we have noted, the arduously conscientious preparation of his definitive edition. These tasks would have sufficed of themselves to check his productivity in sustained fiction, but the break in his health in 1910 and his brother's death were probably the most deterrent causes. He furnished himself, however, with another excuse —and this not of the physical order—for he had come to convince himself that in brevity as he practised it lay greater difficulties and consequently securer triumphs. Shortly after the production of one of these "exquisite trifles"—*The Outcry* (1911)—he wrote in this sense to Mrs Wharton: "You speak at your ease, chère Madame, of the interminable and formidable job of my producing à mon âge another *Golden Bowl*—the most arduous and thankless task I ever set myself. However, on all that il y aurait bien des choses à dire; and meanwhile, I blush to say, *The Outcry* is on its way to a fifth edition (in these few weeks), whereas it has taken the poor old *G.B.* eight or nine years to get even into a third. And I should have to go back and live for two continuous years at Lamb House to write it (living on dried herbs and cold water—for 'staying power' —meanwhile), and that would be very bad for me— would probably indeed put an end to me altogether.

OUTCRIES OR GOLDEN BOWLS

My own sense is that I don't want, and oughtn't to try, to attack ever again anything longer (save for about seventy or eighty pages more) than *The Outcry*. That is, déjà assez difficile—the ' artistic economy ' of that inferior little product being a much more calculated and ciphered, much more cunning and (to use your sweet expression) crafty one than that of five *G.B's*. The vague verbosity of the Oxus flood (beau nom!) terrifies me—sates me ; whereas the steel structure of the other form makes every parcelle a weighted and related value. Moreover, nobody is really doing (or, ce me semble, as I look about, can do) *Outcries*, while all the world is doing *G.B's*—and vous même, chère Madame, tout le premier : which gives you really the cat out of the bag ! My vanity forbids me (instead of the more sweetly consecrating it) a form in which you run me so close. Seulement alors je compterais bâtir a great many (a great many, entendez-vous?) *Outcries*—and on données autrement rich. About this present one hangs the inferiority, the comparative triviality of its primal origin. But pardon this flood of professional egotism. I have in any case got back to work—on something that now the more urgently occupies me, as the time for me circumstantially to have done it would have been last winter, when I was insuperably unfit for it, and that is extremely special, experimental and as yet occult. I apply myself to my effort every morning at a little repaire in the depths of Chelsea, a couple of little rooms that I have secured for quiet and concentration, to which our blest taxi whirls me from hence [the Reform Club] every morning at ten o'clock, and where I meet my amanuensis (of the days of the composition of the *G.B.*), to whom I gueuler to the best of my power."

He had now definitely abandoned Rye for the winter months—" I can no longer stand the solitude and confinement, the immobilisation, of that contracted corner in these shortening and darkening weeks and months. These things have the worst effect upon me, and I fled to London pavements, lamplights, shopping, taxis, and friends; amid all of which I have recovered my equilibrium excellently, and shall do so still more. It means definitely for me no more winters at rueful Rye—only summers, though I hope plenty of *them*."

The Chelsea rooms were only a temporary haven, and Miss Bosanquet, his most competent secretary throughout all these later years, was alert to discover for him some more ample abode, which she ultimately secured, still in Chelsea, at 21 Carlyle Mansions, Cheyne Walk, and which he began to occupy at the beginning of 1913. Here at last his ambitions for major fiction revived, prompted in part by the congenial conditions for work, but partly also by the curious financial apprehensions that on occasion so needlessly possessed him. " My conditions (of situation, etc.) here meanwhile," he writes to his nephew—" I mean these admirable and ample two rooms southward over the River, so still and yet so animated—are ideal for work. Some other time I will explain it to you—so far as you won't have noted it for yourself—how and why it is that I come to be so little beforehand financially. My fatally interrupted production of fiction began it, six years or more ago—and that began, so utterly against my preconception of such an effect, when I addressed myself to the so much longer and more arduous and more fatal-to-everything-else preparation of my ' edition ' than had been measurable in advance. That long period cut dreadfully into current gains—through complete arrest of other current labour ; and when it was at last ended I had only time to do two small books [*The Finer Grain* and *The Outcry*] before the disaster of my long illness of January 1910 descended upon me and laid a paralysis on everything. This hideous Herpetic episode and its developments [a trying attack of vulgar shingles in 1912] have been of the absolute continuity of that . . . dire but departing Climax ; and they have represented an interminable arrest of literary income (to speak of). Now that I can look to apparently getting back to decent continuity of work it becomes *vital* for me to aim at returning to the production of the novel, my departure from which, with its heart-breaking loss of time, was a catastrophe, a perversity and fatality, so little dreamed of by me or intended. I yearn for it intellectually, and with all the force of my ' genius ' and imagination — artistically in short — and only when this relation is renewed shall I be again on a normal basis." To his sister-in-law he is equally expansive. " We have been having, as I believe you have, a blessedly mild winter, and the climax at this moment is a kind of all uncannily premature May-day of softness and beauty. I sit here with my big south window open to the River, open wide, and a sort of healing balm of sunshine flooding the place.

Truly I feel I did well for myself in perching—even thus modestly for a ' real home ' — just on this spot. My beginnings of going out again have consisted, up to to-day, in four successive excursions in a Bath-chair—every command of which resource is installed but little more than round the corner from me ; and the Bath-chair habit or vice is, I fear, only too capable now of marking me for its own. This, of course, not really : my excellent legs are, thank heaven, still too cherished a dependence and resource and remedy to me in the long run, or rather in the long (or even the short) crawl ; only, if you've never tried it, the B.-C. has a sweet appeal of its own, for contemplative ventilation ; and I builded better than I knew when I happened to settle here, just where in all London the long, long, smooth and really charming and beguiling Thames-side Embankment offers it a quite ideal course for combined publicity (in the sense of variety) and tranquillity (in the sense of jostling against nobody and nothing, and not having to pick one's steps). Add to this that just at hand, straight across the River, by the ample and also very quiet Albert Bridge, lies the large convenient and in its way also very beguiling Battersea Park."

He was becoming increasingly selfish of his time as his health and capacity for work increased. At the close of 1912 he had been invited to accept the chairmanship of the English Association, and I dip again into the delightful letters to exhibit the characteristic elaborateness of his refusal of this proffered honour : " When one declines a beautiful honour, when one simply sits impenetrable to a generous

A LETTER OF REFUSAL

and eloquent appeal, one had best have the horrid
act over as soon as possible, and not appear to
beat about the bush and keep up the fond suspense.
For me, frankly, my dear John, there is simply no
question of these things : I am a mere stony, ugly
monster of *Dis*sociation and Detachment.   I have
never in all my life gone in for these other things,
but have dodged and shirked and successfully
evaded them to the best of my power at least, and
so far as they have in fact assaulted me : all my instincts and the very essence of any poor thing that
I might, or even still may, trump up for the occasion
as my ' genius ' have been against them, and are
more against them at this day than ever, though
two or three of them (meaning by ' them ' the
collective and congregated bodies, the splendid
organisations, aforesaid) have successfully got their
teeth, in spite of all I could do, into my bewildered
and badgered antiquity.   And this last, you see, is
just one of the *reasons* (!) for my not collapsing
further, not exhibiting the least demoralisation,
under the elegant pressure of which your charming
plea is so all but dazzling a specimen . . . but the
rough sense of it is that I believe only in absolutely
independent, individual and lonely virtue, and in
the serenely unsociable (or if need be at a pinch
sulky and sullen) practice of the same ; the observation of a lifetime having convinced me that no fruit
ripens but under that temporarily graceless rigour,
and that the associational process for bringing it
on is but a bright and hollow artifice, all vain and
delusive.   (I speak here of the Arts—or of my own
poor attempt at one or two of them ;   the other

83

matters must speak for themselves.) Let me, even while I am about it, heap up the measure of my grossness : the mere dim vision of presiding or what is called, I believe, taking the chair, at a speechifying public dinner, fills me, and has filled me all my life, with such aversion and horror that I have, in the most odious manner, consistently refused for years to be present on such occasions even as a guest pre-assured of protection and efface-ment, and have not departed from my grim con-sistency even when cherished and excellent friends were being ' offered ' the banquet. I have at such times let them know in advance that I was utterly not to be counted on, and have indeed quite gloried in my shame ; sitting at home the while and gloating over the fact that I wasn't present. In fact the revolution that my pretending to lend myself to your noble combination would propose to make in my life is unthinkable save as a convulsion that would simply end it. This then must serve as my answer to your kindest of letters—until at some easier hour I am able to make you a less brutal one.''

This letter to Mr John Bailey proceeds at further length, and the conclusion bidding him welcome at Lamb House is in a like vein of resonant amplitude, so eminently typical of the affectionate and magnifi-cent James, to whom the merest commonplaces of life were matter for generous expansion.

James's seventieth birthday, which fell on 15th April 1913, found him in health and spirits in his Chelsea quarters. To Mrs William James he gives an account of the event which obviously could not be emphasised by a complimentary dinner : " I had yesterday a Birthday, an extraordinary, prodigious, portentous, quite public Birthday, of all things in the world, and it has piled up acknowledgments and supposedly delightful complications and arrears at such a rate all round me that in short, Miss Bosanquet being here, I to-day at least throw myself upon her aid for getting on correspondentially— instead of attending to my proper work, which has, however, kept going none so badly in spite of my last poor fortnight. . . . I send you by this post a copy of yesterday's *Times* and one of *The Pall Mall Gazette*—the two or three passages in which, together, I suppose to have been more probably than not reproduced in N.Y. But I send you, above all, a copy of the really very beautiful Letter . . . ushering in the quite wonderful array of signatures (as I can't but feel) of my testifying and ' presenting ' friends : a list of which you perhaps can't quite measure the very charming and distinguished and ' brilliant ' character without knowing your London better. What I wish I *could* send you is the huge harvest of exquisite, of splendid sheaves of flowers that converted a goodly table in this room, by the time yesterday was waning, into such a blooming garden of complimentary (*sic*) colour as I never dreamed I should, on my own modest premises, almost bewilderedly stare at, sniff at, all but quite ' cry ' at. I think I must and shall in fact compass sending you a photograph of the still more glittering tribute dropped upon me —a really splendid ' golden bowl ' of the highest interest and most perfect taste, which would, in the

85

extremity of its elegance, be too proudly false a note
amid my small belongings here if it didn't happen
to fit, or to sit, rather, with perfect grace and comfort on the middle of my chimneypiece, where the
rather good glass and some other happy accidents of
tone most fortunately consort with it. It is a very
brave and artistic (exact) reproduction of a piece of
old Charles II. plate, the bowl or cup having handles
and a particularly charming lid or cover, and standing on an ample round tray or salver ; the whole
being wrought in solid silver-gilt and covered over
with quaint incised little figures of a (in the taste
of the time) Chinese intention. In short, it is a
very beautiful and honourable thing indeed. . .
Against the *giving to me* of the portrait, presum
ably by Sargent, if I do succeed in being able to sit
for it, I have absolutely and successfully protested
The possession, the attribution or ownership of it
I have insisted, shall be only their matter, that of
the subscribing friends."

The portrait, later to be slashed by a zealous
suffragette and impeccably restored, was painted
in June, and now hangs in the National Portrait
Gallery.   The ten sittings made inroads into the
precious morning hours, but were obviously enjoyed
by the patient. " The thing is, I make out, very
nearly finished, and the head apparently (as I much
hope) to have almost nothing more done to it. It
is, I infer, a very great success ; a number of the
competent and intelligent have seen it, and so pro-
nounce it in the strongest terms. . . . In short, it
seems likely to be one of S.'s very fine things. One is
almost full-face, with one's left arm over the corner

of one's chair-back, and the hand brought round so that the thumb is caught in the armhole of one's waistcoat, and said hand therefore, with the fingers a bit folded, entirely visible and 'treated.' Of course I'm sitting a little askance in the chair. The canvas comes down to just where my watch-chain (such as it is, poor thing !) is hung across the waist-coat : which latter, in itself, is found to be splendidly (poor thing though it also be) and most interestingly treated. Sargent *can* make such things so interesting —such things as my coat-lapel and shoulder and sleeve too ! But what is most interesting, everyone is agreed, is the mouth—than which even he has never painted a more living and, as I am told, 'expressive' ! In fact I can quite see that myself, and really, I seem to feel, the thing will be all that can at the best (the best with such a subject !) have been expected of it. I only wish you and Alice had assisted at some of the sittings—as Sargent likes animated, sympathetic, beautiful, talkative friends to do, in order to correct by their presence too lugubrious expressions. I take for granted I shall before long have a photograph to send you, and then you will be able partially to judge for yourselves."

The glorious summer of 1914 was bringing an un-conscious world daily nearer to the disaster of war, and James was destined never to move out of the shadow. His visionary hope alone could forecast the final victory, and he did not live even to enjoy the moral satisfaction of America's contribution in arms to that event. His letters of that period, as Mr Percy Lubbock says, " tell the story of Henry James's life during the first year of the war in words that make all others superfluous. The tide of emotion on which he was lifted up and carried forward was such as he only could describe ; and week by week, in scores of letters to friends in England and France and America, he uttered himself on behalf of those who felt as he did, but who had no language worthy of the time. To all who listened to him in those days it must have seemed that he gave us what we lacked—a voice ; there was a trumpet note in it that was heard nowhere else and that alone rose to the height of the truth. For a while it was as though the burden of age had slipped from him ; he lived in the lives of all who were acting and suffering—especially of the young, who acted and suffered most. His spiritual vigour bore a strain that was the greater by the whole weight of his towering imagination ; but the time came at last when his bodily endurance failed. He died resolutely confident of the victory that was still so far off."

For a brief time after the outbreak of hostilities he remained in Rye and sought, though vainly, as he soon discovered, to mitigate the strain by the resumption of his interrupted work. He had been fashioning his long-projected American novel, *The Ivory Tower*, to which the inkpot reference in the following extract presumably refers : " My aged nerves can scarcely stand it, and I bear up but as I can. I dip my nose, or try to, into the inkpot as often as I can, but it's as if there were no ink there, and I take it out smelling gunpowder, smelling blood, as hard as it did before."

The outbreak of war found three books or sections of the projected ten completed, a fourth book initiated, and the working scheme that always in his practice prepared the way for serious undertakings fully elaborated. He had built great hopes on this long-pondered American novel which was to draw its vitality from his recently renewed contacts with his native land, but he soon abandoned the effort to deal imaginatively with conditions that the absorbing anxieties and horrors of the day had so falsified. "The subject-matter of one's effort," he wrote, "has become *itself* utterly treacherous and false—its relation to reality utterly given away and smashed. Reality is a world that was to be capable of *this*—and how represent that horrific capability *historically* latent, historically ahead of it? How on the other hand *not* represent either—without putting into play mere fiddlesticks?"

It is fortunate that, despite the fragmentary condition in which he left the work, we can still, with the aid of his confidential commentary, build up our conception of the completed novel. Here everything is planned and noted—the names, the ages, the localities, and pre-eminently the imaginative logic of the theme itself. Difficulties are confronted and solved as they arise, and the scheme aims to leave as little margin as possible for the wasteful overflow of improvisation. Some margin for the happy unforeseen there must of course be, or composition would be a process too arid for delight. "I say these things," he tells us, "after all with the sense so founded on past experience that, in closer quarters and the intimacy of composition, prenoted arrangements, proportions and relations, do most uncommonly insist on making themselves different

89

HENRY JAMES : MAN AND AUTHOR

by shifts and variations, always improving, which
impose themselves as one goes and keep the door
open always to something *more* right and *more*
related. It is subject to that constant possibility,
all the while, that one does prenote and tentatively
sketch; a fact so constantly before one as to make
too idle any waste of words on it. At the same time
I do absolutely and utterly want to stick, even to
the very depth, to the *general* distribution here
imagined as I have groped on; and I am at least
now taking a certain rightness and conclusiveness
of parts and items for granted until the intimate
tussle, as I say, happens, if it does happen, to
dislocate or modify them."

Graham Fielder, when the story opens, has been
summoned across the seas to Newport, where a rich
old childless uncle whom he has never seen lies at
the point of death. Mr Betterman leaves him his
vast possessions, and the remainder of the narrative
informs us of the rapid shrinkage and disappearance
of Graham's wealth through the treachery of a
trusted friend, Horton Vint, to whom he had committed the management of his estate. There are love
complications with two women, Rosanna Gaw and
Cissy Foy, and Mr and Mrs Augustus Bradham are
also drawn into the circle of events.

This sounds bare enough, but we may trust the
resourcefulness of our author to bring richness and
refinement to the material. His first task will be
to create a credible world, and to account, with
accumulation of interest to the reader, for the people
who constitute it. James has never, I think, been
more firmly possessed of his characters, nor launched

90

them to better effect; and if we may accept the existing portion as a criterion of the whole, this would have fallen short of the highest perfection only by reason of the torturing complexities of its syntactical structure.

By insensible degrees the exposition puts us in possession of the requisite preliminaries. What we seem to learn first is that Rosanna's father and Mr Betterman have been estranged for years as the result of Betterman's having attempted to injure Gaw's interests in the days of their partnership. Gaw now haunts the outside precincts of his neighbour's place, perching " like a ruffled hawk, motionless but for his single tremor, with his beak which had pecked so many hearts out visibly sharper than ever, yet only his talons nervous." He is impelled by the grim desire to gloat over his rival's approaching fate, and a savage curiosity to divine, as if mere proximity could reveal it, the extent of the fortune that is now likely to be bequeathed to the astonished nephew.

Rosanna frequently accompanies him on these excursions, though not from filial devotion nor, naturally, for vulgar curiosity. She enjoys access to Mr Betterman himself, whose friendship she had conquered in the interests of the nephew whose arrival is hourly expected. Nineteen years before, these two had met as boy and girl in Dresden, and she condemns herself now for having then, by advice she had given him, irreparably compromised his material prospects. They were a pair of young idealists and both deeply infected with the virus of Europe. The rich and alienated uncle had just

learned of his half-sister's intended second marriage
with a " poor English alien," and he dictatorially
proposes that the boy shall be made over to him
for his education and advancement in America.
Graham, on Rosanna's advice, commits himself to
a refusal of the offer.   In the long lapse of years
he loses both his parents, and by a curious evolution Betterman has come to hate and despise everything associated with the world of business.   It is
at this opportune moment that Rosanna revives his
interest in his pre-eminently cultured but unworldly
nephew of thirty-three.

The second book brings Graham Fielder into the
action, and its three chapters or scenes reveal him
in successive aspects.   Particularly beautiful is the
second chapter, that takes the bewildered young
man into his dying uncle's presence; and of great
" functional value," as James would say, is the third
chapter, that confronts him for the first time with
Rosanna.   She has brought her father home, and
he is actually at the moment dying from the shock of
having heard from Gray's lips and the nurse's that
Mr Betterman is growing visibly stronger !

The method of this novel, save that the author's
comment, disguised as the reflections of the characters, intermingles largely with the dialogue, resembles that of *The Awkward Age*.   In other words,
it proceeds by a series of " successive aspects."   Each
book is a unit controlled by a central figure, and
hence each important character is self-illuminating,
and gathers light from all the other radiating sources.
Since Gray's is the dominating problem it will
be found that light streams in upon him from

every centre. Thus the first book had been specific-
ally Rosanna's, with her father, the Bradhams, and
Cissy Foy subordinately present. In the second book
Gray is the commanding figure, and his play of
contact here is with Rosanna and his uncle.

Let James himself give his account of the last
book he was destined to complete : " I by the same
token see Book III. now as functional entirely for
the encounter of Gray with the two other women
and for the first time with Davey ; and also as
preparing the appearance of Horton Vint, though
not producing it. I see *him*, in fact, I think, as introduced independently of his first appearance to Gray,
see it as a matter of his relation with Cissy, and as
lighting up what I immediately want of *their* situation. In fact don't I see this as Horton's ' Act '
altogether, as I shall have seen and treated Book I.
as Rosanna's, and Book II. as Gray's. By the blest
operation this time of my Dramatic principle, my
law of successive Aspects, each treated from its own
centre, as, though with qualifications, *The Awkward
Age*, I have the great help of flexibility and variety ;
my persons in turn, or at least the three or four
foremost, having control, as it were, of the Act and
Aspect, and so making it his or making it *hers*. This
of course with the great inevitable and desirable
preponderance, in the Series, of Gray's particular
weight."

Book IV. was to give us Gray confronted with
the problem of his inheritance, and other books to
the total of ten were to be distributed between
Horton, Cissy Foy, Davey, Bradham, Gray and
Rosanna. It was a cherished idea with the author

that as the novel had begun with Rosanna, so it should end with her. The alternating localities provided in the scheme were Newport; New York, where the main elements of the plot were to be evolved; Lenox; and about fourteen months from the inception of the action it was to be rounded off to its close again in Newport.

One is left perforce in the dark as to certain subordinate details. Rosanna is, of course, destined to play the part of Gray's good angel. Her twenty-odd millions of contaminated money distress her as much as Gray's fleeting millions had at once amused and embarrassed him, and I do not think it likely that anything so obvious as that Rosanna should reward him in the end with a second fortune and her hand had been hovering in James's mind as the conclusion of a book that so emphasises the malodorousness of ill-gotten gains, even when they have passed into innocent possession. She is in love with Gray—no mistaking that—but the logic of the book points to Gray's infatuation for the much more brilliant and fascinating Cissy. This episode was destined to thread its way through the whole romance, and it would have developed very sinister aspects. So far as Cissy has been adumbrated she reminds one forcefully of a calculatingly selfish and charming woman in another book, Kate Croy, who so devastatingly crosses Milly Theale's path in *The Wings of the Dove*. Kate devises the hateful scheme of her lover's simulating love for the fated woman and inheriting her millions. There was to be the same sort of calculation between the designing pair, Horton and Cissy, in the present book, though when

Cissy finds that Horton has turned Gray's pockets inside out, the latter will discover to his cost where her affections are really engaged.

The author's undertaking to represent aspects of the moneyed world in the States confronted him with the necessity of dealing intelligently with affairs of the street and market, and from this compulsion his inexperience and inexpertness shrank alarmed. We find him facing his dilemma and confessing the " enormous difficulty of pretending to show various things here as with a business vision, in my total absence of business initiation; so that, of course, my idea has been from the first *not* to show them with a business vision, but in some other way altogether; this will take much threshing out, but it is the very basis of the matter, the core of the subject, and I shall worry it through with patience. But I must get it, plan it, utterly right in advance, and that is what takes the doing. The other doing, the use of it when schemed, is comparatively easy."

His device of making old Betterman abhor the arts by which he had climbed to wealth, and of making Gray so inexpert in matters mercenary, helped him across some of these difficulties. Without forcing technicalities to aid him he has made us feel the whole weight of the monstrous pressure that money exerts in the New World that confronts his hero. This was his design, and even in his fragment he has achieved it.

At the close of September 1914 James returned to London, and there remained with few intermissions for the brief remainder of his life. If he

was not in the centre of events as events were then
reckoned, he could still feel there most responsively
the alternating enthusiasms and depressions tha
flowed in from the source of action, and aid the
cause most effectively while his strength served
him. He interested himself actively in the American
Volunteer Motor-Ambulance, which had been organ
ised by the son of his old friend, Charles Eliot Norton
and was constant in his devotion to the welfare o
the Belgian refugees in Chelsea. But though he
found some solace in these charitable exercises he
realised how negligible in the universal ruin were
the efforts he could put forth, and confessed to
feeling " like the chilled *vieillards* in the old epics
infirm and helpless at home with the women, while
the plains are ringing with battle."

Eight months before his death Henry Jame
gave formal expression to his profound attachmen
to England by becoming a naturalised subject. He
felt that some explanation of this step was owing to
his family, and to that end wrote to his eldest
nephew on 24th June 1915 : ". . . My feeling
about my situation here has under the stress o
events come so much to a head that, certain par
ticular matters further contributing, I have ar
ranged to seek technical (legal) advice no longe
hence than this afternoon as to the exact *modu
operandi* of my becoming naturalised in this country
This state of mind probably won't at all surpris
you, however ; and I think I can assure you that i
certainly wouldn't if you were now on the scen
here with me, and had the near vision of all th
circumstances. My sense of how everything mor

and more makes for it has been gathering force ever since the war broke out, and I have thus waited nearly a whole year ; but my feeling has become acute with the information that I can only go down to Lamb House now on the footing of an Alien under Police supervision—an alien friend of course, which is a very different thing from an alien enemy, but still a definite technical outsider to the whole situation here, in which my affections and my loyalty are so intensely engaged. I feel that if I take this step I shall simply rectify a position that has become inconveniently and uncomfortably false, making my civil status merely agree not only with my moral but with my material as well, in every kind of way. Hadn't it been for the war, I should certainly have gone on as I was, taking it as the simplest and easiest and even friendliest thing ; but the circumstances are utterly altered now, and to feel with the country and the cause as absolutely and ardently as I feel, and not offer them my moral support with a perfect consistency (my material is too small a matter), affects me as standing off or wandering loose in a detachment of no great dignity. I have spent here all the best years of my life—they practically have *been* my life ; about a twelvemonth hence I shall have been domiciled uninterruptedly in England for forty years, and there is not the least possibility at my age, and in my state of health, of my ever returning to the U.S., or taking up any relation with it as a country. My practical relation has been to this one for ever so long, and now my ' spiritual ' or ' sentimental ' quite ideally matches it. I am telling you all this because I can't not want exceedingly to take you into my confidence about it, but again I feel pretty certain that you will understand me too well for any great number of words more to be needed. The real truth is that in a matter of this kind, under such extraordinarily special circumstances, one's own intimate feeling must speak and determine the case. Well, without haste and without rest, mine has done so, and with the prospect of what I have called the rectification, a sense of great relief, a great lapse of awkwardness, supervenes. . . . Regard my proceeding as a simple act and offering of allegiance and devotion, recognition and gratitude (for long years of innumerable relations that have meant so much to me), and it remains perfectly simple."

His four sponsors for naturalisation were Mr Asquith, Mr Gosse, Mr J. B. Pinker, and Mr G. H. Prothero, and by the 26th of July the process was effected.

" In a twelvemonth," so ran his hopes, he would have been " domiciled uninterruptedly in England for forty years." But fate had not ordained this rounded symmetry. On the evening of 1st December, in the second year of the war, he was turning over the manuscript leaves of *The Sense of the Past*. On the following morning he had a stroke, quickly followed by another which, after a brief rally, laid him prostrate. He lingered on until 28th February 1916, thus dying within two months of his seventy-third birthday.

In the distribution of New Year honours for 1916 Henry James was granted the signal distinction of the Order of Merit, which George Meredith had borne before him, and which was soon afterwards to be conferred on the one man worthy to challenge his supremacy in letters, Thomas Hardy.

His most devoted contribution to the war had been the sacrifice of his artistic life. Three unfinished productions and a volume of war essays, *Within the Rim*, were the fruit of these blighted years. The third production, not yet named, was *The Middle Years*, planned as a continuation of the two semi-autobiographical volumes which he had produced after his brother's death. But the letters of the period deserve to rank as a literary achievement, and I have been privileged also to see a curious document, now in Miss Bosanquet's possession, which he dictated to her in a semi-conscious interval of his last illness. Psychologically the fragment is of unique interest, revealing as it does the strange and powerful workings of his dormant brain. He summoned her one day and bade her bring her now famous "Remington" to his bedside. He then proceeded to dictate as of yore what purported to be an autobiographic relation of episodes in the great Napoleon's life. The fragment contains a letter couched in the genuine Imperial style, succinct and dictatorial, with comment in the most highly developed Jamesian manner on the complexities of the Napoleonic problem. If Miss Bosanquet and his literary executors can be induced to publish this it will rank among the curiosities of literature.

I pass now to a consideration of James's non-American productions of modest compass.

III

SHORT STORIES : GENERAL GROUP

THREE stories, *Brooksmith*, *The Marriages*, and *The Chaperon*, all of the year 1891, may be dismissed in a few words. The first is narrated by an habitué of Mr Oliver Offord's house, which, for years, had been a centre of quiet but brilliant hospitality. Brooksmith, the butler, took his share in making these gatherings run smoothly, and the narrator does not fail to see how dependent for his part this estimable man has become on the stimulating conversation of his master's dining-room. Mr Offord falls ill, but the chronicler of the story returns to the house frequently, sometimes in the hope of seeing the master, but always with the expectation of having conversation with the servant. The master dies, and Brooksmith loses all the savour of existence. The narrator encounters him here and there as butler, finally as a casual hired waiter, and ultimately learns from Brooksmith's aunt that he had mysteriously disappeared one evening on his way to some social function in Kensington.

The confidential butler was a case eminently worthy of treatment by the historian of London drawing-rooms, and the dispirited Brooksmith fading out of existence with the disintegration of his milieu—for we are made to feel how emphatically it was his—has his place in the catalogue of social specimens. The poor man was at the best of times never vociferously alive—the quiet dignity of his office forbade this—but he is distinguished as the only representative of the servant class whom James ever thought worthy to commemorate.

The Marriages is faintly premonitory of *The Altar of the Dead*, though spoiled as to its finer effect by the melodramatic incident of Godfrey's wife. Reverence for the dead in a society that refuses to remember is the *motif* of either book. Adela Chant continues to cherish sacred memories of her mother, and is distressed by the apparent absence in others of this obligation of grief. Hers " wasn't the way people usually felt in London, she knew, but strenuous, ardent, observant girl as she was, with secrecies of sentiment and dim originalities of attitude, she had already made up her mind that London was no treasure-house of delicacies. Remembrance there was hammered thin—to be faithful was to make society gape. The patient dead were sacrificed; they had no shrines, for people were literally ashamed of mourning. When they had hustled all sensibility out of their lives they invented the fiction that they felt too much to utter."

Adela is much distressed by the growing suspicion that her father, Colonel Chant, is contemplating a second marriage with a rich, vulgar and unprepossessing widow. The marriage never takes place, but this was not owing to Adela's blundering efforts to frustrate it. In the event it was loyalty to the living daughter rather than to the dead wife that forestalled it.

Pandora Day we have already met as the effective

American girl—"the self-made girl," her creator calls her—who, in all kindness but firmness, refuses to allow her parents to encumber her social progress. Rose Tramore on the contrary sacrifices all the advantages of her free position, and *The Chaperon* reveals to us the manner in which she launches her discredited mother in society.

Her father, who has just died, had been separated for many years from his wife because of her infidelity (she had gone off to the Continent with a lover who had died before he could marry her), and in his will he recommends that his son and two daughters shall continue to allow their mother to lead her separate life. Rose's grandmother, old Mrs Tramore, sounds the girl as to her intentions, and makes it clear that she will not see her again if she goes to live with her mother. Bertram Jay of the Royal Engineers, devout and shy and formal, who has once been refused by Rose, adds his solicitations in vain, and the girl drives away from her grandmother's house in her mother's victoria.

What Rose chiefly suffers from in the months that follow are the efforts made by some of her old friends to show her attention while ignoring her mother. Lady Maresfield, for example, knowing Rose as pretty and clever and with a competence, wishes her to dine and go on to a big party, in the hope that her son, Guy Mangler, may make a favourable impression upon her. This offer is rejected, as is a similar proposal by Mrs Donovan.

Bertram Jay runs across Mrs Charles and her daughter in Milan, and finds his way to Rose's heart by his kindly attentions to her mother. He accompanies them to Venice, where Lady Maresfield notes the familiar footing on which he appears to stand. She makes a final effort on Guy's behalf, calls on the mother, and prevails on Mrs Vaughan-Vesey to invite her with Rose to lunch on her yacht. Mrs Tramore's next London season's success is assured, for people are stimulated by the curiosity of seeing a charming young girl bringing out her no less charming mother. Bertram's reward for his share in the triumph is the hand of Rose.

One sometimes wonders whether after all James gains by his cunning eliminations, his " foreshortenings " and other cherished devices, the maximum of intensity that he aims at. *The Altar of the Dead* (1895) is a story that will serve to answer our question as well as any other. It is a composition of exceptional beauty, and in it everything is subordinated to the achievement of a particular effect, which in the present instance is the representation of a morbid state of mind. Even in the longer novels one does not experience the sense of the exuberant variety of life, and in the shorter pieces James compels himself still more rigorously to the exhibition of characters conceived in one particular relation. It is in this direction that his eliminations always operate, and it may well be that the artificial kind of intensity he achieves is the negation of reality. There is certainly no abounding play of life in George Stransom, the hero of our present piece, and one idly questions what manner of life he leads when he is not sunk in meditation before his altar-fires, or communing with his fellow-worshipper through the length of weary years. A man of few but profound attachments, he feels himself an alien in a world where pleasures are so lightly earned and griefs so cheaply valued. Realising that other people are incapable of cherishing in the present and projecting into the future the deeper emotions of the past, he is the more determined to perpetuate his own hallowed memories. He has built, as it were, a mystic temple in his mind, where he solemnises the rites of his sacred dead. But presently he is moved to a more concrete embodiment of his passion, and dedicates an altar in a dim suburban church to their hallowed memory, with for each a lighted candle.

James is as conscious as his sophisticated critics that this is an act which lifts his hero out of all relation with our rough breathing world, but he felt himself as much at liberty to erect his monument to his idea as Stransom to elevate his altar to the dead. To its further embellishment he complicates his extravagance and endows his hero with a fellow-worshipper who finds Stransom's shrine congenial to her kindred devotions. As month by month and year by year he holds his mystic communion almost always the same mourning woman is there, and his altar serves her purpose too. The cluster of candles grows larger with the years, but he has never lighted one for Acton Hague, the friend of his youth who had basely dealt with him.

He has come to know his companion in sorrow, and frequently now they walk away from the church together. It is thus that he makes the discovery that her devotions were dedicated to the memory of Acton Hague, whom she loved though he had abandoned her, and that all the glimmering lights were concentrated into a single flame that burned for him.

They can now meet no longer in the church, and Stransom, deprived of his consolation, draws near to his inevitable end. With a fallacious renewal of his strength he visits his altar for the last time. Here she finds him, and here in her arms he dies with the forgiveness of his lost friend on his lips.

The blemish in this story is the unconvincingness of its central character, of whose capacity to inspire so many friendships we must remain stubbornly dubious. I turn now to a story, *The Spoils of Poynton* (1896), whose central figure, Fleda Vetch, is as interesting as she is attractive.

It behoves a prudent criticism to indulge but sparingly in superlatives. In claiming perfection for this story I incur the charge of rashness, but all extravagance is eliminated from the assertion when I admit that if there are not many degrees there still are many kinds of perfection. After their own kind, therefore, Shelley's *Ode to the West Wind* and James's *Spoils of Poynton* may be considered " perfect," but this statement does not imply equality of value in the two productions. Bentham introduced the elements of intensity and duration into his felicific calculus which, designed by him as an instrument of precision, had only this defect, that it never existed. I am not more certain of the existence of an æsthetic calculus, but were it available, and on the same terms, I still could not satisfy myself that I had reached a final result by weighing one kind of pleasure against another—a work of poignant brevity, for example, against a work of sustained and deliberate calm.

Perfection, then, is of admittedly various kinds, but even in its most consummate form it is not necessarily the mark of supreme greatness. Narrowly considered, there is more perfection of finish and design in half-a-dozen of the masterpieces of Racine than in any of Shakespeare's plays, yet we are satisfied to sacrifice something of the harmony of the one for the abundance and energy of the other. Now the perfection that James wrought for and not infrequently achieved is more Racinean than Shakespearean. Soft flowing contours and harmonies of line distinguish it—a disciplined energy, a temperate warmth, and a refinement of execution that suggest rather deliberation than spontaneity. In either writer, too, a like fastidiousness prevails, which in the interests of concentrated effect clears the stage of all superfluous figures and defines strictly the limits within which the action is permitted to develop. I do not wish to involve myself in a prolonged comparison of two writers whose methods exhibit such obvious affinities, for their dissimilarities would necessitate as copious a discussion. There is this remark, however, to make, that whereas Racine, who chooses his themes for their rich human implications, seems never to concern himself with manipulating them so as to produce the illusion of reality, James, on the other hand, selects subjects which do not appear, save to himself, to hold the promise of germination, but develops them in accordance with the strictest logic of life.

CLUMSY LIFE

It was his theory that the artist is privileged to give the law to Life, and to submit her haphazard processes, her waywardness, her profuse extravagance, or even her occasional meagreness, to a control more severe than the discipline she herself imposes. A dinner-party neighbour gives him the germ of his present story, which she proceeds to amplify in accordance with the facts. He tries vainly to check her narrative, for he sees " clumsy Life again at her stupid work." In shaping the story, therefore, he was at pains to avoid the ineptitude of its actual development, and sought to exhibit the ideal possibilities of the situation as they would be present to an imagination that was the master and not the slave of reality.

The germ of the story, then, was the recorded fact of a dispute between a mother and son concerning some furniture which had accrued to the latter under the father's will. James does not tell us how " clumsy Life " shaped this incident, but presumably the lawyers, and perhaps the police, were brought into requisition—vulgarities which of course were to be got rid of at any cost. James never avails himself of such episodical resources if he can find a human way out of his difficulty. His stories move of their own volition from the moment that he has obtained a clear vision of the central characters. He momentarily played with the idea of making the " old things " of Poynton almost personally take possession of the action, but he shrank from the inventorial exactitude that such a scheme demanded, and preferred to have the spoils gleam with vague suggestions of splendour through the narrative.

He probably first projected the mother, and just as Wordsworth created his Michael to express the tenacious love of the soil in a peasant's nature, so Henry James created Mrs Gereth to represent the more refined but no less tenacious passion for beautiful possessions. He was ultimately to divert himself with tracing in her the aberrations which the possessive instinct engenders, but he put a great deal of himself into his initial conception of her, for his sensibilities, like hers, had often winced at ugliness, and thrilled at the touch and sight of humanly ordered beauty. The son is naturally conceived to be, for the desired contrast, entirely indifferent to the treasures his mother had collected with such eager discrimination, a stupid, handsome, good-natured, sport-loving young Englishman, whose private rooms, adorned with trophies of the chase and the hunting-field, bewray his character. Very early in his testing-out process James discovered that he could produce no interesting conflict from the opposed contact of such a mother with such a son. Summoning his genius to the task he invented Fleda Vetch, and with her discovery all the elements of his story fall into their proper place. She is the one person competent to understand Mrs Gereth's pride in Poynton, but her love of the beautiful has not, as with the latter, restricted her humanity. Mrs Gereth comes very near to being an æsthetic monster, and it is not the first time—let the name of Gilbert Osmond suffice for confirmation—that James has emphasised the dangers of the dilettante spirit. Gilbert saves his intelligence but loses his character. Mrs Gereth has not his meanness nor his calculating cruelty, but her love of beauty has warped her moral sense, and confined her naturally alert mind into a narrow channel. Fleda, who has intelligence and character, and whose feeling for beauty enriches rather than restricts her sympathies, is at once the complement and corrective of the pair. James was probably less concerned with making her a lovable personality, which she inevitably is, than he was grateful for her extreme usefulness. He had not yet found, nor would he in the future discover, a more adequate recorder of facts and impressions than the register of her clear and honest mind. She becomes quite naturally involved in the action at its beginning, she participates in it throughout its progress, and with her the action concludes.

Mrs Gereth seeks her out instinctively at Waterbath, recognising in her a fellow-sufferer from the ugly vulgarities of the Brigstock establishment. A few words suffice to establish sympathy between them, and to put us in possession of the initial situation. With her son still unmarried Mrs Gereth lives on at the Poynton her own genius had created, but she faces with terror the possibility of Owen's entanglement with some girl as criminally unperceptive as himself. The handsome hoyden, Mona Brigstock, is the particular form this terror at the moment assumes, and the story indeed has not proceeded far before Owen announces his engagement. This occurred shortly after Mona had been taken by the young man on a visit of inspection to Poynton, where Fleda is at the time his mother's guest. Communications are now at an end between mother and son, and Fleda becomes the intermediary for all negotiations. Owen concedes his mother, through her, the privilege of removing to the dower-house at Ricks any few things at Poynton that might be her "peculiar property," but Fleda quite understands that everything must now be subject to Mona Brigstock's approval. In the sequel Mrs Gereth takes a very inclusive view of her "peculiar property," and sweeps the choicest contents of the Poynton house to Ricks. Fleda, who is horrified at the act, comforts the helpless and Mona-driven Owen with the hope that she might prevail upon Mrs Gereth to set the packers at work in a reverse direction.

What is happening all the time is that Fleda is falling in love with Owen, and we may note it as one of the minor triumphs of the book that James has succeeded in making this process plausible. That Owen should drift into a similar state demands less explanation, for Mona, cross, inflexible and issuing perpetual ultimatums, fills him with apprehension for the future, whereas Fleda, by contrast, is so comfortable a person, whose cleverness even is conciliatory, and whose domination would always issue from her charm. There is apparently ample justification for Fleda to yield to Owen's pressure, for Mona refuses to set a day for the marriage, and makes that event contingent on the restoration of the spoils. In view of Mrs Gereth's present temper their restitution short of violence seems improbable, and when the mother divines that only on those terms will Mona consent to marry, her justification of her *coup de main* is complete. For Fleda alone would the restitution be made, and Mrs Gereth has convinced herself that if Fleda would only

" let herself go," every difficulty would be resolved. There are two scenes where Owen declares his passion, and in the last of these Fleda's reserve is broken down. It is here that the story takes a curious and characteristic turn. The temptation would have prevailed with the ordinary writer to allow Fleda to capture her prize under the enemy's guns. But the word from her that would have achieved the result is never spoken. Vibrant and strong as her own emotions are, she lacks the romantic aptitude to make her passion her law. Her imagination embraces Mona's position, and though she hopes, she still cannot assure herself that her rival has ceased to love Owen, or has relinquished her claim upon him.

At the close of their last interview Owen begins ruefully to understand Fleda's conception of decent behaviour: " 'You can take it from my honour, you know,' he painfully brought out, 'that she quite loathes me.'

"Facing him, waving him away, she had taken another upward step; but he sprang to the side of the stairs and brought his hand, above the banister, down hard on her wrist. 'Do you mean to tell me that I must marry a woman I hate?'

"From her step she looked down into his raised face. 'Ah, you see it's not true that you're free!' She seemed almost to exult. 'It's not true, it's not true!'

"He only, at this, like a buffeting swimmer, gave a shake of his head and repeated his question: 'Do you mean to tell me I must marry such a woman?'

"Fleda gasped too; he held her fast. 'No. Anything's better than that.'

" 'Then in God's name what must I do ? '

" 'You must settle that with Mona. You mustn't break faith. Anything's better than that. You must at any rate be utterly sure. She must love you—how can she help it ? I wouldn't give you up ! ' said Fleda. She spoke in broken bits, panting out her words. ' The great thing is to keep faith. Where's a man if he doesn't ? If he doesn't he may be so cruel. So cruel, so cruel, so cruel ! ' Fleda repeated. ' I couldn't have a hand in that, you know : that's my position—that's mine. You offered her marriage. It's a tremendous thing for her.' Then looking at him another moment, ' I wouldn't give you up ! ' she said again. He still had hold of her arm ; she took in his blank dread. With a quick dip of her face she reached his hand with her lips, pressing them to the back of it with a force that doubled the force of her words. ' Never, never, never ! ' she cried ; and before he could succeed in seizing her she had turned and, flashing up the stairs, got away from him even faster than she had got away at Ricks."

Irony is invoked to carry the action to its next stage. Fleda receives a telegram from Mrs Gereth telling her to join her at once in a London hotel. Arriving there, the girl finds Mrs Gereth tired but cheerful. They will go abroad for a year to make a decent interval, and Owen will join them at his earliest convenience. Fleda is surprised at the definiteness of these proposals, for ten days had passed since her interview with Owen and she had

had no word from him. Mrs Gereth's positiveness
is based on a visit from Mrs Brigstock, who had
nformed her very definitely that Owen was infatuated with Fleda, and had begged her to intervene.
' ' Don't fail me now ! ' Fleda heard her say.

" It sounded so like a menace that, with a full
divination at last, the poor girl fell weakly into a
chair. ' What on earth have you done ? '

" Mrs Gereth stood there in all the glory of a
great stroke. ' I've settled you.' She filled the
room, to Fleda's scared vision, with the glare of her
magnificence. ' I've sent everything back.'

" ' Everything ? ' Fleda wailed.

" ' To the smallest snuff-box. The last load went
yesterday. The same people did it. Poor little
Ricks is empty.' Then, as if for a crowning splendour, to check all deprecation : ' They're yours, you
goose ! ' the wonderful woman concluded, holding up
her handsome head and rubbing her white hands.
But there were tears none the less in her deep eyes."

Mrs Gereth is angrily amazed that Fleda has
failed to take advantage of her opportunities, and
that she does not now even know where Owen is.
Telegrams are dispatched to discover his where-
abouts, but soon they learn that Mrs Gereth's
restitution of the spoils has placated Mona, and
that a near date is fixed for her marriage ! Mona
evidently is the one who has " let herself go."

The date of *The Spoils of Poynton* is 1896. James
had just emerged from his rather devastating
theatrical experiences, and there is every indication
that his new book was written with the greater
relish in virtue of the fact that he had only his own

conscience and not a crudely critical audience to please. He told his brother that in so far as technique was concerned—" the comparatively poor and meagre, the piteously simplified purposes of the English stage "—he had made it absolutely his own—" put it into my pocket " is his actual phrase. This was balm for the smart and the ache, but he was not eager to make a new application of his sovereign remedy. In his laboratory of fiction there were still undiscovered compounds, and they would not prove so dangerously explosive. Here he was content to devise new tests and combine new experiments. To W. D. Howells he had written in the previous year : " I mean to do far better work than ever I have done before. I have, potentially, improved immensely, and am bursting with ideas and subjects—though the act of composition is with me more and more slow, painful and difficult. I shall never again write a long novel ; but I hope to write six immortal short ones—and some tales of the same quality."

The long novels of course were to be written, but the formula that made them possible was first elaborated in *The Spoils of Poynton*, one of the six " immortal " short ones he proposed to write. Our examination of the longer stories written before this period will reveal Henry James seeking for a method of expression which should be not only congenial to his own genius, but adapted also to the exigencies of the novel. He did not solve his problem to his own satisfaction ; and then followed, after the publication of *The Tragic Muse* in 1889, a succession of years during which he confined himself to dramatic writing and to the composition of short stories. These latter are frequently fine in quality, but it is obvious that within their brief compass the problems incidental to length could not emerge. The *Spoils of Poynton* is, however, long enough to present all the difficulties of an extended composition, and for that reason, and because here James reached the kind of perfection he had long been striving for, the book occupies a position of special importance in the series of his works. Let us note the dates once more. In 1889 we have *The Tragic Muse*. Seven years follow of short stories and dramatic writing, which bring us to the year 1896 and *The Spoils of Poynton*. Four other half-length novels—*The Other House, What Maisie Knew, The Awkward Age* and *The Sacred Fount*—and various short stories represent his activity until 1901, and then in 1902 with *The Wings of the Dove* is ushered in another period of long novels, in which the famous " latest manner " is firmly established.

Perhaps a latest manner is too elusive a thing to analyse and almost too shadowy to apprehend. The enigmatic Hugh Vereker in that amusing parable of the literary life, *The Figure in the Carpet*, refused the eager questers after his secret any expository hint, and referred them to his works with the serene prevision that they would never discover it. " Give it up, give it up," was the echo of his advice. If people got from his books " the sense of something or other," that was as much as an intelligent writer was justified in expecting from an undiscerning public. James has happily been more communicative, and has given us outside the compass of the books themselves, in his letters and his prefaces, hints of his general intention. His first advice to us is precisely to discover this "author's intention," and to measure our approbation by its intrinsic importance and by the greater or less degree of competence with which it is fulfilled. A book must obviously be estimated on the basis of its form and content, and if there is a complete fusion of these two elements the author will be secure of his artistic result. Art is an affair of the conscience no less than of the mind. Effects are achieved at the cost of perpetual vigilance, and success is merely the evidence of infinite difficulties overcome.

When the young critic of *The Middle* asks Vereker for an illuminating hint, the author answers :

" ' My whole lucid effort gives him the clue—every page and line and letter. The thing's as concrete there as a bird in a cage, a bait on a hook, a piece of cheese in a mouse-trap. It's stuck into every volume as your foot is stuck into your shoe. It governs every line, it chooses every word, it dots every *i*, it places every comma.'

" I scratched my head. ' Is it something in the style or something in the thought ? An element of form or an element of feeling ? '

" He indulgently shook my hand again, and I felt my questions to be crude and my distinctions pitiful. ' Good-night, my dear boy—don't bother about it. After all, you do like a fellow.'

" ' And a little intelligence might spoil it ? ' I still detained him.

" He hesitated. ' Well, you've got a heart in your body. Is that an element of form or an element of feeling ? What I contend that nobody has ever mentioned in my work is the organ of life.'

" ' I see—it's some idea *about* life, some sort of philosophy. Unless it be,' I added with the eagerness of a thought perhaps still happier, ' some kind of game you're up to with your style, something you're after in the language.' "

Vereker's hint is broad and his advice sound. The formal element so fascinates us in James that we are tempted to explain his whole excellence in terms of style and composition. He carries to an unwonted pitch fastidiousness for the pregnant expression, and has more regard than all, save a few of his contemporaries, for the musical fall and resonance of his periods. A like fastidiousness governs his control of the larger compositional principles, and our critical vocabulary has not yet invented the terms which will explain his manifold devices for securing the perfect articulation of his theme. What we fail too often to perceive, or perceiving fail to emphasise, is that life and character are after all his paramount concern, and that though he may delight, as every artist should, in beauty for its own sake, yet his search for perfection is governed by the desire to give to life and character their fullest expression. Such a statement may appear to lose its efficacy if it is subjected to an immediate qualification, but I must hasten to add that James does not look upon life as an arena where gross and violent actions come into conflict. Civilisation has done its full work upon him, but if it has dashed his relish for the cruder forms of energy, it has not dulled but rather quickened his appreciation of the permanent elements in human character. We should be rash to conclude that he has lost his sense of values. Conduct is no longer estimated in the rough, but tested on a very finely graduated scale that registers the minutest fluctuations of the spiritual flame.

Defeat and victory are words whose meaning must be closely scanned if not reconstituted when applied to the fortunes of Fleda and Mona in our present story. Mona in a sense triumphs. She is represented as a maiden who plants a solid foot upon the firm foundation of facts. " The will that rides the crisis quite most triumphantly," James writes, " is that of the awful Mona Brigstock, who is *all* will, without the smallest leak of force into taste or tenderness or vision, into any sense of shades or relations or proportions." Hers is a success " the world's coarse thumb and finger " can measure—a triumph of the will James has called it, of the coarse energy that suffers no impairment from " taste or tenderness or vision." We see in the story no tangible evidences of Fleda's victory, nor has James proclaimed her as an example of the will triumphant. But unless we can follow him into the impalpable regions of our moral nature where the real values reside, and if we cannot realise that by " willing " her defeat she has gained her victory, we have not appreciated the significance of Vereker's complaint, and have failed in consequence to credit Henry James with anything beyond an artistic interest in the problem of human conduct.

The *Spoils* was promptly followed by *What Maisie Knew* (1897). The preliminary draft of this

story—such a candid, rambling, confidential conversation of the author with himself as is preserved
for us by chance for his two unfinished novels—
would have been singularly useful, for it would
have resolved many of the difficulties that a reader
coming fresh to this book encounters. Such a reader
might readily be pardoned for his failure to reconcile
himself to immoralities whose only justification
would have lain in their comic exaggeration, and
to accommodate himself to the author's evidently
serious intention of making a child the innocent
centre round whom these multiplied immoralities
revolve. These are considerations of which we may
be sure the author was fully aware, and our interest
would have been deeply engaged to discover how
in his preliminary draft he proposed to make provision against this obvious misinterpretation of his
purpose. Rightly considered, the book does not
fail of its desired effect, but we are at liberty to
regret that our appreciation is achieved only by
the conquest of our initial prejudice.

Maisie is the child of two morally damaged
parents who have secured a divorce at the moment
the story opens. Both parents claim custody of the
small girl, but the Court decrees that she shall remain with each for a period of six months. Neither
parent has any love for the child, and each receives
her when the time arrives, "not for any good they
could do her, but for the harm they could, with her
unconscious aid, do each other." In other words,
she is the innocent vessel into which are poured
alternate floods of vilification and slander. The
mother is the first to weary of the arrangement,

for Maisie has developed a faculty of silence tha
passes for stupidity, and Ida gains from her bu
scanty knowledge of the irregularities of Beal
Farrange's household. " The day was at hand
and she saw it, when she'd feel more delight i
hurling Maisie at him than in snatching her away
so much so that her conscience winced under th
acuteness of a candid friend who had remarke
that the real end of all their tugging would be tha
each parent would try to make the little girl
burden to the other."

When Maisie is eight and living at her mother's
Miss Overmore is installed as governess, and he
sprightliness and beauty make a deep impressio
on the child. They had met the handsome Beal
Farrange in the Park, and Maisie is not surprise
that her father appears to be no less influenced b
her governess's charm. When the father's si
months' turn arrives Miss Overmore feels that sh
cannot part with the child, and in spite of Ida'
stringent injunctions she, too, becomes a membe
of that queer household.

The next half year marks the ascendancy of Mr
Wix, whom Ida Farrange had engaged to save he
from the bother of Maisie. She is a worthy soul
with marked Dickensian oddities, in no wise prudish
but with a moral sense that seems robust by re
ference to the standards of easy virtue that prevai
in the Farrange households. The child forgets th
initial terror of her appearance in the warmth o
her motherly tenderness, and the parting from he
is a grief mitigated only by the excitement of he
papa's arrival, accompanied by Miss Overmore, in

brougham. This young lady has apparently never moved away from Mr Farrange's house, and Maisie's impulsive nature rejoices in her evident happiness. The extent to which she had advanced in the proprieties under Mrs Wix's instruction is revealed in the question—" Did papa like you just the same while I was gone ? " It will be observed that one of the delightful characteristics of Maisie is always to find her pleasure in other people's happiness.

The six months' term with her father is protracted much beyond its due limit, and Miss Overmore permits the child to suspect that her mother is not anxious for her return. " She has other people than poor little *you* to think about, and has gone abroad with them ; so you needn't be in the least afraid that she'll stickle this time for her rights." She tells the child, too, what a comfort it is to have her in the house : " I don't know what in the world, darling, your father and I should do without you, for you just make the difference, as I've told you, of keeping us perfectly proper." This of course makes Maisie very happy, but she still wonders whether if she returned to her mother she might not have her mother's " gentleman friend " for a tutor. It seems to be in her mind that this would keep them perfectly proper. Miss Overmore lapses from her usual correctness so far as almost to giggle while informing the child that the cases were very different, and that her mother's friend was much too young to make such an arrangement possible. This is an intimation to us that Miss Overmore knew already a good deal about him, but Maisie first hears of him definitely from Mrs Wix, who presently arrives to announce her mother's pending marriage with Sir Claude. Miss Overmore treats Mrs Wix with more than the haughtiness even of a rival governess, which is explained by the trump card that she eventually plays in announcing that she is *already* married to Mr Beale Farrange.

The situation, as we see, even at this point promises to take a good deal of working out, but James finds his satisfaction in still further multiplying the complications. The new Mrs Farrange is represented as very quickly neglected by her volatile husband, and as compensating herself just as quickly by a rapidly growing intimacy with the young Sir Claude, who, arriving one day to claim Maisie on her mother's behalf, promptly makes a conquest of the child's heart and that of her susceptible step-mother. " I've brought you and her together," the child delightedly cries.

To provide us with an ideal complexity of design all that is required now, and we have not long to wait, is a succession of new love affairs to maintain Lady Claude's interest in existence, and a similar succession to provide Mr Beale Farrange with a fitting revenge on his wife. Lady Claude (*i.e.* the first Mrs Beale Farrange) is provided in rapid sequence with Mr Perriam, Lord Eric, the Captain, and Mr Tischbein (I may have forgotten someone), and Mr Farrange has, after much experimentation, centred his affections upon Mrs Cuddon, the un-speakable Countess. He is of the two not more fastidious but perhaps less grasping.

This is a monstrous dose of iniquity for the reader to swallow, and seems like the travesty of burlesque. Yet James, while deriving some amusement out of his extravagance, has set a definitely serious purpose before him, and he has not been so pointedly and designedly moral in any other of his books. We are perhaps misled by the title, which falsely suggests a pruriency that has no lodgment in Maisie's mind. The real theme of the book is How Maisie developed a Moral Sense, and James is particularly anxious to give a true account of the way in which childish innocence might react in the midst of irregular and impure surroundings, and how childish *naïveté* may acquire a sense of the distinction between the right and the wrong of conduct while still retaining its serenity of outlook unimpaired.

The effect of an innocent and forthright mind upon people of devious intention was to be more systematically studied in *The Wings of the Dove* and *The Golden Bowl*. In our present book the father and mother are so committed to their course as not to be capable of deviation. Merely feeling the discomfort of Maisie's presence they exercise their blunt wits in fastening the child upon one another. Her stepmother, while not wholly insensible to her charm, uses the child only as a convenience and as a flimsy pretext of propriety, and is too completely under the sway of her infatuation for Sir Claude to open her mind to anything so dull as a moral influence. Mrs Wix being already the embodiment of every tradition of decent behaviour, there remains only Sir Claude to be impressed, and no parts of the book are more charming than the passages that exhibit Maisie's irresistible appeal to his better nature. His adhesion in the end to Mrs Beale, involving as it does the sacrifice of Maisie, looks like the weakness of excessive amiability, but I think we are intended to interpret as an act of strength his encouragement to Maisie to depart with Mrs Wix from the contaminating presence of two people whose association the child at last has begun to see in its true light. It is not probable that she will continue to boast that she has "brought them together," and one closes the book with the inevitable feeling that she will ultimately bring them apart, and that a more radiant Sir Claude, freed from all the agitations his weakness had engendered, will one day look in upon Mrs Wix and Maisie in some quiet English retreat, and remain.

I have suggested a clumsy alternative title for this story ; yet on reflection we can get on very well with the existing one, for it is after all what Maisie ultimately knew that permitted her to act, not as a child on impulsive instinct, but as a maturing mind on reasoned grounds. Mr Beach, in his excellent book, *The Method of Henry James*, inclines to treat Maisie's moral sense even to the end as rather a joke. But there is always more pathos than amusement in the child's estimates of conduct, and still more irony than pathos, and it would seem to have been consciously the author's opinion that childhood ends where morality begins. Maisie the child could never have reconciled herself to parting with Sir Claude whom she loves, but Maisie ceases to be a delightful creature of instinct, or in other words, her childhood dies, when she recognises that duty may sometimes compel a painful choice. It is James himself who furnishes us with the phrase " the death of her

childhood," and who tells us that then " her
situation will change and become another affair,
subject to other measurements and with a new
centre altogether."

The subject of the child in literature is a theme
at once fascinating in character and boundless in
extent. But it had no particular attraction for our
author, and few indeed are the convincing children
one encounters in his pages. Apart from Maisie
there are only four children whom I remember, and
each is presented to us as an abnormality. There is
first that obnoxious specimen of American boyhood,
Master Randolph C. Miller, and his successors are
the preternaturally precocious and prematurely
diseased Morgan Moreen of *The Pupil*, and Miles
and Flora, the perverted and haunted children of
The Turn of the Screw. Maisie also is obviously
not an ordinary child, and the environment that
her creator has designed for her is not conducive to
natural growth. That under such circumstances he
preserves her innocence and her charm is matter
for astonishment, but his triumph would have been
greater and more congenial to the reader had he
allowed her delightful nature to assert itself under
more normal conditions. The play instinct is curiously stifled in her. She has dolls, it is true, but
neither she nor the author knows quite what to do
with them. Sir Claude provides her and Mrs Wix
with complicated games that they cannot understand, but no one ever seems to have thought of
giving her another child to play with, and she is
perpetually moving about in a world not realised.
It may be said that her only childish playmate is

the little dead Matilda Wix, and when that topic of conversation is exhausted Mrs Wix has nothing to talk about with the child save the gross misdemeanours of her elders. It is indeed a matter for congratulation that Maisie at last developed a moral sense!

Other authors—and one imagines for example how George Eliot would have treated the subject—would have sought to enter more completely into the child's mind, and we should have had a much fuller registration of her varying moods. A few sentences of the preface inform us of the way in which James regarded his problem. He wishes to make Maisie the shining centre of his story, and everything that happens is to focus itself upon her attention. This is the accustomed method of his later time, but he is ordinarily careful to choose as his radiating centre a mind that is fully competent to gather and record impressions. Maisie's immaturity of course constitutes the difficulty of his present experiment, for he must reflect all the events in the mirror of her consciousness without subjecting her childish intelligence to an exaggerated strain. " Small children have many more perceptions than they have terms to translate them their vision is at any moment much richer, their apprehension even constantly stronger, than their prompt, their at all producible vocabulary . . . it is her relation, her activity of spirit, that determines all our own concern—we simply take advantage of these things better than she herself. Only, even though it is her interest that mainly makes matter interesting for us, we inevitably note this in figures hat are not yet at her command and that are nevertheless required whenever those aspects about her and those parts of her experience that she understands darken off into others that she rather tormentedly misses. All of which," James continues, " gave me a high firm logic to observe ; supplied the force for which the straightener of almost any angle is grateful while he labours, the sense of pulling at threads intrinsically worth it—strong enough and fine enough and entire enough."

To keep within prescribed bounds, to make a virtue of necessity, and to secure the maximum of intensity with the minimum of licence—these restraints did not constitute for James a self-denying ordinance, but were the law under which now and henceforth his genius could alone find its freedom. In the interests of fuller utterance he has in the case of Maisie permitted himself the luxury of some slight relaxation of rigour ; but he is exploring the limited consciousness of a child, and his amplifications are only the interpretation of what is already there. The pressure of weight he exercises is never excessive, and his footsteps leave no rude imprint upon the delicate pathways of her mind. But as we close the book we are in the same predicament as Mrs Wix, and ask ourselves what, after all, did Maisie really know.

In the Cage (1898) is the product of the early fertile years at Lamb House, and belongs therefore to the same happy creative period that engendered *The Spoils of Poynton, The Awkward Age* and *What Maisie Knew.*

A young girl in the postal and telegraph " cage "

at Cocker's, a small grocer's shop in Mayfair, employs her wits and imagination in piecing together the adventures of the idle rich as she gleans there from the multitudinous but cryptic messages they dispatch over the wires. Cocker's not being a receiving station, she sees only one side of the story. Her interest is more particularly kindled by an apparent intrigue in which a certain Captain Everard and Lady Cissy are involved. Captain Everard's distinguished appearance and manner fascinate the girl to the point that she cannot reconcile herself to the unromantic proposals of Mr Mudge to settle down with him in his grocer-shop at Chalk Farm. Her infatuation compels her to haunt the street where Everard lives, and one evening, wandering homewards by this circuitous route, she encounters him, and her cup of bliss is full when he greets her affectionately and leads her into the Park. James stops short of the ordinary amorous adventure, although he allows us to feel that the air is charged. Everard resists the temptation to compromise her, and she walks away from the bench on which he remains more than ever determined to devote herself to him in the complicated conduct of his affairs. She feels herself now completely initiated, and can afford to despise the rather second-hand information concerning the intimacies of the Mayfair world which her friend, Mrs Jordan, has gleaned in the course of her professional attentions to the floral accessories of pompous dinner-tables.

One day Everard comes to the office and asks in agitation for an old telegram that is not on the files. She holds him in suspense for a time, realising her advantage, and then gives him the important contents from memory. But for all her cleverness she has failed to piece together the whole story of Everard's and Lady Cissy's relations, and in her chagrin at learning the full details from Mrs Jordan, who had them from so vulgar a source as Lady Cissy Bradeen's new butler, she decides that there is nothing better left for her to do than to settle down as Mrs Mudge of Chalk Farm.

I must find space here for the author's account of how the idea of this superb little story was generated : " The postal-telegraph office in general, and, above all, the small local office of one's immediate neighbourhood, haunt of one's needs and one's duties, of one's labours and one's patiences, almost of one's rewards and one's disappointments, one's joys and one's sorrows, had ever had, to my sense, so much of London to give out, so much of its huge perpetual story to tell, that any momentary wait there seemed to take place in a strong social draught, the stiffest possible breeze of the human comedy. One had of course in these connections one's especial resort, the office nearest one's door, where one had come to enjoy in a manner the fruits of frequentation and the amenities of intercourse. So had grown up, for speculation—prone as one's mind had ever been to that form of waste—the question of what it might ' mean,' wherever the admirable service was installed, for confined and cramped and yet considerably tutored young officials of either sex to be made so free, intellectually, of a range of experience otherwise quite closed to them. This wonderment, once the spark was kindled, became an amusement, or an obsession, like another; though falling indeed, at the best, no doubt, but into that deepest abyss of all the wonderments that break out for the students of great cities. From the moment that he *is* a student, this most beset of critics, his danger is inevitably of imputing to too many others, right and left, the critical impulse and the acuter vision—so very long may it take him to learn that the mass of mankind are banded, probably by the sanest of instincts, to defend themselves to the death against any such vitiation of their simplicity."

James appears to have provided for everything in his story but the name of his heroine. It seems to scant her deeply cherished dignity to call her the cage-girl, and yet we have no alternatives available but this and the meagrely designating feminine pronoun. Whatever we call her she is made for our delight. The Cockney shading off into the genteel is what she would have remained to the end had Wells or Dickens fashioned her. James has given her the attributes of her station not so extravagantly but quite as convincingly as these masters of the comic vulgar would have done, but he has made her peculiarly his own by the gift with which he has endowed her of darting her mind's rays abroad. It is imagination doubtless of no highly poetic order, and sometimes, for the ironic amusement that her failure involves, her divination strikes wide of the mark; yet her effort to live in two worlds—the dazzling empyrean of the Olympians and the drab reality of Mr Mudge, Mr Buckton, and the counter clerk—bespeaks her a living mind and a genuine Jamesian subject.

Our author has often told us that one of the greatest pleasures a writer can experience is to triumph over difficulties. If that is true, his pleasure and his triumph in *The Awkward Age* (1899) are alike complete, for he would here appear to have achieved the physical impossibility of making something, and even a great deal of something, out of nothing, and to have done this, moreover, with the most facile ease in spite of the self-imposed rigours of method to which he subjected himself. Mr Wells has spoken to us with intentional playfulness rather than malice of the elephant picking up peas with a satisfied flourish of his trunk, and Mr Desmond MacCarthy has reported the great man's admission that art would lack its motive power if grace were not accorded to the artist to make mountains out of molehills. This was perhaps only an amiable conversational way of insisting upon the intensity of the creative process which constantly elaborates the significance of hidden values. James himself certainly did not on this occasion realise the expansive capacity of his simple-seeming subject until he tried his hand at it. He wanted to give a brief and amusing account of a dilemma that often confronts the smart London hostess : what, namely, will become of the conversational ease of her free-ranging and lively circle when her daughter's skirts lengthen and she takes her place beside the teapot ? This intention soon became complicated with another contemporary problem, and he found himself launched upon a rather elaborate study of the change of manners that had converted the mid-Victorian child into the modern girl—now again how antiquated—of 1890. His enlarged scheme therefore demanded a series of representative characters and the necessary complication of incident to exhibit their idiosyncrasies, with the result that the projected sketch insisted upon becoming a novel. It is right to observe, however, that this mid-way change of design has in no way impaired the quite exquisite proportions of the story we are considering, which shows no signs of the misplaced middles and huddled extremities that James complains of in some of his pieces where he had failed to take the precise measure of his original intention. The admirer of James will be under no compulsion, therefore, to defend the work as a rare product of art. On that ground its detractors merely reveal their incompetence. But such an admirer might find the elephant and pea charge a difficult one to answer, and this book affords us as good an opportunity as any other for a consideration of the question of our author's alleged triviality.

It is not the first time that a great writer has been submitted to this test, but I am not aware that Jane Austen's reputation, for example, has been sensibly diminished by Charlotte Brontë's strictures, nor more recently by the late Mrs Meynell's. That observing young lady, Miss Austen, did not seem to be aware that great European issues were pending as she wrote; the names of Nelson, Napoleon and Wellington do not grace her pages; and it would almost seem that for her placid world the French Revolution had never occurred. It has been her

sufficient justification with posterity that she had
taken the most accurate measure at once of her
capacity and her limitations, and that within the
latter she had the good sense to include the
preacher's and the prophet's rôle. The same considerations hold true, but on a vastly extended
scale, for Henry James. The one writer had competent knowledge of English country life, the other's
scope was more amply bounded by the circumference of the civilised world, but both were alike
impatient of ultimate problems, or considered, it
might be safer to say, that the ultimate problem
for the writer of fiction is to make a true and entertaining report of a group of persons who, for the
purposes of the story, are supposed to be interested
in the same theme and in one another. Even for
the reader who makes scientific demands upon the
novel such a representation will not be without
its value, for, compared with the writer of fiction,
the professional sociologist or psychologist or other
cacophonous person has a vastly inferior opportunity of laying bare the springs of human action.
We may conclude, therefore, with Euclidean assurance, that if James performed this function well,
the importance of his subject-matter is sufficiently
guaranteed.

If the charge of triviality can thus confidently be
dismissed, it is more difficult to justify the unrelaxed
tightness of his technique, which is nowhere better
exemplified than in *The Awkward Age*. Of course
life's fluidity must be regulated by the artist and
its multitudinous variety subjected to control, but
Henry James refuses to satisfy our vagrant mind in

its craving for relief, and compels the same concentration in the reader that his characters and their creator display. His bow is never unbent, his muscles are always tense, and his eye for ever straining at the centre of a shining mark. His fixed belief being that discursiveness is the supreme vice of English fiction, he determined to draw a firm circle round his theme and never to wander beyond the limits of its circumference. Variety was to be obtained by an interchange of the scenic or dramatic and the pictorial method, and by recourse to the author's valued privilege of " going behind " his characters—in other words, permitting us to participate in the working of their minds. In *The Awkward Age* he rejects these legitimate expedients and multiplies his difficulties for the sheer amusement of the experiment. He does not bind his eyes, but he moves forward with hands and feet securely shackled. The descriptive element he reduces to the barest minimum, and forgoing every advantage that may be derived from the exposition of his characters' motives, even by the severe method of self-revelation that he imposed upon himself in other books, he depends for his effects wholly upon the interplay of dialogue. We shall see later how low an estimate he set on the current employment of this fictional resource, but he seems to have determined in this book, as later, in *The Other House*, to make a supreme test of its functional value. His own intervention is limited, therefore, to a few brief summaries of appearance and manner, designed to evoke in our mind a concrete image of his people, and he modestly occupies the interspaces of the dialogue for the purpose of linking speech with speech, without such recourse as drama permits to the marginal naming of persons. These transitional fragments are, therefore, a kind of stage direction, with indications by the author and actor-manager of the gestures and the " business " of his mimic world. James, in his later books, gives the greatest care to these small particulars. To a conscience growing ever more severe no item was negligible, and this explains his avoidance here of the monotony of stereotyped forms. Occasionally " Mrs Brook said," or " Mitchy replied," but more ordinarily she " plaintively wondered " or " wonderfully mur- mured," or " her pale interest deepened," while Mitchy " brightly thought " or " visibly wondered " or " stared with his good goggle eyes " or " his great goggle attentively fixed him" or " he turned upon his hostess his sociable glare."

Let these mild Alexandrianisms pass for what they are worth. The interest lies in the care shown to convert the commonplace into the characteristic. Though I would not value this novel so highly as I do for its technical interest alone (if the thing done, that is to say, were not as important as the way of doing it); yet it is the dexterity of execution after all that gives this particular book its high importance. And it is a dexterity also that dazzled even the author, to the extent that he failed to per- ceive how he had deviated from his original plan. James wished to take account " in a circle of free talk, of a new and *innocent, a wholly unacclimatised presence*," and to exhibit the discomfort of the strained accommodations to which such a circle must subject itself. That is a definite and, though slight, a workable theme. But his book lengthened on his hands not only by reason of complications already referred to, but also because he invented an interesting love-relation between Nanda and Vanderbank, to the happy consummation of which there are two impediments—the subtle manœuvring of Mrs "Brook" to keep Van to herself, but more particularly Vanderbank's incapacity to reconcile himself to the degree of initiation to which Nanda— type of the modern maiden—had attained. Nanda throughout preserves her charm, and remains to the end personally untarnished by her wisdom, but the whole drift of the book teaches us that she is emphatically not the "innocent and wholly unacclimatised presence" she was intended to be.

The remaining characters are admirably consistent, but James, who lavished his best work on Nanda, found her a rather troublesome child to deal with. She is never for a moment untrue to her type, but coming to life as vigorously as she does she compels her creator to take her on her own terms. It is Aggie, therefore, who is compelled to play the part of *ingénue*. Her introduction provides a situation that Molière had found rich in comic suggestion, with the difference perhaps that the innocence of Molière's maiden is quite supposititious, whereas Aggie's too excessive emancipation supervenes upon a truly cloistral stage. In each case the husband is victimised, but James could naturally see no fun in the martyrdom of the sympathetic Mitchy, and gives him accordingly enough worldly philosophy to accommodate himself to the matri-

monial failure he had foreseen when he accepted
Aggie for his love of Nanda.

It is clear from the first where Nanda's affections
are engaged, but the author's thesis is rather strained
in the case of Vanderbank. We are inclined to set
him down as an amiable philanderer, but James
works hard to account for his supineness on other
grounds. He implies in him enough affection to
bring him repeatedly to the brink of a proposal,
but checks him on each occasion by imputing to
him a fastidiousness which proceeds, the reader
suspects, rather from the lukewarmness of his
passion than from the native fineness of his mind.
Mr Longdon with characteristic delicacy had informed him that Nanda would receive a handsome
dowry when she married him. There is no grossness in the bribe, but nevertheless it works as an
impediment rather than as an aid. The girl, whom
nothing escapes, makes a shrewd guess at the truth,
and the knowledge introduces an element of self-
consciousness into her encounters with Vanderbank,
who is the only person with whom Nanda is ever ill
at ease. Furthermore, Mrs Brookenham has been
informed by Vanderbank of the proposal, and this
shrewd woman's calculating faculty at once begins
to work on the new situation. Her main concern is
to keep her drawing-room alive, and to preserve
Vanderbank as its most valued ornament ; but her
thriftiness prompts her also to make capital out of
old Mr Longdon's infatuation for her daughter. She
tries, naturally, to attain both ends. The best thing
of course would be for Nanda to marry Mitchy's
millions, but the Duchess, Nanda aiding, defeats her

there. When, as soon happens, Mrs Brook has reason to feel that the Longdon money is safe, even without the original marriage condition, she concentrates her efforts upon preserving Vanderbank for herself. She had begun early by playing on his quality of pride. In Mitchy's presence she takes it for granted that the idea of a bribe is so distasteful to Vanderbank that he will never come to the point. The passing months seem to justify her expectation, for Nanda, constantly in the country with her old friend, seems to have reconciled herself with cheerful philosophy to her fate. If she has been infected by the London atmosphere she is still apparently susceptible of regeneration in a purer air. But Mrs Brook cannot quench a smouldering irritation at the turn which events have taken, and this smothered anger leaps into a dangerous flame one evening in Tishy Grendon's house, when all her set, including Nanda and Mr Longdon, are present. It is rather a puzzling scene, and if we were only certain of what precisely Mrs Brook hopes to gain by it, it would be more effective. She has felt her social ascendancy weakening, and her own valued circle in process of disruption ; but why she should seek thus publicly to complete the demolition is beyond anybody's wit to understand. Vanderbank is puzzled with the rest. Months later Mrs Brook bemoans to him the fact that they had effectively fallen to pieces.

" ' We shall never grow together again. The smash was too great.'

" Vanderbank for a little said nothing ; then at last : ' You ought to know how great ! '

"Whatever had happened, her lovely look here survived it. ' I ? '

" ' The smash,' he replied, ' was indeed as complete, I think, as your intention. Each of the " pieces " testifies to your success. Five minutes did it. . . . It was a wonderful performance. You pulled us down—just closing with each of the great columns in its turn—as Samson pulled down the temple. I was at the time more or less bruised and buried, and didn't in the agitation and confusion fully understand what had happened. But I understand now.' "

The scene in question being so apparently critical, we must regret its enigmatic character. Why does Mrs Brook insist so peremptorily on Nanda's return from the country, and why in the sacred name of motherhood does she develop the incident of the book to expose before a mixed company her daughter's unabashed familiarity with indecent literature ? The book was a free-and-easy French one that Vanderbank had lent to Mrs Brook, and that Nanda had picked up and taken to Tishy Grendon's house, where she was then staying. Tishy is a young married friend of Nanda's, and frankness being so emphatically of the essence of this society it is obvious to all, and in an extreme degree to the fastidious Vanderbank, how thorough must be Nanda's knowledge of the complex relationships that constitute the main topic of conversation of the inner set. Mrs Brook, indeed, has often let Van know that she gets her latest information from her daughter, but on this occasion she surpasses herself, and elicits from Nanda the admission that she had

read this appalling book for the purpose of knowing
whether she could pass it on to Tishy. This is not
the sort of thing a mother usually does, and the
motive—to confirm the never too steadfast Vanderbank in his irresolution—is in like degree un-
motherly. Unfortunately for her she overreached
herself on this occasion. The smash, as Van admitted, was too great, and the first result is his own
defection from Mrs Brook's now fast-waning circle.
Nanda's last efforts are expended in repairing the
damage. There is no apparent desire on her part to
rehabilitate herself, for while she is sufficiently conscious that she has been breathing an infected air,
she knows also that she is competent to withstand
the poison. She is secure now in her new-found
happiness with Mr Longdon, but her mother is
adrift, and she is the weak vessel that must be towed
to harbour. There is a quaint blending of pathos
and irony in Nanda's attempts at a rescue, and her
interviews with Mitchy and Vanderbank, designed
to that end, recall other situations in James in which
he deals, as in *The Chaperon*, with the same predicament of a daughter mothering a mother. One
must not press the resemblance of Maisie's queer
history too far, for in the heroine of *What Maisie
Knew* we are given the spectacle of naïve innocence
serenely unconscious of its disreputable surroundings, whereas in the present case the surroundings
are as evil as you please, but not disreputable,
and Nanda's innocence can scarcely be described as
naïve.

To this point I have been able to speak with
confidence of the effects which our author desired

to produce, but where the ethical emphasis of the book is designed to fall demands a closer scrutiny. James was never enslaved by the Flaubertian heresy of pure disinterestedness, and he sought always to combine the dispassionate with the sympathetic attitude. He quotes approvingly Taine's phrase that "Balzac loved his Valérie," which means of course that an author should learn to value his villains; and his own constant aim was to allow the faultiest among his characters the fullest liberty of self-expression. If they hang themselves with their own rope they are at least their own executioners, and James never puts on the black cap of the condemning judge. In Taine's sense it is obvious enough that James "loved his Mrs Brook" in direct proportion to her power to live in his story.

From his letters we learn that he believed her to be his greatest triumph in characterisation. In this narrowly critical way he would have loved Nanda more only in so far as she achieved a greater intensity of life. But of course he loved her a great deal better on purely human grounds, and he created the index figure of Mr Longdon in order to convey this impression to the reader. The mid-century French dramatists had utilised their *raisonneurs*, and even Molière had employed his Philinte to convey the safe and presumably the author's opinion on men and things. Mr Longdon is James's substitute for the *raisonneur*, but this dear little friendly man, who never argues or expostulates, seems hardly to belong to that logical and formal family. He is, upon a reduced scale, the *alter ego* of his creator, and representing him not in opinions only, he is permitted even to inhabit the enlarged replica of his own Lamb House in Rye. The Longdon view is therefore with minor modifications the Jamesian view. Our author is naturally a much more alert man of the world, less sensitive, therefore, to the tittle-tattle and scandal of the modern drawing-room, and capable on occasion of contributing his own magnificent quota of gossip to the general stock ; yet one is compelled to feel that this apparent acquiescence in the prevailing tone of society only serves to mask his conviction of the actual decay of modern manners. He would have enjoyed much more than Mr Longdon a rattling hour of conversation with Mrs Brookenham, and an interview with the Duchess would not have inspired him with the same terror, but his estimate of these two characters would have revealed a notable correspondence. He would have shared, too, Mr Longdon's affection for Nanda, dear uncorrupted child of a corrupt age, and that is why we too are permitted to find our way at last into the serenity and purity of her essential nature.

James does not often in his letters indulge in minute criticism of his own books. There is fortunately, however, a letter to Miss Henrietta Reubell which contains such valuable references to *The Awkward Age* that I avail myself of it to supplement my own insufficient analysis of the story :

" . . . Your bewilderment over *The Awkward Age* doesn't on the whole surprise me—for that ingenious volume appears to have excited little *but* bewilderment—except indeed, *here*, thick-witted denunciation. A work of art that one has to *explain* fails in so far, I suppose, of its mission. I suppose I

must at any rate mention that I had in view a
certain special social (highly ' modern ' and actual)
London group and type and tone, which seemed to
me to se prêter à merveille to an ironic—lightly and
simply ironic !—treatment, and that clever people
at least would know who, in general, and what, one
meant. But here, at least, it appears there are
very few clever people ! One must point with finger-
posts—one must label with pancartes—one must
explain with conférences ! The *form*, doubtless, of
my picture is against it—a form all dramatic and
scenic—of presented episodes, architecturally combined and each making a piece of the building ;
with no going behind, no *telling about* the figures
save by their own appearance and action and with
explanations reduced to the explanation of everything by all the other things *in* the picture. Mais il
paraît qu'il ne faut pas faire comme ça : personne n'y
comprend rien : j'en suis pour mes frais—qui avaient
été considérables, très considérables ! Yet I seem to
make out you were interested—and that consoles
me. I think Mrs Brook the best thing I've ever
done—and Nanda also much *done*. Voilà ! Mitchy
marries Aggie by a calculation—in consequence of a
state of mind—delicate and deep, but that I meant
to show on his part as highly conceivable. It's
absolute to him that N. will never have him—and
she *appeals* to him for another girl, whom she sees
him as ' saving ' (from things—realities she sees).
If he does it (and she shows how she values him by
wanting it) it is still a way of getting and keeping
near her—of making for *her*, to him, a tie of gratitude. She becomes, as it were, to him, responsible

for his happiness—they can't (*especially if the marriage goes ill*) *not* be—given the girl that Nanda is—more, rather than less, together. And the finale of the picture *justifies* him : it leaves Nanda, precisely, with his case on her hands. Far-fetched ? Well, I dare say : but so are diamonds and pearls and the beautiful Reubell turquoises ! So I scribble to you, to be sociable, by my loud-ticking clock, in this sleeping little town, at my usual more than midnight hour."

The Sacred Fount of the year 1900 is a monstrously overgrown short story upon which the author wasted much excellent writing. My own opinion of its relative inferiority is confirmed by the fact that James excluded it from his supervised edition.

It is a book in which he has been defeated by his own cleverness, and where his determination to do full justice to the germinal idea has resulted in a vicious over-treatment of his theme. He proposed to explore the mystical sources of character, and to examine more particularly the subtle changes to which personality is subject. We feel in ourselves perpetually the ebb and flow of power, and we observe in others the same fluctuations in force. We are to some extent creatures of place and circumstance, occasions develop or depress our energies, and with no two persons are we ever quite the same. To illustrate this range of compass in the individual might have been a difficult but a legitimate task. But James has far transcended the limits of realistic observation, and has converted his material into a fantastic vampire theme.

The nameless observer and narrator is first en-

countered on the Paddington platform, where he is
about to entrain for a week-end visit to the also
nameless proprietors of the matchless Newmarch.
There are numerous other guests, and our friend
occupies a carriage with Mrs Brissenden, whom he
finds astonishingly well preserved for her years, and
with Gilbert Long, whom he had known as a man
of very limited intelligence and surly manners, but
who shines now in the altered light of affability
and brilliance. Arrived at Newmarch, the sight of
the prematurely aged and withered Guy Brissenden
gives him the hint that the wife's strength and
youth and beauty bear some inscrutable relation to
her husband's diminished state. If, however, he
may ultimately hope to succeed with his application
of this theory his success will leave Gilbert Long's
brilliance still unexplained. For coherence sake
there must be some woman who has been similarly
drained of her vitality on his behalf. Our friend is
so obsessed with his morbid imaginings that he
makes himself rather a nuisance to his fellow-
guests during this weird week-end. He wastes no
time in prosecuting his investigations. His first
colloquy had been already at Paddington with Mrs
" Briss," who agreed with him that Gilbert Long
had become another person, and who hazarded the
theory that it was Lady John who had wrought
the change.

" . . . ' Well, you may be right,' I laughed,
' though you speak as if it were cod-liver oil. Does
she administer it, as a daily dose, by the spoonful ?
or only as a drop at a time ? Does he take it in his
food ? Is he supposed to know ? The difficulty for

me is simply that if I've seen the handsome grow ugly and the ugly handsome, the fat grow thin and the thin fat, the short grow long and the long short ; if I've even, likewise, seen the clever, as I've too fondly, at least, supposed them, grow stupid : so have I *not* seen—no, not once in all my days— the stupid grow clever.'

" It was a question, none the less, on which she could perfectly stand up. ' All I can say is then that you'll have, the next day or two, an interesting new experience.'

" ' It *will* be interesting,' I declared while I thought —' and all the more if I make out for myself that Lady John *is* the agent.'

" ' You'll make it out if you talk to her—that is, I mean, if you make *her* talk. You'll see how she *can.*'

" ' She keeps her wit then,' I asked, ' in spite of all she pumps into others ? ' "

Lady John is duly tested, but she is obviously not the Sacred Fount whence Gilbert Long has derived his power. She is still in full command of her resources, and has evidently yielded nothing of her hard and unintelligent smartness. Here the ordinary man would have broken off for a round of golf, but James never permits his victims such easy alternatives. He keeps them with their noses to the scent until they have run the idea to earth. Our analyst is momentarily off the trail, but he casts resolutely about, sniffing the air for renewal, and presently is off full cry again, his quarry at last in sight.

It is only the pathetic figure of May Server, and

our inquisitive friend has not even the full merit of
her discovery. The painter Ford Obert had com-
mented on the tragic way in which her beauty had
outlived her wit. A few years before, when he had
painted her, she had been a stimulating subject,
but now she seems nervously aware of her own
lapsed powers. She is literally all over the place,
" pouncing " on one man after the other in turn,
and masking her insufficiency with her eternal
witless smile. It is only with the similarly smitten
" Briss " that she can enjoy a continuity of
speechless intercourse.

Mrs Brissenden in a second colloquy with our
observer is informed that Lady John will not fit
in with his theory. She then points triumphantly
to Mrs Server as having all the marks and signs,
but the other does not even yet consent to be convinced. Is he momentarily bewildered because of
the bedazzlement of May Server's beauty? Does
he think that his theory demands a diminution of
her physical charms no less than of her intelligence?
Or is he perhaps falling under the influence of a
certain pathetic attraction she exercises on him,
and is eager to shelter her from the imputation of
a former dangerous intimacy with Long? With
somewhat tedious subtlety, and frequently to our
confusion, these teasing problems are pursued in
the ensuing chapters, and the book winds up with
the ineffective climax of a midnight colloquy
with Mrs Brissenden in the deserted drawing-room,
where they fence at cross-purposes and come to
no effective result. We enter a maze at the book's
beginning and are still in a labyrinth at its close.

HENRY JAMES : MAN AND AUTHOR

We should have been more satisfied if James had treated his fantastic theme on a purely supernatural basis, but he thought, mistakenly as the result proves, that he might achieve a more significant effect by organising a highly conventional environment for the abnormal conditions that he was investigating. This is one, and a sufficient, explanation of the book's failure. If we must supply another explanation it lies in its grotesque exaggeration of the central idea. People are influenced by their personal contacts and exert an influence in return. But do such ravaged specimens of the psychical process exist, and are they conceivably to be found in contact with their flourishing counterparts at a week-end gathering in a sumptuous country house ? To think so, is to concede too much to the principle of artistic selection.

The Two Faces is also of the year 1900. Lord Gwyther had been paying marked attention to the beautiful Mrs Grantham, and now returns to London to request that she shall be kind to his young wife, who is nervous at the prospect of her first introduction to English society. The opportunity comes shortly at a country house. Mrs Grantham, looking radiant, makes her appearance when large numbers of the guests are already at tea on the terrace. Lady Gwyther presently follows. The subtle system of revenge had been to betray the innocent young Continental bride into the hands of a dressmaker, with instructions to load her down with vulgar ornaments. First impressions in the London world are difficult to live down.

In the same year appeared *Paste*, which avowedly

148

owes its origin to Maupassant's *La Parure*. There the wife of a subordinate civil servant borrows a string of pearls from a richer friend. Returned from the entertainment she discovers that the pearls are lost. She returns a similar necklace of such value that its purchase impoverishes them for years. After a lifetime of parsimonious toil it is revealed to them by their astonished friend that the original necklace was not genuine.

James ingeniously manipulates the conditions, but he does not, in the process, achieve the same effect of tragic irony. A girl is rather contemptuously given as a memento a lot of apparently worthless trinkets by her cousin, whose stepmother has just died. Among them are some pearls, which he refuses to believe to be anything better than paste, for had the magnificent string been genuine it would have compromised his mother's reputation. She had been a struggling actress when his clerical father had married her. The point is, of course, that they are real, and James works out his further complications on that basis.

James does not often care to confine himself to the extreme brevity of *The Story in It* (1901), a brilliant trifle which gives us perhaps no story after all, but a lively dramatic discussion on the nature of romance between Mrs Blessingbourne and Colonel Voyt, the latter's very special friend, Mrs Dyott, occasionally interjecting a word. The Colonel's contribution, most winningly conveyed, is that romance always implies a developed relation, and that a developed relation cannot consort with innocence. Maude Blessingbourne makes her point stoutly that a book should be written, and she would like to write it, in which a woman's innocence might be preserved precisely because her romance consisted in a suppressed relation. It is conveyed to us at the close that her unavowed love for Colonel Voyt is the shy flower of just such an innocent romance.

It is difficult to credit the fact that *The Birthplace* (1903) went knocking in vain at editors' doors. It is a more entertaining piece, in the lighter sense, than James usually presents to his readers, and its extravagance is a picture of conditions conceivably real.

Through the medium of the influential Mr Grant-Jackson, Morris Gedge and his wife are appointed custodians of the presumptive birthplace of England's greatest poet. They had been poorly established in a northern village, where Gedge had been librarian. They are put through their initiation by their glib predecessor, but Gedge's incurable honesty impairs the fluency befitting his office. He finds much relief in the visit of a young couple from New York, Mr and Mrs Hayes, and to them with utter frankness he expresses the doubts that beset him, and his deep repugnance for the credulous ignorance of the multitudes whom he is paid to dupe. His wife lives in constant fear that his sceptical and even scornful attitude will procure their dismissal. Indeed, Mr Grant-Jackson comes down to administer in person a rebuke from the Board which he would be well advised to regard in the light of a warning.

Gedge sees the humour of the situation, but also

appreciates its dangers. He changes his method, and is now as profuse in comment and positive assertion as he had before been reticent. The Hayes of New York have heard the reverberation of his fame in America, and visiting him again receive the full impact of his eloquence. His wife now fears that his exaggerations will wreck them, and thus interprets a second visit from Grant-Jackson. The latter has come, however, bearing the congratulations of the Board, and announcing their appreciation of his zeal by a considerable increase in his stipend !

The qualities of our author's genius are nowhere more convincingly in evidence than in *The Beast in the Jungle* (1903). The harmonious fusion of all the elements of his theme, the sonorous march of his periods, the subtlety, the tenderness, the futility —all these combine to produce an effect of which James alone possessed the secret. The confluence of meaning and music is such as to compel us at first into a mood of complete surrender. We seem to be listening to the chanting of a full-voiced choir, and we make no effort to discover reasons for our submission to the lulling harmonies that fill our ears.

When the effort of attention is finally roused we shall not fail to discover beyond the emotional an intellectual basis also for our appreciation. James has an infallible instinct that leads him by a safe pathway through the treacheries of his material, and it is a clear gain for the reader if he can but follow in his footsteps and occupy the same firm ground. We must admit that here, as always, James finds abundant interest in working out the

problem of the special case, the man whose life is
haunted by the secret fear that some horrible fate
is destined to overtake him, leaping upon him like
a beast from the jungle. Yet the beauty of the
present theme did not lie for James in the direct
presentation of the morbid consciousness of John
Marcher, but in the *indirect* yet vivid revelation of
May Bartram's personality. When the bereft man
realises all too late that the Beast has made its
fatal leap, it is to the woman who lies beneath the
dumb, cold slab that our sympathy goes out.

The Bench of Desolation is the concluding narrative in the same volume (*The Finer Grain*). The
theme of a James story being not an affair of
multiplied incidents, but of the mind's play about
them, we can afford to be brief in our presentation
of the items that make up the colourless existence
of Herbert Dodd. He is a seller of prints and old
books in a small south-coast town, and we first
encounter him in a bitter and dispirited mood under
the threat of a breach of promise action. He had
admired Kate Cookham for her alert interest in
his intellectual but unprofitable trade; but, aware
of an inexplicable change in her manner towards
him, he seeks to withdraw from an engagement
which had been so markedly of her contriving.
She threatens reprisals in a suit, and to escape the
indignity of an action he compromises for the sum
of four hundred pounds. By the time that two
hundred and seventy of this amount is paid, he is
married and bankrupt. His two children have died,
and presently his wife dies too, with the eternal
complaint on her lips that he should have made

himself sure that the woman had any just claim
against him.

For years he had mechanically dragged his load
of cares to a seaward-looking bench—his bench
of desolation—at the extremest limit of the Marine
Terrace. This bench has almost become conse-
crated to his use, but one day he finds it occupied
by a distinguished-looking person, whose identity
gradually dawns upon him. This encounter with
the woman who had wrecked his life is embarrassing
at first, but Kate Cookham shows so exquisite a
tact that the following Sunday afternoon finds
him drinking tea with her in the fashionable hotel
of the place. She had taken his money because she
recognised her own greater competence to use it to
advantage, and she now brings it back to him with
fivefold interest. If her intentions had been charitable she had grimly left out of her calculations the
stretch of years he had so limpingly traversed.
The thought of this overcomes the man and he precipitately leaves. The following Sunday she again
occupies his bench, and this time the explanations
are forthcoming. She had never ceased to love him,
but had thought that he was transferring his affections to a prettier face, just as he had falsely imputed
a like dereliction to her. Their mutual tenderness
seeks now, like an effacing wave, to obliterate the
past.

The most recent collected edition of James's
works reserves five volumes for short stories that
were excluded from the New York edition, which
the author personally supervised. Three of the
volumes contain chiefly early stories which were

judged too immature for preservation. Most of these have been referred to in our discussion of the American group. Another consists of work of high value that was written too late for inclusion, but which many of us have read in *The Finer Grain.* Still another volume contains stories which, though written in his prime, he saw reason to reject under the special conditions imposed upon him. The stories in question are *Lord Beaupré, The Visits, The Wheel of Time,* and *Collaboration* (which appeared in 1893), *Glasses* (1896), *The Great Condition, The Given Case, John Delavoy, The Third Person* (1900), and *The Tone of Time* (1903). Six of the group therefore fall within the period of his greatest success in this cherished form of expression; the remainder predate *The Spoils of Poynton,* where the matured theories of his art were first systematically applied. To these rejected stories of his maturity we must add *Maud Evelyn, The Special Type* and *The Papers.*

If one were to set up a trial theory in advance as to the motive grounds of rejection it would rest in part on his recognition of the supreme need in all the briefer forms of narration of rigorous compression. A jealous and watchful economy must everywhere prevail—in description, in dialogue, in reflection—and suggestion must frequently do service for full-flowered statement. One thinks of the image that James has supplied us with of an exquisitely chased vessel filled to the brim, and from which not one drop of its precious liquid must be spilled. A situation that develops in length from incident to incident is prolific of looseness and can never achieve the firm rotundity of one that expands by its own informing energy to the limits of its circumference. *Lord Beaupré* is eminently easy to read, and its sparkling contents may be appreciated without injury to an artistic conscience that is not vulnerable to slight affronts; what it lacks, however, is precisely what James most prized—firmness of texture and the irresistible lateral pressure from the centre outwards to the marginal limits of the theme. Beaupré, having recently and unexpectedly come in for his title and its large accessories, is much pestered by designing mothers and aspiring daughters. He had playfully at a former time suggested to his good friend **Mary Gosselin** that a bogus engagement would be a useful aid in such an imagined contingency, and laughingly asks her if she would help him out. In the event it so happens that Mary's assent has been forced by the precipitate action of her mother in announcing the engagement. The complications arising out of this arrangement are deftly related. Lord Beaupré, who has used the charming Mary for his convenience, comes to the realisation that he is in love with her. But he has left out of his reckoning an American invader, Mr Bolton-Brown, who has captured his prize, and has left him only with a charmless cousin as his reward.

The Visits is possessed of even less " inwardness " than *Lord Beaupré*, and tells us of how Louisa Chantry dies from the shame of having declared her love to a man who, out of mere decency, responds to her advances. *Sir Dominick Ferrand* (1890) and *Mona Vincent* (?) are stories of the same

slack-fibred type. *The Wheel of Time* and *Glasses*
deal with the problem of ugliness in women. Each
story, short though it is, requires a notable space
of time for its evolution. The plain girl of the
former is Fanny Knocker. Her parents—the father
a retired army officer from India—are willing to
provide her with a substantial dowry, and Lady
Greyswood, her mother's friend, exerts herself to
interest her son Maurice in the girl. Fanny becomes
clearly much attached, but the young man bolts in
continently before committing himself. Her exces
sive plainness had evidently not been compensated
by her admirable intelligence.

He spends twenty years abroad, and returns with
a motherless daughter, Vera. He had married a
wife for an attractive face, who had lived a year
and left as a legacy this child, who was distinctly
not the heir to her beauty, and stunted into the
bargain. Relations are renewed with the former
Fanny Knocker, now, by extreme poetic licence
a widow of most distinguished appearance and
charm of manner, and the mother of Arthur Tregent.
Maurice falls again under the spell of the widow
whose relation to him had been her secret life
romance, and Arthur's interest in the girl parallels
in closest detail the frustrated episode of his own
youth. Mrs Tregent refuses to marry him, for all
her desires are centred in the girl's happiness. At
the last moment Arthur swerves aside as he had
done, and death closes the chapter for Vera.

The girl in *Glasses* is Flora Saunt, whose main
delight in existence is her beautiful face and what
she can perform with it, and whose chief but most

ecret preoccupation is her defective eyesight, which demands for its restoration that defacing spectacles, with a straight bar across the middle, shall cover her lovely orbs. A painter tells her story. His portrait of her has been an Academy success, and is purchased off the line by Lord Iffley, who is obviously infatuated with her beauty. A more devout admirer has fallen in love with the picture and later with the original, but Flora, flying at bigger game, gives the faithful Geoffrey Dawling scant hope or satisfaction. The painter-man, returning from a long visit to America, is startled at meeting Flora with the grotesque spectacles deforming her face. She is staying with old Mrs Meldrum, whose similar disfigurement she had formerly held in horror, but to whom she now clings in her affliction. Lord Iffley's love for her beauty had not survived its ruin.

After another absence the painter sees her face beaming down upon him, more beautiful than ever, from an opera box. She has evidently recognised him, and as she is momentarily alone he goes to pay her his respects. As he enters the box she turns and smiles on him. " 'Here you are again!' he exclaimed, with her disgloved hand put up a little backward for me to take. I dropped into a chair just behind her, and, having taken it and noted that one of the curtains of the box would make the demonstration sufficiently private, bent my lips over it and impressed them on its finger-tips. It was given me, however, to my astonishment, to feel next that all the privacy in the world wouldn't have sufficed to mitigate the start with which she greeted this free application of my moustache ; the blood had jumped to her face, she quickly recovered her hand and jerked at me, turning herself round, a vacant, challenging stare. During the next few instants several extraordinary things happened, the first of which was that now I was close to them the eyes of loveliness I had come up to look into didn't show at all the conscious light I had just been pleased to see them flash across the house ; they showed, on the contrary, to my confusion, a strange, sweet blankness, an expression I failed to give a meaning to until, without delay, I felt on my arm, directed to it as if instantly to efface the effect of her start, the grasp of the hand she had impulsively snatched from me. It was the irrepressible question in this grasp that stopped on my lips all sound of salutation. She had mistaken my entrance for that of another person, a pair of lips without a moustache. She was feeling me to see who I was ! With the perception of this and of her not seeing me I sat gaping at her and at the wild word that did not come, the right word to express or to disguise my stupefaction. What was the right word to commemorate one's sudden discovery, at the very moment, too, at which one had been most encouraged to count on better things, that one's dear old friend had gone blind ? "

John Delavoy was rightly judged by James to be one of his least successful efforts in literary portraiture. *The Tone of Time* has, like *Glasses*, a flavour of the studio ; but it too is ineffective by comparison with other stories dealing with the painter's craft. Mary J. Tredick is the uncompromising name of the principal woman. She is a copyist of old masters, and a friend—the nameless narrator—has secured her a curious commission to execute for a woman she has never seen or heard of a portrait that is presumably to represent a dead husband. The portrait is to be an idealised effort of pure imagination.

The fantastic coincidences that follow are staggering enough. Mary Tredick puts all her hatred and all her art into the representation from memory of a man she had loved and suffered from. The commissioner, Mrs Bridgeworth, recognises her lover in the portrait, and Mary divines by instinct that she is the woman for whom she had been abandoned. Needless to say, a handsome cheque is refused and the portrait never delivered.

The Third Person is the most harmless excursion that James ever made into the field of the supernatural. Two dear old maids are the heroines, if one must employ that imposing word. They have jointly inherited a pleasant old country house, and in their rummaging have unearthed a box of ancient family papers. The local vicar who deciphers these informs them that an ancestor had apparently been hanged for smuggling. The ancestor in question, evidently made uneasy by the belated revelation of his crime, becomes the old ladies' constant companion, and they are secretly delighted, even to jealousy, at his attentions. But he is obviously troubled, and they seek to exorcise him each in her several way. Miss Susan sacrifices her little hoard of savings to the Chancellor of the Exchequer, and Miss Amy, more greatly daring, smuggles a Tauchnitz volume from France.

IV

THE LITERARY AND ARTISTIC GROUP

A ROUND dozen or more of our author's stories
beginning with *The Author of Beltraffio* in 1884 an
ending with *The Velvet Glove* in 1910, essay to presen
various complications of the literary art and variou
aspects of the literary conscience. These little fiction
—stories in the ordinary sense they can scarcely b
called—constitute a distinctive and distinguishe
group, whose general characteristics I think it wis
to indicate before passing them in separate review.

James is usually able to point us to some sug
gestion of actuality as his source of inspiratior
but he confesses his inability to trace back th
origins of this group to any specific facts encountere
by the way. They have therefore this advantag
for the student of his mind—that they are th
immediate fruits of his own consciousness, and tha
they present what he conceives to be the ide
truth about literature. Though he cannot give u
chapter and verse for his sources, we are not a
pains to see that in the ideal sense which I hav
indicated they strike firm root in his own experi
ence. No author of his day had been more consist
ently haunted by the idea of perfection, and non
assuredly had more reason to realise the isolatio
that such solicitude entailed. Most of these stories

then, are parables designed to embody the idea of perfection sought and isolation achieved, but he occasionally deviates in the interests of a finer irony to exhibit the multiplied vulgarities of popular success, and to contrast the self-satisfaction of mediocrity with the sensitive discontent of genius.

In four of these stories James may be said to reveal with scarce-veiled directness the impulses of his own imaginative life. *The Middle Years* (1893) presents us with the case of Dencombe, " poor Dencombe," who has come to recover his shattered health on the sheltered beach of Bournemouth. He had finished the proofs of his latest book before illness had struck him down, and now that the volume is in his hands he cannot recover its contents. " He couldn't have chanted to himself a single sentence, couldn't have turned with curiosity or confidence to any particular page. His subject had already gone from him, leaving scarce a superstition behind. He uttered a low moan as he breathed the chill of this dark void, so desperately it seemed to represent the completion of a sinister process. The tears filled his mild eyes : something precious had passed away. This was the pang that had been sharpest during the last few years—the sense of ebbing time, of shrinking opportunity ; and now he felt not so much that his last chance was going as that it was gone indeed. He had done all he should ever do, and yet hadn't done what he wanted. This was the laceration—that practically his career was over ; it was as violent as a grip at his throat. He rose from his seat nervously—a creature haunted by a dread ; then he fell back in his weakness and

nervously opened his book. It was a single volume :
he preferred single volumes and aimed at a rare
compression. He began to read and, little by little,
in this occupation, was pacified and reassured.
Everything came back to him, but came back with
a wonder, came back, above all, with a high and
magnificent beauty. He read his own prose, he
turned his own leaves, and had, as he sat there
with the spring sunshine on the page, an emotion
peculiar and intense. His career was over, no
doubt, but it was over, when all was said, with
that.

" He had forgotten during his illness the work
of the previous year ; but what he had chiefly forgotten was that it was extraordinarily good. He
dived once more into his story and was drawn down,
as by a siren's hand, to where, in the dim underworld of fiction, the great glazed tank of art, strange
silent subjects float. He recognised his motive
and surrendered to his talent. Never, probably, had
that talent, such as it was, been so fine. His difficulties were still there, but what was also there,
to his perception, though probably, alas ! to nobody else, was the art, that in most cases had
surmounted them. In his surprised enjoyment of
this ability he had a glimpse of a possible reprieve.
Surely its force wasn't spent—there was life and
service in it yet. It hadn't come to him easily, it
had been backward and roundabout. It was the
child of time, the nursling of delay ; he had struggled
and suffered for it, making sacrifices not to be
counted, and now that it was really mature was it
to cease to yield, to confess itself brutally beaten ?

There was an infinite charm for Dencombe in feeling as he had never felt before that diligence *vincit omnia*. The result produced in his little book was somehow a result beyond his conscious intention; it was as if he had planted his genius, had trusted his method, and they had grown up and flowered with this sweetness. If the achievement had been real, however, the process had been painful enough. What he saw so intensely to-day, what he felt as a nail driven in, was that only now, at the very last, had he come into possession. His development had been abnormally slow, almost grotesquely gradual. He had been hindered and retarded by experience, he had for long periods only groped his way. It had taken too much of his life to produce too little of his art. The art had come, but it had come after everything else. At such a rate a first existence was too short—long enough only to collect material; so that to fructify, to use the material, one should have a second age, or extension. This extension was what poor Dencombe sighed for. As he turned the last leaves of his volume he murmured : ' Ah for another go ; oh for a better chance ! ' "

If James had desired to put on record an estimate of his own career, he need not have altered one word of this avowal, and it is for this scarce-veiled identification that we should value the story. " Poor Dencombe " actually dies, in spite of Doctor Hugh's devotion, curtailed of the margin of time he craves wherein to amplify his vision of perfection; but since that is the fate of every artist, the identification is still complete.

HENRY JAMES : MAN AND AUTHOR

In *The Death of the Lion* (1894) James satirises the predatory curiosity of the vulgar public, and aims a second shaft in his quiver at the unintelligently refined members of the same public who exploit celebrities for their own amusement.

One of the difficulties that confronted James in this series was to present a convincing picture of genius. A mere statement of the fact of superlative ability would not establish the illusion, so he frequently sets in the foreground some intelligent young literary aspirant whose enthusiasms are designed to communicate themselves to the reader. It is accordingly a young journalist, who has learned to abhor the vulgarities of his profession, who tells Neil Paraday's story. He seeks to constitute himself a buffer between his hero and the world, but though he deals effectively enough with the interviewing fraternity, he is incapable of withstanding the onset of society. Paraday's greatness has its hours of weakness and its mood of relaxation, and he launches now upon a furious round of routs and gaieties which culminates in a visit to the country house of Mrs Weeks Wimbush, wife of the " boundless brewer." This energetic hostess has invited a distinguished company, including a foreign princess, to meet him, and he is to entertain them by reading from a projected work. To relieve the strain two eminently popular novelists (Miss) Guy Walsingham and (Mr) Dora Forbes have been asked down for a similar purpose.

Paraday dies in the house before his promised reading had come off. The precious manuscript, though he died without knowing it, had been mislaid by one of the great people, whose valet had presumably left the bundle in a train.

The Next Time (1895) is also narrated by a literary journalist, who holds in the highest esteem the frustrate talent of Ray Limbert. The latter's sister-in-law, Mrs Highmore, has become satiated by the easy popularity of her fiction, and her ambition now is to produce a book so cryptic that it might vie in unpopularity with Limbert's novels. The latter, pressed on by the goad of domestic necessity, is, on the contrary, ambitious to secure a vulgar success. Mrs Highmore's cryptic effort proves commonplace and triumphant, while Ray Limbert's compulsive genius betrays him again into the perfection he so studiously sought to avoid.

Many years of his literary life are covered in the narrative, which illustrates with tragic irony the embarrassments that accumulate on the path of a man of genius. He had married, on his literary prospects of course, the charming Maud Stannace plus her mother, who allows the match on terms of perpetual lodgment. Children follow, who are not still-born like the books. A North British paper makes him London correspondent, and he seeks to prostitute his talent by being chatty and familiar. The editor terminates the engagement because of the high-pitched severity of his articles. The narrator co-operates with him in a more serious publication, which brings him prosperity for a year, when that engagement likewise is terminated.

Limbert leaves his London house, camps out cheerfully in a cheap cottage on the edge of a goose-green, and dies, still confident that the Next Time he will achieve a popular success.

In one of the last letters he penned, James admits a failure as complete as Limbert's, for, like him, though with no unscrupulous concessions to popular favour, he had been the victim of his own genius. His productions bear to him " the grotesque likeness of a sort of miniature Ozymandias of Egypt (' look on my *works*, ye mighty, and despair ! '), round which the lone and level sands stretch farther away than ever. . . . I am past all praying for anywhere; I remain at my age and after my long career utterly, insurmountably unsaleable. And the original preparation of that collective and selective series involved really the extremity of labour— all my ' earlier ' things—of which *The Bostonians* would have been, if included, one—were so intimately and interestingly revised. The edition is, from that point of view, really a monument (like Ozymandias), which has never had the least intelligent critical justice done it—or any sort of critical attention at all paid it—and the artistic problem involved in my scheme was a deep and exquisite one, and moreover was, as I held, very effectively solved. Only it took such time—*and* such taste—in other words, such æsthetic light."

The Figure in the Carpet (1896) is the best-known story of the group. Here, again, it is a young literary critic who presents the case of Hugh Vereker. He is in a flutter of excitement at the prospect of meeting the great novelist at Lady Jane's country house. Meanwhile his friend Corvick has asked

THE FIGURE IN THE CARPET

him to relieve him of an article he had promised
to contribute to *The Middle* on Vereker's last book.
He does the article much to his own satisfaction
and goes down to Bridges. Vereker, not knowing
him to be the author of the review, makes a contemptuous reference to it at dinner, but later,
when he has learned of the authorship, he unburdens himself frankly and kindly to the young
critic. He says that there is an " intention " present
in all his books which has remained a secret only
because no one has had the intelligence to divine
it. This fires the youngster's ambition, and he
devotes himself to the task of elucidating the
secret until, baffled, he takes relief in exasperation
at Vereker and his famous " intention."

Corvick meanwhile, and Gwendolen Erme, whom
he hopes to marry, have caught the contagion.
They work unremittingly at the puzzle, until
eventually Corvick, who had gone on a literary
mission to India, cables that he has discovered
the Figure in the Carpet, the thread of design that
he has woven so cunningly with his pattern. He
leaves India precipitately, visits Vereker at Rapallo,
and confirms his discovery.

Disasters now thicken in the fable. Corvick
marries Gwendolen and is accidentally killed before
he has revealed the secret, save to her. Vereker
dies. Gwendolen marries Drayton Deane, a second-
rate man of letters, and after Gwendolen's death
the baffled critic seeks to gather the secret from
him, only to discover that Gwendolen had not
revealed it.

It is a puzzling little parable, and one is tempted

to say that an artist of Vereker's competence had no business to leave his intention so obscure. The first concern of a novelist must surely be to extricate his subject, and his merit will be measured by his command of the resources of invention and combination. It is James's contention that these elements have rarely been mastered in English fiction. Vereker essayed the task and found himself in James's predicament, with the public indifferent or bewildered and the critics for ever hunting down a vanishing trail—a sorry business this for us who write books about him !

In the remainder of the stories the revelation is not so intimate. *The Author of Beltraffio* (1884) was the fruit of a random remark, of which James saw the dramatic possibilities : " It had been said to me of an eminent author, these several years dead, and on some of the embarrassments of whose life a common friend was enlarging : ' Add to them all, moreover, that his wife objects intensely to what he writes. She can't bear it (as you can, for that matter, rather easily conceive), and that naturally creates a tension——' *There* had come the air-blown grain which, lodged in a handful of kindly earth, was to produce the story of Mark Ambient." Though Ambient faces tragedy in his own house, the flag of his ideals never droops at half-mast. His wife is a moral fanatic, but he suffers the discomfiture of her scorn rather than sacrifice his vision of reality. Henry St George of *The Lesson of the Master* (1888) is as finely gifted but more weak of fibre. A rising novelist, Paul Overt, meets this master of the craft at Lady Watermonth's country

house. The young man is much attracted by a Miss
Fancourt, who is stirred with him by a like enthusiasm for St George's genius. Their admiration is
qualified by a recognition that there is a regrettable
deterioration in his later work, which is presently
explained by St George as due to the operation of
the influence of his wife, who has been for many
years his managing director, and who has launched
him upon a career of worldly success. In a long
midnight colloquy St George drives home the
virtues of perfection and the resolute self-denial
that the literary conscience exacts. Overt, who
has been yielding to the irresistible charm of Miss
Fancourt, and who feels that her intellectual sympathy would stimulate him to a finer quality of
effort, is so impressed by the elder novelist's advice
that he leaves for the Continent and toils for two
years at a book. He returns to find that Mrs St
George has died and that Miss Fancourt is presently
to succeed her as St George's wife.

Another case of worldly success set over against
undeserved failure is to be found in the admirably
written *Abasement of the Northmores* (1900), a story
of such developmental possibilities that James has
called it, in its present condensed form, a miracle
of compression. It is a gratifying thing that a
writer of ability should find a helpmate so discern-
ing and sympathetic as Warren Hope enjoyed in
his wife. One might have liked a fuller measure of
this generous comradeship than James, under his
self-imposed conditions, could give us. Her confidence in his genius, which the world's callousness
intensifies, makes her yearn, after his death, to

establish him in his true dominion. The pompous Northmore, whose shallowness she of all women knew, had gone out in a blaze of journalistic glory, while her husband, her king of men, had died with his worth unrecognised and unrecorded. " His work, unencouraged and interrupted, failed of a final form ; there would have been nothing to offer but fragments of fragments. She felt, all the same, in recognising this, that she abandoned him : he died for her at that hour over again. . . . During the first six months she wondered what she could herself do, and had much of the time the sense of walking by some swift stream, on which an object dear to her was floating out to sea. All her instinct was to keep up with it, not to lose sight of it, to hurry along the bank and reach in advance some point from which she. could stretch forth and catch and save it. Alas ! it only floated and floated : she held it in sight, for the stream was long, but no gentle promontory offered itself to the rescue. She ran, she watched, she lived with her great fear ; and all the while, as the distance to the sea diminished, the current visibly increased."

Her satisfaction is that the voluminous published record of Northmore's life has been a monument to his ineptitude, while she can look forward with serene confidence to the time when, at her death, her husband's brilliant letters to herself will appear.

Greville Fane (1893) is another record of successful incapacity in which, though its author designates it "a minor miracle of foreshortening," the effort of compression has been less successful.

One's sympathetic attention flows out much

more readily to *Broken Wings* (1900), the story of
a woman whose novels had once been popular, and
of a man whose pictures once had sold. Mrs Harvey
and Stuart Straith are, much to their own surprise,
fellow - guests at a distinguished country - house
party. They had known one another well in the
days of their early successes, but an odd shyness
now keeps them apart, and they have no conversation until some time afterwards, when they are
sitting by chance in neighbouring stalls at a play.
He has designed the costumes for the second act,
and she is getting material for her weekly London
letter to an obscure journal.   Such is the extent
of their present fame; but now for the first time
each learns the other's story.   In the sequel she
finds her way to his overstocked studio, and he
returns the visits in her diminished flat.   Like
Browning's lovers in *Youth and Art* they realise
what they have mutually missed ; but, happier
than these, they seize their opportunity of facing
life, or what remains to them of life, together, determined, if need be, to make a joyous community
of failure.

In *The Aspern Papers* (1888) and *The Coxon
Fund* (1894) James permitted himself a fuller
licence of development than in the stories we have
been considering.   In the first, Shelley, and in the
second, Coleridge, may be roughly said to be the
theme, or at least the point of departure.   Jane
Clairmont, Shelley's sister-in-law and the mother
of Byron's Allegra, had lived to a great age in
retirement in Florence, and James's imagination
played with the idea that had he known this fact

it might easily have been his privilege to conjure up the ghosts of a vanished time. " The thrill of learning that she had ' overlapped,' and by so much, and the wonder of my having doubtless at several earlier seasons passed again and again, all unknowing, the door of her house, where she sat above, within call and in her habit as she lived, these things gave me all I wanted ; I seem to remember in fact my more or less immediately recognising that I positively oughtn't—' for anything to come of it '—to have wanted more. I saw quickly how something might come of it *thus* ; whereas a fine instinct told me that the effect of a nearer view of the case (the case of the overlapping) would probably have had to be quite differently calculable. It was really with another item of knowledge, however, that I measured the mistake I should have made in waking up sooner to the question of opportunity. That item consisted of the action taken on the premises by a person who *had* waked up in time, and the legend of whose consequent adventure, as a few spoken words put it before me, at once kindled a flame. This gentleman, an American of long ago, an ardent Shelleyite, a singularly marked figure and himself in the highest degree a subject for a free sketch—I had known him a little, but there is not a reflected glint of him in *The Aspern Papers*—was named to me as having made interest with Miss Clairmont to be accepted as a lodger on the calculation that she would have Shelley documents, for which, in the possibly not remote event of her death, he would thus enjoy priority of chance to treat with her representatives.

He had at any rate, according to the legend, become, on earnest Shelley grounds, her yearning, though also her highly diplomatic, *pensionnaire*—but without gathering, as was to befall, the fruit of his design.

" Legend here dropped to another key; it remained in a manner interesting, but became to my ear a trifle coarse, or at least rather vague and obscure. It mentioned a younger female relative of the ancient woman as a person who, for a queer climax, had had to be dealt with; it flickered so for a moment and then, as a light, to my great relief, went out. It had flickered indeed but at the best—yet had flickered enough to give me my ' facts,' bare facts of intimation; which, scant handful though they were, were more distinct and more numerous than I mostly *like* facts. . . . Nine-tenths of the artist's interest in them is that of what he shall add to them and how he shall turn them. Mine, however, in the connection I speak of, had fortunately got away from me, and quite of their own movement, in time not to crush me. So it was, at all events, that my imagination preserved power to react under the mere essential charm—that, I mean, of a final scene of the rich dim Shelley drama played out in the very theatre of our own modernity."

In the prefatory prelude to *The Spoils of Poynton* James has expressed the same eagerness to escape the indiscriminate welter of facts that life too often thrusts upon the artist's attention. *Beltraffio*, it is curious to note, presents the contrary doctrine. " I want to be truer," Mark Ambient says, " than

I've ever been. . . . I want to give the impression of life itself. No, you may say what you will, I've always arranged things too much, always smoothed them down and rounded them off and tucked them in—done everything to them that life doesn't do. I've been a slave to the old superstitions.'' We can generally trust his logic, but I think in the present instance James would have been better advised to have made either Shelley or Byron his centre of reference rather than a hypothetical American poet of the early century, who neither did nor could exist.

In *The Coxon Fund* he has kept much closer to the Coleridge legend, and has created a very living picture of that rudderless genius, with, unfortunately, all the poetry left out. Mr Saltram is as shiftless as his prototype in life and as copious in the improvisations of his eloquence, but there is no music in his soul, and it was after all these wandering airs from heaven that constituted the miracle of Coleridge's genius.

The Velvet Glove of 1910 is the last and perhaps the most ingenious exhibition of the literary conscience in difficulties. Berridge's curious predicament is that a woman of august lineage and transcendent charm appears to his dazzled senses to be making the most unmistakable love to him in the course of a midnight drive through Paris, to which she has inveigled him. Alas for his high hopes of playing the shepherd to an Olympian goddess ! The Princess, as Amy Evans, is the writer of insufferable books, and her caresses are merely designed to extract from him, as the most distinguished American writer of his day, a charming

commendatory preface. He saves his conscience
and achieves a sweet revenge. With no lack of
tenderness he returns her caresses, and as the car
drives up at her *porte-cochère* he presses his lips to
hers and says good-bye for ever.

The studio stories form a small and distinctive
group, of which it must be admitted that they do
not strike to the centre of pictorial problems with
the same penetration that was displayed for the
sister art of literature. One of the best of these
is the earliest, *The Madonna of the Future* (1879),
which, apart from giving a brilliant impression of
Florence, interests us for its working out of the
problem of Theobald's character—the procrasti-
nating artist of exquisite sensibilities and clear
perceptions, whose appreciation of beauty and sense
of perfection are so acute that he dreams his life
away until the nerve of execution is atrophied.
His idealism is constant. The street-woman who
is his Madonna plies her trade by day, but for
Theobald, who visits her each evening for twenty
years, she radiates purity and beauty. A peddling
artist of cheap statuary is her paramour, and his
vulgar facility brings into still stronger relief the
incapacity which makes Theobald's former friends
deem him a charlatan.

In *The Liar* (1888), a portrait-painter, Oliver
Lyon, has come down to a country house to paint
Sir David Ashmore, a nonogenarian famous in his
day. At dinner he studies the faces of his fellow-
guests, and finds one to be eminently paintable.
His neighbour names him as Colonel Capadose
of the Indian Army. Several places to his left he

catches sight of a beautiful woman, with whom he had once been in love, and who had years before refused him. She turns out to be the Colonel's wife. After the ladies leave, and later on in the smoking-room, Capadose regales Lyon with the most extravagant stories of his adventurous career, and it gradually dawns upon the artist that the woman he had once loved is married to an irredeemable liar. He continues to cultivate their acquaintance in London for the purpose of seeing whether the contamination has involved the wife. He paints the daughter's portrait, and then lavishes all his art on the Colonel's head and figure. At the last sitting a derelict woman makes her way into the studio and tells a tale, inspired by beer and gin. When she leaves, the Colonel weaves one of his usual romances about her, and says that the woman has been persecuting him for years. The portrait is a consummate success, and has " liar " stamped ineffaceably on every feature. It is laid aside for a few weeks in its all but completed state while the artist takes a holiday. He returns unexpectedly in August and learns from his housekeeper that a lady and gentleman are in the studio. Mrs Capadose has evidently not been able to resist the temptation to see the picture. Entering the gallery above his studio he hears violent sobbing, and discovers Mrs Capadose weeping in her husband's arms. He has a momentary triumph, for he realises now that his picture has succeeded, and that he has achieved his further intention of communicating to the wife his knowledge of her husband's weakness. Mrs Capadose goes out of the studio, but the husband returns and slashes the canvas in pieces. When the artist visits them some weeks later they ask him when he is going to have the concluding sittings. They are horrified to learn of the fate of the picture, but Capadose has the ready explanation that the crazy woman who has been persecuting him had revenged herself in that way. The wife admits that they had seen her in the street as they left the studio. This admission proves to Lyon that Mrs Capadose has in fact been contaminated, and his visits to the house come to an end.

The Real Thing (1893) was worked up by James on a hint from his friend Du Maurier. An artist is supposed to tell the story. One day a rather distinguished-looking couple appear in his studio, and he at once concludes that he is to receive a commission to do them singly or as a group. But Major Monarch and his wife, reduced to penury, have come for another purpose. They have learned from Mr Rivet, a landscape painter, that our artist is to undertake the illustration of a fashionable novel, *Rutland Ramsay,* and they are convinced that he will be glad to avail himself of their services in posing for the hero and heroine. They will at least be the Real Thing. He finds them quite unworkable, inflexibly correct in type to the point of monotony. Eventually Miss Churm, a Cockney drudge, and Oronte, a bankrupt fruit vender and ice-cream pedlar, do the refined bits of posing, and the Major and his wife, who had by this time contracted the habit of the studio, perform the common chores— wash up the dishes and serve the models with tea. The situation finally gets on the artist's nerves, and gently but firmly he pays them off and sees them no more.

The Tree of Knowledge (1900) is a story that appealed to its author for the firmness and neatness displayed in the extrication of his theme. The principals are a sculptor who is infatuated with his own execrable art, a wife who conceals from him her knowledge of his mediocrity, and a son to whom this same recognition eventually comes. The story's virtue lies less in the matter than in the telling.

The Beldonald Holbein (1901) is narrated in the first person by an artist to whom Mrs Munden proposes that he shall paint a portrait of her still beautiful sister-in-law, Lady Beldonald. The day for the first sitting arrives, but Mrs Munden announces that her sister-in-law is very disturbed by the illness of her companion, Miss Dadd. The latter dies, and an interval follows, during which Lady Beldonald searches for a successor. She is a woman who lives on her vanity, and, according to Mrs Munden, her chosen companion must be plain enough to serve as a foil to her beauty. The announcement is made that a remote relation, Mrs Brash, has arrived from America to fill that office. The painter gives a reception for Lady Beldonald, who wishes to see his latest things before her picture is begun. A French artist friend, Paul Outrean, is there, and waxes enthusiastic to the narrator over a wonderful face, a perfect Holbein, that he has discovered in the throng. Our artist agrees with his verdict, and congratulates Lady Beldonald on the superb ageing beauty and character of her

companion's face. Mrs Brash becomes the " rage "
of all the art circles of London, but she stoutly
refuses to sit to anyone. Lady Beldonald ultimately
ships her home, where she presently dies, having
tasted a year's draught of intoxicating triumph.
Her successor is inanely pretty, and Lady Beldonald
again proposes to sit. The artist, we are assured,
will reveal all the secrets of her face.

In *Mora Montravers* (1910) James has essayed
the task of conveying an impression of the completest self-assurance combined with the maximum
of charm. Mora is a dashing, handsome girl of
artistic leanings, and of a temperament as romantic
as is consistent with the cultivation of advanced
modern views. She has at the moment precipitated
a crisis in the quiet Traffle household by her migra-
tion to Puddick's studio. Her Uncle Traffle has
just returned from an interview with the artist,
who repudiates all responsibility for Mora's action,
but will marry the girl if they insist and if he can
bring Mora to that point of view. But he asserts
that if he does marry her he will probably lose all
his influence over her, and the responsibility will
rest on them.

Mrs Traffle, in all her lachrymose arguments
with her husband, sees nothing beyond the conventional aspects of the situation: the girl has
compromised herself, and until Puddick has re-
instated her there can be no question for them of
recognising her in any way. Traffle is more liberally
disposed, for, while acknowledging the advantages
of combining a sense of decency with a sense of
life, he is not certain in his own mind that if one

of these must be sacrificed it might not be well
to strain the conventions and indulge oneself in
the luxury of living. Mora must certainly have
found life extremely dull with them.

Resolving to carry things with a high hand Mrs
Traffle summons Puddick to her house, asks him
bluntly if he is Mora's lover, and bids him tell Mora
that she will settle four hundred and fifty a year
on her when they marry. Puddick naturally asserts
Mora's complete innocence, and shows genuine
embarrassment at the intrusion of the money
question into the affair. A month later Traffle
meets Mora in the National Gallery and learns
that she is now quite unromantically Mrs Puddick.
She is frank and pleasant with her uncle, but makes
no concealment of her resentment at the imputa-
tions against her innocence. Her chief concern
now is that her uncle should undertake to have the
settlement made over to her husband, for she herself wishes only to be free. A hint of the reason is
offered by the appearance of a distinguished-looking
man, with whom Mora presently walks away.

On his return home Traffle finds that his wife
has had a visitor and is still under the excitement
of her interview. Puddick had been the caller, and
she has evidently lavished on him all her sympathy
in his present embarrassment. So far as she is
concerned the money will be safe for him, and
Mora may make all necessary arrangements to
unmarry herself again, and unite her fortunes with
Sir Bruce Bagley, Bart.

Like all its companion stories in *The Finer Grain,*
this one is treated with a rare perfection of finish.

MORA MONTRAVERS

Mr Traffle's is the consciousness most delved into, and he rewards us, though in a minor way, like Strether of *The Ambassadors*. James evidently is rather fond of presenting a case of frustrate sensibilities which are suddenly, but too late, given their opportunity to expand. Woolett had been a dull forcing-ground for the passions and the imagination, and emancipation for Strether begins only with Chad Newsome and Paris. Traffle has been saddled all his days with a Philistine wife, but this monotony of dullness is broken at last by the advent of Mora, who is evidently competent to create her own current even in the most stagnant pool. I have noted her precipitate behaviour down to its last perplexing phase. What James, however, wishes us to follow is the interesting reaction of her conduct on her uncle, and the counterpoise which his quickened perceptions find in his wife's so self-satisfied dullness. She is devoid of any faculty of discrimination, but this does not prevent her from developing a pitying contempt for her husband's lack of discernment.

V

THE SUPERNATURAL GROUP

THE Jamesian spook has a character entirely his own. He is only by exception lurid or spectacular, and is quite unencumbered by the clumsy paraphernalia with which tradition has invested the ghostly tribe—the sheet, the groan, the clanking chain. James has preferred to see him in his essential ghostliness as a haunting presence, and he has succeeded so well in his representation because he more than half believed in him. There is a vulgar sense in which a house may be haunted, and a great deal of spectral machinery may be brought into play with no effect of conviction upon us. But there is a truer way for ghosts to inhabit, for what are the memories that seem to cling to the very walls of ancient houses but pale, impalpable presences which, under the sympathetic pressure of imagination, may live again ? *The Turn of the Screw* passes for the most ingeniously contrived supernatural romance that James has given us, but equally suggestive and convincing are *The Jolly Corner* and the unfinished *Sense of the Past*. In both of these stories the strong compulsion of imagination is used to make the vanished time yield up its secrets, and they have the curious feature in common that the living man waylays and haunts the dead.

THE JOLLY CORNER

I cannot discover where or when *The Jolly Corner* first appeared, though James refers to it as already being in print when he introduced it into his New York edition. Any attempt to recapitulate the weird midnight adventures of Spencer Brydon would leave with the reader only a strong impression of his insanity. He occupies himself nightly in the empty house of his youth with stalking his own wraith, but as we read we are so satisfied with the credibility of this performance that we become sharers in the excitement and terror of his chase. He had left New York at twenty-three, and now at fifty-six is returning there from Europe to look after some private business affairs. He finds New York much altered and most of the old links severed, his only pleasant contact with the past being through Miss Staverton, who still lives in the old style and with her old things about her. In their conversation he frequently wonders with her what he would have been had he never uprooted himself—had he, for example, embraced a business career, as would have been his inevitable fate if he had remained at home. The horror of the idea fascinates him, and it is this phantasmal projection of what he seemed destined to become that he hunts down and encounters in the deserted home of his youth.

James, at the turn of the century, had some interesting correspondence with Howells on the subject of a story the latter had asked him to write on the theme of an " international " ghost. By the merest chance James had been endeavouring to work out just such a theme, but was momentarily

held up by the difficulties it presented. We know
that it was these difficulties that caused it to be
laid aside for fourteen years, when he took it up
again precisely because of its difficulty and of its
utter disconnection with conditions engendered
by the war. "The beauty of this notion of *The
Sense of the Past*, of which I have again, as I tell
you, been astride, is precisely that it involves, without the stale effect of the mere bloated bugaboo
the presentation, for folk both in and out of the
book, of such a sense of gruesome malaise as can
only—success being assumed—make the fortune,
in the ' literary world,' of everyone concerned. I
haven't, in it, really (that is, save in one very
partial preliminary and expository connection) to
make anything or anybody ' appear ' to anyone
what the case involves is, awfully interestingly
and thrillingly, that the ' central figure,' the subject
of the experience, has the terror of a particular
ground for feeling and fearing that he *himself* is,
or may at any moment become, a producer, an
object of this state of panic on the part of others
He lives in an air of malaise as to the malaise he
may, woefully, more or less fatally, find himself
creating—and that, roughly speaking, is the essence
of what I have seen. It is less gross, much less banal
and exploded, than the dear old familiar bugaboo
produces, I think, for the reader, an almost equal
funk—or at any rate an equal suspense and unrest;
and carries with it, as I have ' fixed it,' a more
truly curious and interesting drama—especially a
more human one."

It was when he abandoned *The Ivory Tower* that

THE SENSE OF THE PAST

James bethought him of this tale of sheer phantasy
that had defeated him years before by its inherent
difficulty. He hoped now that its theme might be
remote enough from current reality to permit him
to work upon it, and he writes to Mrs Wharton in
this sense : " I have got back to trying to work
on one of these books begun and abandoned—at
the end of some 30,000 words—fifteen years ago,
and fished out of the depths of an old drawer at
Lamb House (I sent Miss Bosanquet down to hunt
it up), as perhaps offering a certain defiance of
subject to the law by which most things now
perish in the public blight. This does seem to kind
of intrinsically resist—and I have hopes. But
I must rally now before getting back to it. So
pray for me that I do, and invite dear Walter to
kneel by my side, and believe me, your faithfully
fond—Henry James."

Ralph Pendrel, a young New Yorker of English
descent, has a difficult alternative presented to
him by the young widow he wishes to marry.
Aurora Coyne has just returned from Europe,
where she seems to have had some curious psychic
experience, as a result of which the husband she
marries must bind himself to life in perpetuity in
America. She knows that these are impossible
conditions to impose on Ralph, for whose passion for
the past America would afford too lean a pasture.
He had abstained from visiting Europe because of
his mother's illness, but her death had now removed
the only impediment to his desire. When he
returns home from this strange interview he finds
a letter from a firm of English solicitors announcing

that an old Pendrel cousin, who had read with interest an historical brochure he had written, had died, bequeathing to him his family house in London. An early boat takes Ralph across the sea, and the house that is now his—a Bloomsbury mansion, with all the flavour of the eighteenth century hanging about it—begins to exercise a disconcerting influence over his imagination. For him it becomes the audible palpable past, and the furniture and the portraits seem to people it with living presences. One portrait is especially intriguing. It is of a smartly dressed young man of the Waterloo period, who, for some freak or wager, had had himself painted in reverse. It is with this Ralph Pendrel of the older time that our hero exchanges identities, for the earlier Ralph had as greatly yearned to live into the future as his modern double was desirous to live into the past. The weird circumstances of this interchange are admirably contrived and they are one of the numerous treacherous bridges over which our author was compelled to pass.

Ralph takes the precaution, before bidding farewell to the modern world, of visiting his Ambassador, who is, without any effort at concealment, James's valued friend, Lowell. The Ambassador thinks him amiably and interestingly mad, but humours him to the extent of going down to the cab where the other Ralph Pendrel was presumably waiting. But he had escaped to his own modern adventures in Piccadilly, and the Ambassador contents himself with accompanying his strange young friend to his house. When the door closes upon him his experiences of a hundred years ago begin. He is another Ralph new landed from America, who has come up post-haste from Plymouth to greet his English cousins and claim his bride. His marriage was to seal the family reconciliation, for a long estrangement had prevented him from seeing any of its members, even the charming Molly whom he was to marry. Here was another treacherous bridge to cross, and admirable is the skill with which James permits Ralph to feel his way into his new surroundings. Everything comes to him from divination, from sympathetic contact, and it is when these contacts are imperfect, as particularly with Perry and Sir Cantopher, that he from time to time betrays himself, and produces in the others the malaise of which James has spoken.

I need not enter into all the complications of the story, for some of them are not unravelled even in the working scheme we have to aid us. The main thing to note is that Ralph finds his real affinity in a sister whose existence he had not suspected, and when " sweet Nan " appears he is overcome with horror at the idea of being walled up in the past for ever with the unsympathetic Molly. From time to time his *alter ego*, who is enjoying himself hugely in the present, revisits him in menacing fashion, and seems to be angered at his impending rupture with Molly. It is all at this point rather confusing, but we may be sure that the methods of release would have been engineered with a cleverness no less ingenious than that with which the main dilemma was conducted. The Ambassador and Aurora will naturally be involved in the rescue, and sweet Nan will expedite it by some unselfish sacrifice.

In *The Turn of the Screw* (1898) James fulfilled the essential conditions of the good ghost-story. He has invented a " new shudder," which can only mean that by achieving his effect of horror without recourse to the conventional expedients for attaining this result he has produced a work that will stand in permanence as a model of its kind. The story is concerned with the malign influence exercised on two exquisite and brilliant children, Miles and Flora, by two dead servants, the valet, Peter Quint, and the governess, Miss Jessel. It is conveyed to us through the written record of the new governess, who has been engaged in London by the uncle of the orphaned pair under somewhat strange conditions. She is to take up her duties at the country house of Bly with the understanding that she must never communicate to him any complaints or difficulties. When her gruesome experiences begin it is only her love for the children and the knowledge that she alone can save their innocence from pollution that keep her at her post. The grim battle for the mastery goes on for many months, and, fortunately for the young woman's sanity, she promptly enlists the sympathy of Mrs Grose, the housekeeper, a good, stout, comfortable person, who naturally is never aware of the spectres, but vouches for their villainy when alive. Most impressively are these ghostly appearances presented, and skilful to a degree the representation step by step of the struggle for possession. We might have desired less innocent victims than the helpless children, who, despite their natural loveliness and purity, show evidence of the evil contamination whose fascination they cannot escape. Love alone might save them, but Flora has already passed beyond this refuge. Over her Miss Jessel's mastery is complete. With Miles our young woman's victory seems assured, but when at the supreme moment he defies the monstrous Quint, he dies from terror in her arms.

The conditions imposed upon James in the most famous of his supernatural stories forbade anything beyond the most rudimentary characterisation. I am not aware that the young woman whose harrowing adventure we have followed is even named, and, save for courage and devotion, she has no discussable attributes. In *Owen Wingrave* (1893) James gives us a more recognisable world, in which forces purely human collide. In *The Turn of the Screw* the abnormal is of the essence ; here it is superimposed and merely extraordinary. The result is an agreeably written story, which owes too little for a successful specimen of the type to the element of suspense. Owen Wingrave is a brilliant young man of a family from time immemorial wedded to the army. He is coaching with Spencer Coyle for his examinations, and the latter is much perplexed and perturbed at his announced decision not to write. He has conceived an invincible distaste for the profession, which he considers brutal and brutalising. Lechmere, a youth of his own years, realises that an imputation of cowardice might lie against him, but realises also, as does his tutor, that no small measure of courage is necessary to withstand the pressure of his family, who resent his decision as a stain on their honour.

He is called home, and with him Coyle and young Lechmere are invited. His aunt, Miss Wingrave, does what she can in her hard military way to influence him, and that stern old soldier, his grandfather, lets him measure quite clearly the extent of his financial sacrifice unless he should recover his senses.

There is also in the house a girl, Kate Julian, who has the family honour much at heart, and for whom Owen has in the past shown an affection that would easily ripen into love. Her taunts are the hardest thing he has to bear. There is a room in the house where, long ago, an ancestor had mysteriously died, who had killed a child by an angry blow. It is still spectre-haunted, and no one ventures to sleep there. The girl says he lacks the courage to test its terrors. Owen replies that he had slept there the night before, but Kate Julian will not credit this from a man of his proved cowardice. Lechmere speaks of the interview to his tutor, and says that Owen, in spite of his disclaimer, had had a weird experience. Stung by the girl's taunts Owen tells her to lock him in the room that night herself. Spencer Coyle is too perturbed to go to bed, but dozing in his chair he is roused by cries of a woman in terror. " He rushed straight before him, the sound of opening doors and alarmed voices in his ears, and the faintness of the early dawn in his eyes. At the turn of one of the passages he came upon the white figure of a girl in a swoon on a bench, and in the vividness of the revelation he read as he

SIR EDMUND ORME

went that Kate Julian, stricken in her pride too late with a chill of compunction for what she had mockingly done, had, after coming to release the victim of her derision, reeled away, overwhelmed, from the catastrophe that was her work—the catastrophe that the next moment he found himself aghast at on the threshold of an open door. Owen Wingrave, dressed as he had last seen him, lay dead on the spot on which his ancestor had been found. He was all the young soldier on the gained field."

Sir Edmund Orme (1892) is an exceptionally refined ghost who has adopted an original way of avenging himself upon the woman who had jilted him. Whenever he finds Mrs Marden's daughter unduly interested in a young man he appears promptly at her side, though only the mother can see him. His method serves the double purpose of alarming the mother and protecting the interests of the prospective suitor. The narrator, falling in love with Charlotte, also becomes aware of the disconcerting presence. He sees him repeatedly and with intense vividness, and this effects a community of nervous interest between him and the mother. When Charlotte eventually gives her hand in her mother's presence, Sir Edmund Orme bends menacingly over Mrs Marden, and this time the girl too sees the sinister figure. It was his last appearance, for the mother's death had appeased him.

The remainder of the group have less value. *Maud Evelyn* (1900) gives us an anæmic hero who prefers to marry a ghost rather than the charming

girl he might have had, and *The Friends of the
Friends*, published in 1896 in *The Chap Book*, under
the title *The Way it Came*, is a subtler elaboration
of the same theme. *The Private Life* (1892) deal
with certain mysterious facts of personality some
what in the fashion of *The Sacred Fount*. The
genesis of the idea is interesting. Having met Robert
Browning at various times, James was impressed
by his failure to exhibit in his person any evidence
of the power his books revealed—they so subtle and
obscurely complex and the man so forthright, so
sane and so commonplace. An artist at the same
time inhabited London—may we venture to name
Lord Leighton ?—whose dazzling presence and pre
eminent social quality seemed an equally antitheti
counterpart of the masterpieces in which his prolific
studio abounded. The story is a too ingenious
attempt to explain these mysteries.

The Great Good Place (1900) is Henry James'
Land of Cockayne, the somewhat lethargic paradise
he could conceive as a refuge from the rude assault
of the world. George Dane, encumbered with
engagements and clogged with success, faces a new
day and its multiplied responsibilities with incurable
distaste. His butler reminds him of his various
duties, and more particularly that some young man
will presently arrive for breakfast. His unknown
admirer appears, and in a very few moments
strange thing happens. Dane finds himself trans
ported to " The Great Good Place," where every
thing is pleasantly ordered, tranquil and beautiful
We are to understand some sort of mesmeric charm
exercised by the young visitor on a tired brain

THE GREAT GOOD PLACE

At the close of the day Dane awakens with the consciousness of having passed weeks in his beautiful
retreat, and the face the young man turned upon
him " was the face turned to him by the good
Brother there in the portico while they listened
together to the rustle of the shower."

VI

CONVERTED DRAMAS

OUR survey of the short stories is complete with
the consideration of three pieces which James converted from their dramatic original. *Covering End*
has a complicated history. Originally written as
a one-act play, it appeared first as a short story
in *The Two Magics* (1898), and then as *The High
Bid* it was produced in three acts by Sir J. Forbes-
Robertson at Edinburgh in 1908, and repeated in
London in the following year for a few afternoon
performances at His Majesty's Theatre.

The elation of James at the Edinburgh performance shines through the letters of the period, and his
conviction of the " consummate " art of the piece
was an unhappy preparation for the flatness of the
London production, of which his letters breathe
never a word. He was now more philosophically
disposed to failure on the stage than at the time of
his earlier harsh experiences of the British public's
density of perception. The story is mildly farcical,
but we are not disposed to blame the British public
severely for its failure to find its amusement in
the farce. The characters, as the play-bills would
say, in the order of their appearance are Chivers,
the perfect old family butler, a dashing young
American widow, later to be known as Mrs Gracedew,
Mr Prodmore, a vulgar city man, his stuffy, good-

hearted daughter Cora, Clement Yule, the captivating but impoverished heir to the property of Covering End, and some roaming groups of nondescript sightseers making the customary rounds of the antiquities of Britain. The complication of the action arises from the fact that Prodmore holds all the mortgages on the estate, which he is prepared to sacrifice on one condition, that Yule shall abjure his radical opinions, stand for Gossage in the Conservative interest, and marry his daughter Cora! Events are controlled by the all-prevailing Mrs Gracedew. She compels Yule to fall in love, first with his own house, which he had never seen, and then with herself, whom he sees for the first time. We may note in passing to what sacrifices of his usual leisurely developments the exigencies of drama compelled our author. Yule is subdued to the point of abjuring his principles, and also, as the young widow fears, to acceptance of Cora, who was the other element in the bargain, when, hey presto! we find that Cora has settled her own affairs with someone else while walking from the station. Mrs Gracedew puts down seventy thousand pounds for the mortgages, which, with herself, she presents to the astonished and delighted Yule. We ask ourselves in wonder what the grave and careful James could have to do with such a hocus-pocus. He has left his evident mark only in a few descriptions of the old house, which, necessarily, the dramatic version lacked.

The Outcry (1911) is in every way a more successful affair. When the theatrical people had importuned him for plays in 1908 he freshened up his two

HENRY JAMES : MAN AND AUTHOR

earlier pieces, *The High Bid* and *The Other House*, and wrote a new one, *The Outcry*, which, like its companions, he converted into fiction. It was probably the failure of the first of these which kept the others from the boards, but his illness in 1910 was, in Mr Percy Lubbock's opinion, the prevailing reason. Firmness of handling and swiftness of movement are qualities for which *The Outcry* must thank the original dramatic intention. The style too is as swift and firm as the matter, though I have for animadversion quoted elsewhere a passage from its text which does not stand on its own two feet or even four. The hubbub or outcry has its source in the projected sale to an American dealer of a picture of national importance. The storm directs its fury upon the unbending figure of its owner, Lord Theign, who takes his stand upon his individual rights as a Briton. "The picture is mine, and I can do what I damned well please with it," is a vernacular rendering of his attitude. Indeed it is only the opposition to his will that justifies his own action to himself, for the Theigns have never had the habit or the need of bartering their personal possessions. Lady Kitty, his eldest daughter, is chiefly responsible for the dilemma. She is in debt for cards to the tune of thousands to the Duchess. The latter's son, Lord John, is eager to marry Lady Grace, the younger sister, with the resultant compromise that the gambling account will be rescinded. Unfortunately for the scheme, Lady Grace has a mind and a heart of her own, and with both of these she warmly espouses the interests of Hugh Crimble, the young

196

connoisseur who had set in motion the agitation about the picture. He came to the Theign house by her invitation to examine its treasures at the same moment when Bender, a vulgar rich American dealer, is appraising its contents. Bender's avowed purpose is to get the great Reynolds, but when young Crimble pronounces a supposed Moretto portrait to be a genuine and rare Mantovano he transfers his aspirations to the latter picture. Such are the bare elements out of which the interests of the story are created. The love episode between Hugh and Lady Grace is effectively treated with a minimum of passion, and the explosive movements of the outraged peer, her father, supply the needful infusion of comedy, with, at the same time, innumerable strokes of sure, incisive, ironic characterisation.

The Other House reads like an Ibsen play with Jamesian amplifications. It is a study in morbidity and passion, and he has not elsewhere ventured to sketch a character of such tragic possibilities as Rose Armiger.

VII

THE LETTERS, THE PREFACES AND LITERARY CRITICISM

THE reader may decide for himself how competent our author is in the region of the short story, and I am not disposed to quarrel with him if he thinks Maupassant or Tchekoff a greater practitioner of the craft. These attempted rankings lead us to no satisfactory conclusion, whereas the effort to appreciate an author's intention and to measure his success in achieving it has common sense and interest to commend it. James here comes generously to our assistance, and I propose to levy tribute on his letters, his prefaces, and his critical papers for what they can reveal to us of his conception of sound workmanship. This chapter therefore, the author so potently aiding, should be a valuable prelude to our consideration of the major novels that still lie before us.

The four hundred letters of Henry James that Mr Percy Lubbock has recently given to the world are apparently but a small proportion of those that have been preserved, but he has skilfully organised his material to constitute a fully rounded document with a beginning, a middle and an end, that leaves the reader with no sense of incompleteness, though with a lingering regret that he might have enjoyed a still ampler feast. They reveal, as

genuine letters should, the qualities of mind and
heart of the writer, and if they exhibit his range
of interests as somewhat narrow, this restriction is
compensated by his intense preoccupation with the
matter in hand. They lack the familiar pleasant
ease of Cowper and Fitzgerald, the sardonic fury
of Carlyle, the wit and vivacity of Byron, and the
glancing playfulness of Stevenson; but this admission is a platitude that might be hazarded of any
letters from any pen. What constitutes the virtue
of any correspondence these letters pre-eminently
possess—they are a frank communication from
mind to mind and from heart to heart. They are
the abundant overflow of an affectionate nature,
and it is precisely their combination of human
qualities with a discriminating sense of values
where the arts of expression are concerned, that
will give them permanent rank in our epistolary
literature. What the letters of Keats are for the
lovers of poetry, the letters of James are for the
student of fiction, in spite of Mr Lubbock's contention that they fail to reveal the master interests of
his mind.

They are edited with the intention of illustrating
the novelist's life from the moment when his own
autobiographical notes fail us. *A Small Boy and
Others* had covered, in its majestic and circum-
ambient way, the period of childhood ; *Notes of a
Son and Brother* had revived the memories of his
early maturity ; and *The Middle Years*, suspended
in mid-course when the war, as it seemed to him,
made all personal revelations an impertinence,
brings us forward to his London life of the seventies

and early eighties. The letters from this last period are consequently few in number, and are all addressed to his family or to American friends. His only literary correspondent of this time is W. D. Howells, and one realises from these letters that James in those early days was indulging his cosmopolitan fervours at the cost of a good deal of loneliness. His initiation into the social world of London was not to be long delayed, and he soon could flourish forth the news that he had " dined out during the past winter 107 times," and could meet his brother's rebuke on the insufficiency of his reading by urging the importance of social dissipations in an observer's life. His earliest literary connections were formed not in London but in France, and we find him for a time seriously canvassing the advisability of making his centre in Paris, though deciding ultimately that the French temperament does not yield its secrets to a stranger. His London literary friendships were of slower growth. Sir Edmund Gosse dates his intimacy with him from the year 1882, and James's first letter to Stevenson, evidently before he met him, was written in 1884. From this time on the literary letters abound, and it is these letters that make his correspondence so remarkable, and constitute it so far as English literature is concerned, a unique record of a great artist's intellectual activity and development, with plenty of scope left for the expansion of the sympathies and affections, which in James were of no stinted growth, and for the expression of innumerable subtleties and fine discriminations on the theme of modern civilisation.

What interests us throughout is his thrilling response to life, and his consummate faculty for enjoying it on his own terms and in his own peculiar way. He was never a man of cliques or movements, and scarcely even a disinterested observer of public affairs until the crisis of 1914 imperilled the civilisation he so passionately loved. But with all an artist's unconcern for the things he cannot use he lived intensely at every moment of his existence, and every experience precipitated an imaginative reaction, the ripe fruit of which is preserved for us in his fiction and in his letters. He always maintained that only the artist can live at this high pitch of intensity, and this, if any excuse were necessary, is his sufficient apology for his preoccupation with art. He happened also to arrive upon the scene at a time when the novel had established itself as the most necessary, if not the most important, form of literary expression, and he seemed to perceive that our English writers, even the greatest, had an imperfect vision of what the true scope and direction of fiction should be. His many sojourns in Paris, in active commerce with the Daudet, Flaubert, Goncourt and Turgénief group, had convinced him that there was a goal of perfection towards which the conscientious artist should aspire, and that the talent is wasted that does not discover, at the cost perhaps of painful experiment and failure, the particular aspect of perfection it is constituted to reveal.

The spontaneous artist who plucks perfection ripe upon the bough is rare, and James always mistrusted his own uncontrolled faculty of improvisation.

In his later years it played him many tricks, turning his shorter pieces into stories of middle dimension, and constraining him by laborious excision to compress his longer stories within their fitting measure. In the experimental seventies he was already aware of the dangers of amplification unfortified by method, and refrained from launching upon themes of major importance, confident as he was in his power to reach ultimately a method that should permit him to move securely within a circle of the broadest circumference. His brother William had spoken slightingly of the " thinness " of *The Europeans*. " I don't trust your judgment," James replies, " about *details*; but I think you are altogether right in returning always to the importance of subject. I hold to this strongly ; and if I don't as yet seem to proceed upon it more, it is because, being very ' artistic,' I have a constant impulse to try experiments of form, in which I wish not to run the risk of wasting, or gratuitously using, big situations. But to them I am coming now. It is something to have learned how to write, and when I look round me and see how few people (doing my sort of work) know how (to my sense), I don't regret my step-by-step evolution."

Learning how to write did not involve for James merely the felicitous and correct use of the English language. Balzac was not a good writer in point of harmony and purity of phrase, yet he was the greatest master of " composition " that the craft of fiction has produced. Gautier and Flaubert and George Sand were more subtle manipulators of words, divined more haunting cadences, evolved more sonorous rhythms, but in the capacity to organise their material to produce the maximum of effect they were markedly Balzac's inferiors. The letters, the prefaces and the criticisms inform us inferentially that James proposed to himself to combine, so far as his powers would permit him, the virtues of masterly composition with the merits of impeccable style.

We gather few hints from him that would find their place in a rhetorical text-book. But in default of rules and formulas we have copious evidence of his solicitude for expression. The author of *Beltraffio*, a transparent disguise for the man who wrote the tale, speaks with the irritable accent of Flaubert of his just finished book. " This new affair must be a golden vessel, filled with the purest distillation of the actual ; and oh, how it worries me, the shaping of the vase, the hammering of the metal. I have to hammer it so fine, so smooth ; I don't do more than an inch or two a day. And all the while I have to be so careful not to let a drop of the liquor escape ! Ah, polishing one's plate —that's the torment of execution ! . . . The effort to arrive at a surface, if you think anything of that decent sort necessary—some people don't, happily for them ! My dear fellow, if you could see the surface I dream of as compared with the one with which I've to content myself. Life's really too short for art—one hasn't time to make one's shell ideally hard. Firm and bright, firm and bright is very well to say—the devilish thing has a way sometimes of being bright, and even of being hard, as mere tough frozen pudding is hard, without being firm. When I rap it with my knuckles it doesn't give the right sound. There are horrible sandy stretches where I've taken the wrong turn because I couldn't for the life of me find the right. If you knew what a dunce I am sometimes ! If I knew I should be publicly thrashed else I'd manage to find the right word. The people who can't— some of them don't so much as know it when they see it—would shut their inkstands, and we shouldn't be deluged by this flood of rubbish ! "

The solicitude for precision and harmony guarantees the artist's respect for the scope of his instrument of expression, but as an exclusive doctrine it has its dangers. If it operates to the destruction of variety, vigour and spontaneity, if it substitutes the literary for the characteristic phrase, degenerates into preciousness or swells into grandiosity, we have a fallacious perfection pur- chased at too great a price, and one that James was certainly not willing consciously to pay. A novelist is well advised to make expression a luxury rather than an agony. " Why feel, and feel genuinely, so much about ' art,' " James says of Flaubert, the classic instance of the torment-ridden stylist, " in order to feel so little about its privileges ? Why proclaim it on the one hand the holy of holies, only to let your behaviour confess it on the other a temple open to the winds ? Why be angry that so few people care for the real thing, since this aver- sion of the many leaves a luxury of space ? . . . How can art be so genuine, and yet so unconsoled, so unhumorous, so unsociable ? When it is a religion, and therefore an authority, why should it not be like other authorities, a guarantee? How can it be such a curse without being also a blessing?"

For the first twenty years of his literary life the style of James bore no strong marks of individuality. It was correct, nervous, pure, but his severe later taste condemned it as inadequate. *The American* is "wretchedly written," and *Roderick Hudson* has become insufferable to his more fastidious sense of verbal perfection. Sir Edmund Gosse has amusingly told us of the check his temerity received when he ventured to suggest the inadvisability of tampering with a book that was so admirably conceived and written, and afforded such good material for the student of his evolution. "What was my dismay, on reaching the breakfast table next morning, to see my host sombre and taciturn, with gloom thrown across his frowning features like a veil. I inquired rather anxiously if he had slept well. 'Slept!' he answered with dreary emphasis. 'Was I likely to sleep when my brain was tortured with all the cruel and—to put it plainly to you—monstrous insinuations which you had brought forward against my proper, my necessary, my absolutely inevitable corrections of the disgraceful and disreputable style of *Roderick Hudson*?'" It cannot be said that the corrections were radical enough to bring these books into harmony with his later work. This would have demanded a breaking of the mould and the infusion of a richer ore. He contented himself, therefore, with mere mechanical readjustments, involving principally the elimination of commonplaces and the substitution, where possible, of the characteristic for the obvious phrase. The result is that the revised *Roderick Hudson* gives us an example of his simpler manner in perfection, without the polyphonic harmonies and the megaphonic amplifications that developed when he substituted the voice for the pen in the act of composition.

Undue stress has been laid on the surface mannerisms that are alleged as a marring element in his later developed style. The discriminating admirer will consider himself at liberty to be amused at certain lovable oddities, but he will find a refreshment that no other contemporary author gives him in the fastidious " perfection of surface " of such stories as *The Beast in the Jungle, The Altar of the Dead, The Great Good Place, Flickerbridge* or *The Middle Years.* Good phrase-makers we have in abundance among us, manipulators of smart dialogue, and competent craftsmen in reflective or descriptive passages, but none who can sustain comparison with James in the harmonious blending of his material, none who can use such profusion of wealth to such economic advantage.

The parodists have found sport among his adverbs and far-flung parentheses. It is not to be disputed that the game abounds. " I'm glad you like adverbs," he wrote to one correspondent, " I adore them—they are the only qualification I really much respect, and I agree with the fine author of your quotation in saying—or in thinking —that the sense for them is the literary sense." " I never said," he wrote to his brother, " in announcing George Sand's death, that she was ' fearfully shy ' : I used no such vile adverb, but

another, I forget which." As likely as not it was
" portentously," but I forbear to accumulate
references under this head. The most casual reader
can gather them from page to page. An odd use
of the auxiliary is frequent in James, and this, it
would appear, the parodists have not yet discovered :
" The place where he would be to be heard of " ;
" That's exactly why—if one could have done it—
you'd have been to be kept ignorant and helpless " ;
" It would have been to be found " ; " What was
this at bottom but what had been to be arrived
at ? " ; " Would she be after all to be squared ? "
Characteristic also is the use of " whatever " in
phrases or sentences like the following : " For the
glory of Woollett or whatever " ; " There are
people who are supposed interesting or remarkable
or whatever." The interlocutors in James are all
such highly civilised beings that careless naturalness of speech is not frequently encountered, though
the conversations of his later books exhibit a growing approximation to reality. The parenthetical
habit of his own mind is a contagion that few of
his characters escape, and so far as their speech
is concerned they are in consequence imperfectly
differentiated. This partly explains James's increasing distrust of dialogue. " She surely would
be sorry to interfere with the exercise of any other
affection which I might have the bliss of believing
you now to be free, in however small a degree, to
entertain." A schoolmaster would say that this is
not incorrect, but infelicitous. " Tell my father,
please, that I'm expecting Mr Crimble, of whom
I've spoken to him even if he doesn't remember,

and who bicycles this afternoon ten miles over from where he's staying—with some people we don't know—to look at the pictures about which he's awfully keen." This extract from *The Outcry* is a good example of the loose laboriousness which James too frequently mistook for naturalness of dialogue.

It is not necessary to give more space to the mere manipulation of phrases, which in James leave generally nothing to be desired for deftness or precision. Manner and matter are hard to disengage from one another in any writer of power, and enough has been said of the surface peculiarities that developed in the course of a long career. By any standard of appraisement save that of consistent clearness he is one of the great masters of our English speech, and, needless to say, his obscurities never develop out of slovenliness of thought, nor from the converse desire to be brilliant at his readers' expense. At times he makes us work laboriously to fill out the interstices of his thought or read meanings into the capacious silences of his characters, who traverse sometimes between their speeches more space than our labouring minds can compass ; but more usually his obscurity arises from his multiplication of subtle discriminations. In his eagerness to leave no shade of meaning unexpressed he often makes the sentence groan under a paragraph's burden. That the result of all this should be a loss of readers is less to be deplored than that those who give him the " attentive perusal " that he demands should so often find their best efforts unavailing, even while obeying his injunctions to chant his passages in order that the rhythms may elucidate the sense. He grew too lavish of his verbal wealth and clothed his later books in tissue of cloth-of-gold. But this muffled magnificence encumbers the free movement of the limbs of the story, and compels us to ask whether he would not more frequently have realised his vaunted economy of action had he been more studious of economy of utterance.

James was a generous but jealous admirer of the work of his fellow-craftsmen of the past and present time, and a courageously dispassionate judge of his own productions. He realised, as definitely I think as any of his contemporaries, the effects that fiction is competent to attain, but more definitely and more philosophically than they he also recognised the insinuating faults of method that tend to compromise the result. It is a perilous thing to formulate laws of imagination, and James is at frequent pains to emphasise the virtues of freedom for the artist. He held that Besant had laid down too strict conditions for the novel, and he made his rejoinder in *The Art of Fiction* : " The good health of an art which undertakes so immediately to reproduce life must demand that it be perfectly free. The only obligation to which in advance we may hold a novel, without incurring the accusation of being arbitrary, is that it be interesting. That general responsibility rests upon it, but it is the only one I can think of. The ways in which it is at liberty to accomplish this result (of interesting us) strike us as innumerable, and

such as can only suffer from being marked out or
fenced in by prescription. They are as various as
the temperament of man, and they are successful
in proportion as they reveal a particular mind,
different from others. A novel is, in its broadest
definition, a personal, a direct impression of life ;
that, to begin with, constitutes its value, which
is greater or less according to the intensity of the
impression."

Besant, we may remember, had been laying down
rules governing the author's choice of subject, and
in the sacred name of reality had been advising
the feminine aspirant to fame not to thrust herself
for example into the barrack-room. The rejoinder
is obvious. You take the risk of an unfamiliar
subject at your peril, and a saturation with your
theme is at least an initial guarantee of your competence to treat it. But there are impressionable
beings who can measure life as exquisitely and as
truly by the inch as by the yard, and it is not
necessary to throw a gross volume of experience
into the scales if the weight of a hair can cause the
balance to vibrate. Life may sometimes be too
prodigal for the uses of art, and her casual hints
are frequently more operative for the imagination
than the fully documented story. *The Spoils of
Poynton* sprang from ten words at a dinner-table.
" There had been but ten words, yet I had recognised in them, as in a flash, all the possibilities of
the little drama of my *Spoils*, which glimmered
then and there into life; so that when in the next
breath I began to hear of action taken, on the
beautiful grounds, by our engaged adversaries, I saw

clumsy Life again at her stupid work. . . . The
stray suggestion, the wandering word, the vague
echo, at touch of which the novelist's imagination
winces as at the prick of some sharp point : its
virtue is all in its needle-like quality, the power to
penetrate as finely as possible. This fineness it is
that communicates the virus of suggestion, anything
more than the minimum of which spoils the operation. If one is given a hint at all designedly, one
is sure to be given too much ; one's subject is, in
the merest grain, the speck of truth, of beauty,
of reality, scarce visible to the common eye—since,
I firmly hold, a good eye for a subject is anything
but usual."

It is difficult to form a clear picture of James's
point of view in connection with the choice of
subject for fictional purposes. One is lucky or un-
lucky in one's choice, but the subject must always
yield in importance to the skill with which it is
presented, and our quarrel must be with the treatment rather than with the selection. We have
found James admitting to his brother that a novelist
may be favoured or hampered by his theme, and
that he, for purposes of experimentation, was
limiting himself to subjects that would not run
away with him. Elsewhere he ruefully laments
his inability to estimate in advance the expansive
qualities of his material. *The Awkward Age* was
meant to be a brief, incisive, ironical illustration
of a simple social instance—the emergence of a
daughter from the nursery to the drawing-room.
A tale was projected, but a book resulted, and
our author found his career bestrewn with like

experiences. " They were projected as small things, yet had finally to be provided for as comparative monsters—the little ideas one wouldn't have treated save for the design of keeping them small, the developed situations that one would never with malice prepense have undertaken, the long stories that had thoroughly meant to be short, the short subjects that had underhandedly plotted to be long, the hypocrisy of modest beginnings, the audacity of misplaced middles, the triumph of intentions never entertained—with these patches, as I look about, I see my experience paved ; an experience to which nothing is wanting save, I confess, some grasp of its final lesson."

Every subject is possessed, then, of an ideal length, the neglect to observe which, by over-compression or expansion, is prejudicial to the artistic integrity of the work. Compression is the lesser evil, and James recognises with satisfaction the richness of effect that he attained in *The Abasement of the Northmores* and *The Middle Years,* in which closely wrought stories the problems of elimination were solved to his entire satisfaction. In his longer stories he aimed constantly at the same effect of concentrated interest, but he seemed to himself perpetually to be betrayed, despite every effort to avoid it by cunning excisions, into the vice of disproportion. The inventive mind so rejoices in its capacity to go on and on that subordination and salience too rarely play their part in the creative process. Immersion in life, the complete saturation with their subject-matter of such full and flowing writers as Mr Wells and Mr

THE STRUCTURAL CENTRE

Arnold Bennett, is an antecedent advantage of uncontested value to an author who can invest his wealth at the highest rate of interest, but these abounding artists are so confident of the inexhaustible funds they control that percentages of return do not concern them. If you cannot spend your interest, you can afford to live on your capital. Such triumphant rashness made no appeal to James, in whose book-keeping the ledger balance was always struck before the account was closed. If any pennies went astray he conscientiously charged himself with a debit item. The leakage of interest that he found most difficult to control was one which he congratulated himself the ordinary reader could not detect. But his own fastidiousness was offended by his failure to find the centre of his theme, or, having found it, to set it in the true middle of his circumference. " Again and again, perversely, incurably, the ' centre ' of my structure would insist on placing itself *not*, so to speak, in the middle. It mattered little that the reader with the idea or the suspicion of a structural centre is the rarest of friends and of critics—a bird, it would seem, as merely fabled as the phœnix : the terminational terror was none the less certain to break in and my work threaten to masquerade for me as an active figure condemned to the disgrace of legs too short, ever so much too short, for its body. I urge myself to the candid confession that in very few of my productions, to my eye, has the organic centre succeeded in getting into proper position. Time after time, then, has the precious waist-band or girdle, studded and buckled and placed for brave outward show, practically worked itself, and in spite of desperate remonstrance, or, in other words, essential counterplotting, to a point perilously near the knees—perilously, I mean, for the freedom of these parts. In several of my compositions this displacement has so succeeded, at the crisis, in defying and resisting me, has appeared so fraught with probable dishonour, that I still turn upon them, in spite of the greater or less success of final dissimulation, a rueful and wondering eye. These productions have, in fact, if I may be so bold about it, specious and spurious centres altogether, to make up for the failure of the true. As to which in my list they are, however, that is another business, not on any terms to be made known."

James has borrowed an expression from the vocabulary of painting to express the process of dissimulation that an artist must practise in order to arrive at the illusion of reality. A space-time necessity circumscribes him, and he must resort to a species of " foreshortening " that the various planes of his narrative may appear in their proper relation. Sometimes, as in the huddled second half of *The Wings of the Dove*, this stratagem is too impudently applied. James admits that he has here had recourse to endless dodges for " disguising the reduced scale of the exhibition, for foreshorten-ing at any cost, for imparting to patches the value of presences, for dressing objects in an *air* as of the dimensions they cannot possibly have." Legitimately applied, as Balzac pre-eminently applied it, this art of foreshortening is the govern-ing principle of composition, and by its aid alone can one cope with the treacherous " space-hunger and space-cunning " of one's theme. The prefaces emphasise James's opinion that the skilful handling of space and time presents difficulties that few novelists succeed in mastering — indeed that few novelists appear even to recognise. Foreshortening he describes as " the particular economic device for which one must have a name and which has in its single blessedness and its determined pitch, I think, a higher price than twenty other clustered loosenesses ; and just because full-fed statement, just because the picture of as many of the conditions as possible made and kept proportionate, just because the surface iridescent, even in the short piece, by what is beneath it and what throbs and gleams through, are things all conducive to the only compactness that has a charm, to the only spareness that has a force, to the only simplicity that has a grace—those, in each order, that produce the rich effect."

The preliminary drafts of *The Ivory Tower* and *The Sense of the Past* attest the efforts of the author to adjust his time-scheme with the utmost nicety, so that the days and weeks might float upon the current of the story. Here Balzac is again invaluable. " No one begins, to my sense, to handle the time-element and produce the time-effect with the authority of Balzac. . . . That study of the fore-shortened image, of the neglect of which I suggest the ill consequence, is precisely the enemy of the tiresome procession of would-be narrative items, seen all in profile, like the rail-heads of a fence ; a substitute for the baser device of accounting for

the time-quantity by mere quantity of statement.
Quality and manner of statement account for it
in a finer way—always assuming, as I say, that
unless it is accounted for, nothing else really is."
Blank spaces or rows of stars, like kisses in a servant's
letter, are a cheap evasion of the difficulty, and
Mr Wells, who in his *Time-Machine* plays such
masterly tricks with time, descends too frequently
to this easy stratagem. It is a matter of surprise
that James, in his effort to say something com-
mendable of the work of Mr Arnold Bennett, has
omitted to note the skill with which in *The Old
Wives' Tale* the illusion of the irresistible yet
almost imperceptible flow of time is created. James
strives to inform himself of what meaning lies
behind the prodigious mass of life this story presents, and fails to discern that the central theme
is precisely the passage of the years.

A more ambitious device for confronting the
time-difficulty is the inordinate use of dialogue,
and Gissing in this respect is a typical offender.
He " overdoes the ostensible report of spoken
words ; though I hasten to add that this abuse is
so general a sign, in these days, of the English and
American novel as to deprive a challenge of every
hope of credit. It is attended visibly—that is,
visibly to those who can see—with two or three
woeful results. If it had none other it would still
deserve arraignment on the simple ground of what
it crowds out—the golden blocks themselves of the
structure, the whole divine exercise and mystery
of the exquisite art of presentation. The ugliest
trick it plays at any rate is its effect on that side

USE AND ABUSE OF DIALOGUE

of the novelist's effort—the side of most difficulty
and therefore of most dignity—which consists in
giving the sense of duration, of the lapse and
accumulation of time. This is altogether, in my
view, the stiffest problem that the artist in fiction
has to tackle, and nothing is more striking at
present than the blankness, for the most part, of
his indifference to it. The mere multiplication
of quoted remarks is the last thing to strengthen
his hand."

In our examination of the novels we shall find
plentiful occasion to note the skill with which
James conducts his dialogue element. In the
interests of experimentation, and following in his
own original way the lead of Gyp and Lavedan,
he has in rare cases based his construction on the
conversational method alone. *The Awkward Age*
is executed almost throughout under this stringent
law. In this book he made it his aim to secure vividness of presentation while forgoing the
privilege, dear to the psychological analyst, of
" going behind " any one of the characters, and
sacrificing the " golden blocks of narrative " and
multiplied touches of the descriptive brush that
serve to educe the meaning and compose the picture.
Such a technical *tour de force* cannot give us a
formula of general application, and interests us
mainly, as it interested the writer, by virtue of
difficulties overcome. He has reared his edifice
without bricks or mortar, and has proved that,
other resources failing, the spoken word is tough
and malleable material that may be wrought into
form to withstand the pressure of superimposed

217

weight. *The Outcry* and *The Sacred Fount* are
largely conversational, but in his normal practice
he tended to confine dialogue within much narrower
limits than it occupies in the work of our best
writers of fiction. Where books are so much an
affair of perspective, each word must be focused
upon the centre of the theme, and discursiveness
is fatal to a symmetrical design. He sacrificed live-
liness, eloquence and wit in the interests of this
higher economy, but it cannot be denied that the
studied uniformity of utterance that he achieved in
his later books is responsible for a lack of salience
in his characters. Differentiation may be secured
in a variety of ways, but James at an early date
abandoned the cheap and easy device of oddity of
gesture and eccentricity of speech. He apologises
for the delightful Henrietta Stackpole of 1880, and
says no good word for the discursively brilliant
Gabriel Nash, to whom *The Tragic Muse* owes so
much for the vivacity of his fancy and the audacity
of his wit. He invokes again the authority of Balzac
for his discreet employment of the conversational
resource, yet Balzac, who from the fullness of his
documentation could afford to subordinate dialogue
and still preserve the salience of his multitudinous
figures, perpetually finds the revealing word that
flashes a character upon us and lights up its most
hidden tracts. Balzac has recourse to dialogue
to illuminate a situation and to reveal character,
though heaven knows he takes full advantage elsewhere in his books of the author's privilege to vent
his own opinions. Flaubert's mind, to mention
another authority invoked by James, was not rich

in general views, and he had not Balzac's temptation to make his characters talk at random and at large ; yet his conversations repeatedly drift beyond the limits of the central situation. The apothecary Homais is a part of Emma's mean and narrow world, but his divagations have nothing whatever to do with her particular problem. Their sole yet ample justification is that they solidly establish the character and exhibit the vanity and pompous insincerity with which the author's ironic vision chose to endow him. Turgénief was, in James's view, the " perfect novelist," and Turgénief's range in dialogue is still freer from restraint. It does not usurp the function of narrative, but it does everything of which dialogue is legitimately capable. It marks character and illuminates a situation of course, but also it is a well-grooved channel through which flows a brimming river of ideas. So long as the ideas are in character their utterance infringes no conceivable law of art, and Turgénief satisfied this condition by introducing into his books voluble talkers, whose expansiveness is their temperamental sign. To return to James. While his conversations are generally, as we say, " in character," we have noted that he avoids the accent that marks the tonic difference of one individual from another. His interlocutors are merged in the monotony of their high civilisation, and they are so subtle that it is often by reticence rather than by speech that they are betrayed to us — a peculiarity well exemplified in the pleasant game of hide-and-seek we play throughout *The Golden Bowl*. His reverence, too, for the dominant theme does not allow him even in the reflective passages the author's licence of variegated comment in which Balzac so freely indulges himself, and I can think of no character like Flaubert's Homais who is permitted to reveal himself in terms and by actions that do not chime with the particular intention of the book. It is his solicitude for tone and atmosphere that has compelled this reserve, and James probably felt that the business he had in mind, the necessity of exhibiting the interrelations of his chosen group, was matter large enough to occupy and to repay his full attention. *The Tragic Muse*, whose theme is art, and *The Princess Casamassima*, whose theme is socialism, are the only full-length novels in which, thanks to the subject-matter, the conversations are allowed a flexible range.

We may now estimate the degree of co-operation between the practice of James and his critical theory. Representation of life, the revelation of human relations in a given situation, is his supreme concern as a novelist. A social case is posited, and an interested group of persons is established whose varying reactions from the series of situations in which they are involved are the " golden joints," the noiseless, well-oiled hinges on which the story turns. One's first business is to " condition " the characters—establish them substantially, that is to say, in their environment. Since it was James's usual practice to launch his stories from an initial conception of character, the environment creates itself spontaneously in a normal relation to the tastes and habits of his groups. They are not like Hardy's major or minor personages rooted in the

THE ELEMENT OF DESCRIPTION

soil, nor like the men and women of Balzac huddled within the walls of some provincial town. They are unencumbered wanderers where interest and beauty invite them, and " fixedness " is the characteristic that least denotes them. The function of description is limited therefore to an impressionistic brushing in of the general aspects of sumptuous country houses, world capitals, or towns unsoiled by commerce and rich in the accumulated beauties of the past. James abounds in admiration for the localising faculty of Balzac and his French disciples, but he is himself not subjugated to their passion for externals. The restless habits of his people abstract them from the influence of a settled locality, and the further consideration prevailed with him that the inner drama is prone to be sacrificed when a writer makes the physical environment his supreme concern. It is essential to establish such a happy interrelation of the moral and physical worlds that they mutually support and play into one another. Stevenson cheated himself wilfully of his painter's privilege. " I read with unrestricted relish the first chapters of your prose volume (kindly vouchsafed me in the little copyright-catching red volume), and I loved 'em and blessed them quite. But I *did* make one restriction—I missed the *visible* in them—I mean as regards people, things, objects, faces, bodies, costumes, features, gestures, manners, the introductory, the *personal* painter-touch. It struck me that you either didn't feel—through some accident—your responsibility on this article quite enough, or, on some theory of your own, had declined it. No theory is kind to us that cheats us of *seeing.*" And in a later letter to R.L.S., after reading *Catriona* : " The one thing I miss in the book is the note of *visibility*; it subjects my visual sense, my *seeing* imagination, to almost painful underfeeding. The *hearing* imagination, as it were, is nourished like an alderman, and the loud audibility seems a slight the more on the baffled lust of the eyes; so that I seem to myself . . . in the presence of voices in the darkness—voices the more distinct and vivid, the more brave and sonorous, as voices always are—but also the more tormenting and confounding by reason of these bandaged eyes. I utter a pleading moan when you, *e.g.*, transport your characters, towards the end, in a line or two from Leyden to Dunkirk, without the glint of a hint of all the ambient picture of the eighteenth-century road. However, stick to your own system of evocation so long as what you positively achieve is so big. Life and letters and art all take joy in you."

Stevenson, as we know, had vowed " death to the adjective and destruction to the optic nerve." His eliminations, therefore, were designed and deliberate. The copiousness of evocation in his younger successors—Mr Wells and Mr Bennett, for example—received the fullest commendation from James, who noted, in reservation merely, that they were possessed of a greater abundance of life than they could artfully organise. If one must discriminate between the too little and the too much of seeing, James inclines to the view that safety lies for the novelist in the fuller quantity, provided always that the material is harmoniously disposed to intensify the drama of motives and multiply the vibrations that proceed from the inner life of the characters.

Turning to the books of James we realise that, in so far as concerns the " conditioning " of his characters, his theory outruns his performance. He has a wonderful faculty of evocation, but within closely defined limits. In obedience to his theory, and after the gropings of his experimental youth had pointed the better way, he developed his characters by a process of progressive revelation : his major figures are never, after the manner of Balzac, Dickens or Bennett, sharply discriminated and set solidly on their feet at the outset, but take shape and substance with the gradual unfolding of the story. Much, too, as he favoured the method of analysis, he abstained from such anticipatory dissection of character as marred, in his opinion, the novels of Bourget ; and he avoided with equal solicitude the " omniscient author's " comment after the event that has baffled or infatuated the readers of George Sand or Meredith. But however gradual the process of revelation may be, he does not fail to mark the identity of his characters, and it is a graceless reader who does not recognise their vivid sufficiency. He is more forthright with his subordinate figures. Our knowledge of Kate Croy and Milly Theale is a leisurely and luxurious affair, but we are suddenly possessed of all the items in Mrs Lowder's capacious register. Kate's courage is not easily daunted, but living in her aunt's house and on her aunt's bounty " she compared herself to a trembling kid, kept apart a day or two till her

turn should come, but sure sooner or later to be
introduced into the cage of the lioness. The cage
was Aunt Maud's own room, her office, her counting-
house, her battle-field, her especial scene, in fine, of
action, situated on the ground floor, opening from
the main hall, and figuring rather to our young
woman on exit and entrance as a guard-house or a
toll-gate. The lioness waited—the kid had at least
that consciousness—was aware of the neighbourhood of a morsel she had reason to suppose tender.
She would have been meanwhile a wonderful lioness
for a show, an extraordinary figure in a cage or
anywhere; majestic, magnificent, high-coloured,
all brilliant gloss, perpetual satin, twinkling bugles
and flashing gems, with a lustre of agate eyes, a
sheen of raven hair, a polish of complexion that
was like that of well-kept china and that—as if
the skin were too tight—told especially at curves
and corners." Her moral items are presently totalled
up for us by Merton Densher—the Car of Jugger-
naut is his figured designation of the portentous
lady—and thus, with no expenditure of comment
from the author, Mrs Lowder is rapidly revealed to
us in feature, form and moral stature.

Vagueness of representation is not a defect, then,
of the major novels, and it exists in the shorter
pieces only where ample characterisation would ex-
tend the theme beyond its designed range. I have
spoken, however, of certain limits imposed upon his
faculty of evocation, and Henry James admits
his embarrassment when, as so often happens, he
finds a man of the American business world upon
his hands. His prefaces deal amusingly with his

perplexities in this regard, and he conjures away his difficulties by simply refusing to face them, or turns them deftly to his advantage by an evasion of the intractable items. Such an evasion is the device of endowing Maggie Verver's father, the retired merchant prince, with an energetically developed æsthetic sense. We still feel that his notation is incomplete, and that Balzac would have made it a matter of conscience to provide him with the necessary documents of authentication.

The limitations of our author may be considered from another point of view when we turn to his method of establishing the physical environment of his characters. We shall seek in vain in his later pages for passages of detached description, his early misdemeanours not being in question here. A paragraph that might be eliminated without impairment of the complete design is such a paragraph as James resolutely refused to write. His sketches of travel reveal his abounding facility in reproducing the features of a scene that interested him, but no novelist of repute has subjected his natural copiousness to such restraint. If this is a limitation, it is incurred in the interests of a theory of art that valued subordination and proportion at a higher appraisement than the writers of a romantic generation had been willing to accord them. There is room for regret that his characters react only from the ordered beauties of nature as man has fashioned them, from formal gardens, clipt yews and lordly terraces, or from cities where the ages have lodged their treasures. Masterly as is his evocation of the tone of the Continental centres through which his characters march in monotonous procession, we miss the lyric charm of Meredith and Hardy, and Conrad's wide horizons. Susceptibility to the elemental forces that move through the world is a revelation of temperament as interesting to note as impressionability from a more sophisticated source, and here it is that we must indicate a positive limitation of James's observant faculty. His appreciation of wild nature was as imperfect as his apprehension of significance in the untrained mind of man.

A faint sense of missed opportunities occasionally visited him, and an early letter to Miss Grace Norton betrays a twinge of conscience for inspirations deliberately forgone in the abandonment of his native country: " It would seem that in our great unendowed, unfurnished, unentertained and unentertaining continent, where we all sit sniffing, as it were, the very earth of our foundations, we ought to have leisure to turn out something handsome from the very heart of simple human nature."

The home-keeping Hardy managed to do this for England, but James thought the miracle operable only in an undeveloped country, and its achievement after all not worth the rigours of sacrifice it would entail. He preferred to remain where life was organised and its accretions rich. In any other scene a novelist's outlook must be pinched and provincial. Such was the case with Hawthorne, as James was at some pains to show in his account of a writer whom in other respects he greatly valued. Howells demurred at the imputation of provincialism to Hawthorne, and protested against the contention of James that it takes an old civilisation to set a novelist in motion—" a proposition," replied James, " that seems to me so true as to be a truism. It is on manners, customs, usages, habits, forms, upon all these things matured and established, that a novelist lives; they are the very stuff his work is made of; and in saying that in the absence of those ' dreary and worn-out paraphernalia ' which I enumerate as being wanting in American society, ' we have simply the whole of human life left,' you beg (to my sense) the question. I should say we had just so much less of it as these ' paraphernalia ' represent, and I think they represent an enormous quantity of it."

A sentence from *The American Scene* restates this view with epigrammatic point : " It takes a great deal of history to make a little tradition, a great deal of tradition to make a little taste, and a great deal of taste to make a little art." Again, we come back to the question of an author's good or ill fortune in his environment, and his consequent good or ill fortune in the choice of subjects that lie ready to his hand. While the treatment of a subject must always weigh more in our esteem than the subject itself, it is a sufficiently elementary truth that a good theme well treated must always outweigh in value an indifferent theme executed with like power. Flaubert execrated the themes that modern life afforded him, and established his faith in the redeeming virtues of superior craftsmanship. But his ironic detachment from his characters is not an adequate substitute for the sympathy that should flow from an author to the world of his creation. Repellent or gracious, a character can never take on the hues of life unless the generating mind has warmed it with passion. To assert with Taine that Balzac " loves his Valérie " does not imply a fund of virtue in this unlovely person, but is a guarantee that her creator will not by his capricious ill-will or warping irony frustrate her of her freedom to develop.

This is sound doctrine, but we cannot subscribe without reserve to our author's insistence that characters are interesting only in so far as they are aware of the predicament in which they stand. It is Don Quixote's bewildered state that attaches us to him and endeared him to Cervantes. The blundering confusion of Monsieur Jourdain is more fun-provoking than the subtle machinations of Mascarille, and the unconscious generators of humour—the Dogberrys, the Slenders, the Silences, the Coggans and the Cantles—are not jeopardised of their immortality by virtue of their muddled wits. James is perhaps not qualified to speak of mirth-provoking characters, and his theories are barren of reference to them. He makes some concessions to the vulgarities and ineptitudes of minor personages, but on the need of luminosity at the centre he is adamant. Flaubert's art is compromised by his neglect of this law, and it required the prodigious virtuosity of Ibsen to arouse our interest in the passions of his *bourgeois* world. James is curiously reticent of reference to Mr Hardy, whose mastery of the resources of his art has been so rarely challenged : but we may safely surmise that his lack of sympathy derives from the same cause.

ON CENTRAL CHARACTERS

If I am interpreting his silence aright, his judgment was that Hardy, no less than Flaubert and Ibsen, is in bondage to the mediocre, and that his imperfectly civilised beings are, at the best, but broken registers and cracked reflectors of the passions that sway them. Ideas in the highest sense they cannot possess; all subtlety is denied them; and to endow them with significance the author is forced to levy tribute upon his own mind, an expedient which, if rashly resorted to, is fraught with disaster to the artistic integrity of the work.

We must not understand James as implying the necessity of setting a Lear or a Hamlet in the centre of his action. " Where a light lamp will carry all the flame," he inclines " to look askance at a heavy "; but his invariable practice is to choose central characters who are capable of bearing their whole dramatic burden without shifting it to the shoulders of the author. His severest experiment in centrality was in *The Ambassadors*, where the whole story is sifted through Strether's mind. He felt that in this book, more than in any other, he had approximated to his ideal of compactness, having " sat on it," as he wrote to Mr Hugh Walpole in Germany, " with that intending weight and presence with which you probably often sit in these days on your trunk to make the lid close and *all* your trousers and boots go in."

He is satisfied usually with a looser concentration, lighting his subject, as in *The Golden Bowl*, from the consciousness of two persons, and allowing himself the privilege in other books of " going behind " the minds of several of his major characters.

His opinions as to the right use and abuse of this privilege form the subject of an interesting letter of advice to Mrs Humphry Ward, who had submitted her novel, *Eleanor*, to his criticism. The letters also to Mr Wells are full of the friendliest and wisest advice as to how a story may be conducted to the best advantage. He had the frankest admiration for Mr Wells's " cheek " and his brimming sense of life. His uncontrolled fluidity alarmed him, but as we read the kindly letters we realise that James was never so completely the slave of formal doctrines as to forfeit his right to enjoy work that does not proceed from a rigid theory of art. " Strange to me—in his affair—" he writes to Mrs Humphry Ward on the subject of Mr Wells's *Marriage*, " the co-existence of so much talent with so little art, so much life with (so to speak) so little living ! But of him there is much to say, for I really think him more interesting by his faults than he will probably ever manage to be in any other way ; and he is a most vivid and violent object-lesson."

The main thing is to possess a sense of life and the gift to represent it with entertaining vividness. The virtue of art resides in the economy of power it generates, and the one ineluctable law imposed upon the artist is that he shall dominate the prodigal wastefulness of life. " Life," said Stevenson, " is monstrous, infinite, illogical, abrupt and poignant ; a work of art, in comparison, is neat, finite, self-contained, rational, flowing and emasculate." Save for the last word James might have written this, and the two craftsmen mingle their theories at many points. But Stevenson is wholly wrong in his assumption that James proceeds by a fixed law and is the same from book to book. "The life of man is not the subject of novels, but the inexhaustible magazine from which subjects are to be selected : the name of these is legion ; and with each new subject—for here again I must differ by the whole width of heaven from Mr James—the true artist will vary his method and change the point of attack. That which was in one case an excellence will become a. defect in another ; what was the making of one book will in the next be impertinent or dull."

James, on the contrary, held that variety of attack and treatment is a constant obligation. Mrs Humphry Ward, like Stevenson, had entertained a false view of his position. "As to there being but *one general* 'hard and fast rule of presentation,' I protest that I have never had with you any difference, consciously, on any such point, and rather resent, frankly, your attributing to me a judgment so imbecile. I hold that there are five million such 'rules' (or as many as there are subjects in the world—I fear the subjects are *not* five million !), only each of them imposed, artistically, by the particular case—involved in the writer's responsibility to it ; and each *then*—and then only —'hard and fast' with an immitigable hardness and fastness. I don't see, without this latter condition, where any work of art, any artistic *question* is, or any artistic probity."

VIII

THE MAJOR NOVELS

JAMES never consented to regard *Watch and Ward*, which appeared in *The Atlantic Monthly* in 1871, as his first novel. An artist with the principle of growth in him is often severer than the critics with his own insufficiency. The time was to come when he would speak of *Roderick Hudson* as vilely written ; but it was with every intention of producing a genuine book that in the spring and early summer of 1874 he settled himself in Florence to fulfil his serial contract with his friend Howells of *The Atlantic Monthly*. When the book appeared in the course of the following year Henry James became, after ten years of earnest amateur scribbling, a professional novelist.

Like many another first novel, *Roderick Hudson* (1875) is too ambitiously planned, but its author has more art than the ordinary beginner to make a failure interesting, and to beguile his readers with a fallacious sense of effortless ease when he was really floundering through difficulties and labouring for breath. His design was to portray a man of genius, and to reveal him to us in his formative period, in the moment of his success and in the decline of his intellectual and moral nature. Fiction shows few examples of artistic or literary genius convincingly displayed, and for a young writer to attempt the task and complicate it by a representation of the decay of these abnormal powers was to invite almost inevitable failure.

The peculiar distinction of James in his maturer work is his competence to occupy the whole scope of his design. His books are so planned that his intentions are amply fulfilled; and though he may drive his road through hazardous country, he never advances without a preliminary survey and measures taken for the surmounting of all engineering difficulties. In *Roderick Hudson*, by throwing pontoon bridges across the rivers and rope ladders across the gorges, he gets us precariously to the end of our journey; but lest these metaphors should mislead us into the assumption that the book is complicated by dangers of flood and fire and sword, I hasten to add that the processes of Roderick's decay are attended with singularly few incidents of an adventurous kind. He escapes from Rowland Mallet's oppressive company, but his borrowing of a few hundred pounds is our only indication that he has enjoyed himself in Baden-Baden. There he meets the balefully beautiful Christina Light, who completes what Rome had already begun — his alienation from his native country, and his abnegation of all the sentimental ties that bind the ordinary man to his home. Rowland seeks to redeem his friend in the early stages of his dereliction by compelling him to send for his mother and Mary Garland, who had engaged herself to him on the eve of his departure. Their appearance produces the contrary of the desired effect, and Christina's fascinations are more strongly exercised by reason of her simple

rival's presence. Christina's mother had engineered
her betrothal with the wealthy Prince Casamassima.
On the threshold of the wedding the girl precipitates
a rupture, and everything seems to point to an
elopement with the brilliant young sculptor. Her
mother brings unusual pressure to bear on her, and
bends her will to the repugnant marriage and the
wealth and splendid station in the world it secures.
Rowland suspects that the pressure was nothing
less than the hint that her father was the abject
Cavaliere Giacosa, and that Christina was merely
making a choice of horrors in preferring marriage
to a publication of this indignity. It is thus in-
auspiciously that the ceremony takes place. A few
months later the Princess encounters the Hudson
group in Switzerland, and further complications
are saved by Roderick's death at the bottom of a
cliff.

James deals somewhat tenderly with this firstling
romance in his review of forty years later. His
kindly attitude towards the book was not prompted
by any consideration of its merits, which he thought
meagre, but because to renew contact with its pages
was to revive the ambitions of his youth and to
rekindle memories of the pleasant places with which
those ambitions were associated. He felt that he
had failed in vividness on the American side of the
picture, but, after all, the volubly vulgar Mr Striker
and Mary Garland hemming her coarse kitchen
towel sufficiently meet the realistic demands of the
reader. More important is the failure of perspective
he notes in the abruptly foreshortened account of
Roderick's moral collapse. Revolutions of character

are not often so catastrophic as James has made
this particular one appear, and the author further
involved himself in the equally difficult task, which
confronted him later in Miriam Rooth, of accounting also for the sudden development of power that
preceded the decay. Genius is a word to conjure
with, but even genius requires some preparation,
and must use ladders like the humblest talent. If,
for Roderick's development, we are willing to accept
mere affirmations for demonstration, the process of
sudden decay is still to be accounted for. James
has recourse in his dilemma to the old convention
of the wild irregularity of genius, its inborn contempt of prescription, its rudderless reliance on
impulse. Artistic conscience is allowed also to
exercise its pressure, and Roderick is given us as
an example of a creative genius whose technique,
however wonderful, is incompetent to register his
dreams of ideal perfection. But the great instrument
of his moral decay was a woman of devastating
beauty and diabolic charm, and James exerts himself to the utmost to represent the personality and
influence of the enigmatic Christina Light. It was
reserved for a later book to reveal her more completely. In the early novel, not only was his knowledge of the sex less profound, but his hands were
tied by his method, since we are dependent for our
knowledge of her complexity on Rowland Mallet's
unsupported testimony, and Rowland does not
impress us as possessed of the requisite subtlety
or depth for his task. A letter from him to his
cousin Cecilia gives us the situation when the story
is half-way advanced to its conclusion : " I wish,

235

heaven forgive me, that he were less of a genius and more of a charlatan. He's too confoundedly all of one piece ; he won't throw overboard a grain of cargo to save the rest. Fancy him thus, with all his brilliant charm, his handsome head, his careless step, his look as of a nervous nineteenth-century Apollo, and you'll understand that there's mighty little comfort in seeing him spoil on the tree. He was extremely perverse last summer at Baden-Baden, but he finally pulled together and was for some time steady. Then he began to knock about again, and at last toppled over. Now, literally, he's lying prone. He came into my room last night miserably the worse for liquor. I assure you it didn't amuse me. . . . About Miss Light, it's a long story. She's one of the great beauties of all time, and worth coming barefoot to Rome, like the pilgrims of old, to see. Her complexion, her eyes, her step, the planting and the mass of her dusky tresses may have been seen before in a goddess on a cloud or a nymph on a Greek gem, but never in a mere modern girl. And you may take this for truth, because I'm not in love with her. On the contrary, I sometimes quite detest her. Her education has been simply infernal. She is corrupt, perverse, as proud as a potentate, and a coquette of the first magnitude ; but she's intelligent and bold and free, and so awfully on the look-out for sensations that if you get rightly to work you may enlist her imagination in a good cause as well as a bad. . . . I've come to the conclusion that she's more dangerous in her virtuous moods than in her vicious."

THE AMERICAN

It was James's recognition of Christina's undeveloped possibilities that prompted him to resurrect her and subject the baffling contrariety of her nature to a more competent analysis. Rowland Mallet luckily drops away from her in the book that bears her name, but the good Grandoni, shorter of breath and ampler of girth, is revived with her and justifies her resurrection. The duenna has taken very actually the measure of Christina's tainted idealism, and recognises precisely to what extent this magnificent creature is the dupe of her own theatrical enthusiasms. Madame Grandoni's ultimate desertion of this beautiful wrecker of souls is the only clue the author provides for us in this moral labyrinth.

The American, like *Roderick Hudson,* was subjected by James to a rigorous verbal revision before being admitted into the New York edition of his works. I have noted elsewhere the angry outbreak amusingly reported by Sir Edmund Gosse when the latter questioned the propriety of tampering with the early books. The remonstrance cannot be pressed too seriously. Since these early books, after all, remain for reference, we may, if the evolution of the author is in question, spend a profitable half-hour in the collation of phrases and passages. There is hardly, I imagine, a page in either book that was allowed to remain precisely as it was written. For purposes of comparison I shall select passages from *The American* almost at random, and the reader may reach, independently of me, his own conclusions.

Early Edition	*New York Edition*
1. And yet he was evidently not a man to whom fatigue was familiar ; long, lean, and muscular, he suggested the sort of vigour that is commonly known as " toughness."	1. And yet he was evidently not a man to whom fatigue was familiar ; long, lean, and muscular, he suggested an intensity of unconscious resistance.
2. The gentleman on the divan was a powerful specimen of an American. But he was not only a fine American ; he was, in the first place, physically, a fine man.	2. The gentleman on the divan was the superlative American ; to which affirmation of character he was partly helped by the general easy magnificence of his manhood.
3. His eye was of a clear, cold grey, and save for a rather abundant moustache he was clean-shaved.	3. His eye was of a clear, cold grey, and save for the abundant droop of his moustache he spoke, as to cheek and chin, of the joy of the matutinal steel.
4. As the little copyist proceeded with her work, she sent every now and then a responsive glance toward her admired.	4. As the little copyist proceeded with her task, her attention addressed to her admirer, from time to time, for reciprocity, one

Early Edition	*New York Edition*
	of its blankest, though not of its briefest, missives.
5. At last he rose abruptly, put on his hat, and approached the young lady.	5. At last he rose abruptly, and putting on his hat, as if for emphasis of an austere intention, approached the young lady.
6. The truth is that circumstances had done much to cultivate in Mrs Tristram a marked tendency to irony.	6. The truth is that circumstances had done much to cultivate in Mrs Tristram the need for any little intellectual luxury she could pick up by the way.
7. Her clear grey eyes were strikingly expressive ; they were both gentle and intelligent, and Newman liked them immensely ; but they had not those depths of splendour—those many coloured rays—which illumine the brow of famous beauties.	7. Her wide grey eyes were like a brace of deputed and garlanded maidens waiting with a compliment at the gate of a city, but they failed of that lamp-like quality and those many-coloured fires that light up, as in a constant celebration of anniversaries, the fair front of the conquering type.

Early Edition	*New York Edition*
8. Madame de Cintré was rather thin, and she looked younger than probably she was. In her whole person there was something both youthful and subdued, slender and yet ample, tranquil yet shy; a mixture of immaturity and repose, of innocence and dignity.	8. Madame de Cintré was of attenuated substance and might pass for younger than she probably was. In her whole person was something still young and still passive, still uncertain and that seemed still to expect to depend, and which yet made, in its dignity, a presence withal, and almost represented, in its serenity, an assurance.
9. M. de Bellegarde was a foreigner to his finger-tips, and if Newman had met him on a Western prairie he would have felt it proper to address him with a " How-d'ye-do, Mosseer ? " But there was something in his physiognomy which seemed to cast a sort of aerial bridge over the impassable gulf produced by difference of race.	9. M. de · Bellegarde was a foreigner to the last roll of his so frequently rotary r; and if he had met him out in bare Arizona he would have felt it proper to address him with a " How-d'ye-do, Mosseer ? " Yet there was that in his physiognomy which seemed to suspend a bold bridge of gilt wire over the impassable gulf produced by difference of race.

THE AMERICAN

A glance of the eye assures us that James, as time went on, required more words to express his meaning, and from the resultant charge of verbosity he can be exonerated only if he has more meaning to express. Perhaps that is really the truth of the situation. The accretion of words often gives the effect of making his phrases seem not more prolix, but more tightly packed. I will not say that every alteration in my random extracts makes for improvement. There is a hint, for example, of preciousness in the " matutinal steel " of the third passage. It was inevitable, perhaps, that in his eagerness to escape banality he should sometimes pay the penalty in an unpardonable ponderosity of phrase. But numbers one and two are a clear improvement. Number four, where one might prefer the flat to the mannered, is open to question, and probably the preference might also be given to the simple early number seven over the weird Cyrano de Bergerac substitution. My specimens have been of the author's descriptive comment, but the dialogue has been no less markedly modified, and here there has been an unquestioned advance in point and naturalness. The whole of chapter seven would reward the attention of a reader determined to deal teutonically with the processes of James's style.

The situation that our author works out in this book he carried in his mind for years before he had the courage to attack it. In so far as the surmounting of difficulties is concerned he might as well have tackled the theme in the first flush of his invention, or have given himself the luxury of a longer incubation. He admits the falseness of the central conception—that is, the ascription of a dastardly and motiveless crime to Madame de Bellegarde and her eldest son ; but he flatters himself that he has made a merit of his defect by creating for his book an atmosphere of romantic mystery and suspense. Now James, and to his ultimate advantage, was very imperfectly endowed to explore the possibilities of adventurous romance—the romance of the dagger and the cowl, of dark, mysterious chambers and subterranean caves. His earliest efforts, and weak and groping they were, abound in melodramatic situations and overflow with effusive descriptions ; but a chastening process gradually mitigated this exuberance, and by the time *The American* was written he had already achieved his emancipation from romantic extravagance. Christopher Newman has no impulse, for example, to scale the walls of the convent of the Rue d'Enfer, but paces the streets instead like an ordinarily disappointed man. The virtues or demerits, therefore, that attach to romanticism are not in question here, and we accept the crime as a somewhat clumsy expedient for precipitating the crisis that his plot demanded. Let us reach this crisis swiftly and draw our conclusion.

Christopher Newman is represented as an American in the early forties of his life, who, having made a large fortune in wash-tubs, leather and kindred enterprises, conceives a sudden disrelish for the further amassing of coin, and forgoes even an opportunity for honourable revenge upon a business rival, which would have, made him richer by an added half-million. Instead of carrying out this quite legitimate transaction he comes to Europe to improve his mind and to find a wife, and his baffled efforts in both directions are the story's theme. It was not difficult to exemplify his failure to achieve culture, for, granted his sufficient yet unæsthetic mind, a meagre measure of success in that direction was inevitable. He would grow as emancipated as you please, but expert never. His matrimonial adventures therefore constitute the main problem, and here James demands more concessions than the reader is disposed to give. He has, for sponsors in society, only Mr and Mrs Tristram; and since the problem was to provide a contrast between the honest, shrewd yet naïve American and certain polished, corrupt and sophisticated specimens of an older civilisation, the first difficulty was evidently to establish relations for Newman in the great world. To this end the out-at-elbows device of a convent friendship had to be adopted, and we are to understand that after the lapse of years, and having been unhappily wedded and happily widowed, Claire de Bellegarde refused to let her childish intimacy with the present Mrs Tristram die. When Newman, therefore, communicates to Mrs Tristram his eagerness to marry and his determination to marry with splendour—a piece of snobbery, I may remark, that does not chime in with his character—the lady is quick to suggest the still young and beautiful Madame de Cintré as the woman in all Europe who will suit him best. A meeting takes place at the Tristram house, but Newman has no further opportunity of pressing his suit until his return from a Continental tour—that inevitable and pathetic resource of the Jamesian American in search of culture.

Up to this point the book is sufficiently commonplace, and is only inadequately relieved by the subordinate episode of the Nioches, which has the slenderest connection with the main story. The saving element that now enters is Claire's younger brother, the superlatively attractive Valentine, in whose life the book lives, and in whose death it dies. And truly the book was in full need of enlivenment, for Christopher was not born under the planet Mercury, and tradition and authority have set their killing weight on any natural spirits that Claire might normally have had. But her brother is not benumbed by chilling contacts, and his resiliency is proof against all the casual troubles of existence. His recklessness courts disaster at every turn, and he would have died as he had lived, gaily, if he had not learned of the perfidious breach of faith of which his mother and his brother were guilty. It is the stain on his family honour that darkens his dying hours. He drags from the reluctant Newman the admission that Claire's family have used some strange compulsion upon her to break off the engagement to which they had given their consent. Valentine has a grim suspicion of what this compulsion may be, and acting on his hint Newman acquires possession of a document that places his enemies at his mercy. It is nothing less than an ante-mortem statement of the old Marquis, in which he accuses his wife of murdering him.

With Valentine out of the story, James falls back for the sustainment of interest upon the elaboration of his original first conception—a guileless yet strong-willed American, the suitor of a woman of high birth, infamously rejected by the family that has accepted him, and presently possessed of information that would utterly discredit them. The theme is not adapted to his genius, yet working with alien material he does not wholly fail of his effects. A dozen contemporary writers could have manipulated more skilfully the element of suspense, but we cannot be certain that they would have divined the quite special value that might be elicited from the ultimate renunciation of revenge. This and the Valentine portrait are the redeeming features of a faulty book. I rank it for importance not above *The Bostonians*, and its reperusal satisfies me that the alteration of manner and method that begins to be so marked towards 1890 was prompted by an instinct wholly sound. James was not completely himself until he discovered that he was totally unlike everybody else. It has happened before in literary history that sincerity and naturalness have suffered rebuke as pose and affectation. The truth about James is that his particular form of sincerity and naturalness has never formed a working alliance with simplicity.

We now arrive at *The Portrait of a Lady* (1880), which is a book fortunate amongst its fellows in having enough of the obvious to recommend it to the casual reader, and enough subtlety to recompense attentive perusal. Of all novelists the one who has most to gain from the discernment of his public, James permits himself least the satisfaction of expecting it. " The artist may of course, in wanton moods, dream of some Paradise (for art) where the direct appeal to the intelligence might be legalised ; for to such extravagances as these his yearning mind can scarce hope ever completely to close itself. The most he can do is to remember they are extravagances . . . he is entitled to nothing that can come to him from the reader as a result on the latter's part of any act of reflection or discrimination. He may enjoy this finer tribute —that is another affair—but on condition only of taking it as a gratuity ' thrown in,' a mere miraculous windfall, the fruit of a tree he may not pretend to have shaken."

This seems sufficient sanction for glancing first at the superficial interests of the story, which, as I have said, abound for the casual reader, before venturing upon an analysis of the calculated subtleties that reveal the author's more deep-lying intention, and which for him at least constitute the book's claim to be considered as a work of art.

Isabel Archer is discovered by her eccentric aunt, Mrs Touchett, in her apparently dull Albany home, and she eagerly succumbs to the latter's invitation to accompany her to Italy. James divides Americans into two broad groups — an intelligent class, that yields readily to the lure of Europe and the larger life, and an unintelligent class, that travels miserably and under the compulsion of habit or example. Isabel is at once impressionable and intelligent, but if any further motive were necessary to win her consent to her aunt's proposal, we may discover it in her desire to escape the too masterful attentions of Caspar Goodwood. Isabel does not wish to sacrifice her liberty before she has begun to live, and marriage with Caspar offers her no prospect of the enlarged experience her imagination craves.

We meet her first in her new surroundings at Gardencourt, where Mrs Touchett, *en route* for Florence, occasionally looks in upon her valetudinarian husband and Ralph, her invalid son. Gardencourt is a sumptuous place, and Isabel promptly fascinates its inhabitants by her quick response to its varied charm. Ralph quizzes her in true cousinly fashion, but makes no concealment of his more than cousinly interest in her. Old Mr Touchett likewise falls under the spell, and Lord Warburton, with remarkable alertness, offers marriage to the penniless girl. Him she refuses for much the same reasons that had before prevailed with her, but he clings to the hope that her rejection of him is not final.

Ralph persuades his father during his last illness to make over half his own share of the estate to Isabel, and she is now launched upon the second stage of her career as a very considerable heiress. We follow her fortunes presently to Italy, whither she has accompanied her aunt. Madame Merle, an enigmatic nomad American, has begun to exercise a certain ascendancy over Isabel's free spirit, and it is through her mediation that the girl meets Gilbert Osmond. Caspar is still pursuing her, Ralph is attentively watchful, and Warburton is as faithful as ever ; but the nonchalant fastidiousness

of Osmond and his noble poverty, so exquisitely
defeated by his unerring taste, prevail over the
more solid virtues and the more substantial claims
of the other suitors.

Her married life is a process of bitter disenchant
ment, and eventually she learns that her step
daughter Pansy is the fruit of an old *liaison* between
her husband and Madame Merle. With her newly
gained knowledge she realises that Madame Merle
had engineered her marriage with a view to her
daughter's interests. She still retains her fondness
for the girl, whose love affairs introduce a new and
final complication between Isabel and her husband.
Pansy and a rather ineffective young man named
Rosier are in love with one another, but Gilbert
aspires to a loftier connection. Lord Warburton
has again begun to frequent their Roman house
and appears to be captivated by Pansy's innocent
charms. Gilbert relies on Isabel to bring the affair
to an issue. At first she works with some willing
ness to that end, until, from a hint of Ralph's, she
discovers what her own quick perceptions should
have divined, that Lord Warburton's pursuit of
the girl was actuated by his old infatuation for
herself. From that moment her intervention ceases
and Osmond's resentment develops into a positive
hatred, from which there appears to be no issue or
escape. An avenue of escape does, however, seem
to open with a summons to come to Ralph's death
bed. She leaves for England in defiance of her
husband's wish, and has a final interview with
Ralph in which all her tenderness for him finds
vent and all her concealed suffering is revealed to

him. Caspar Goodwood, whom she had dismissed from Rome, makes a final appeal to her to sever her relations with her husband. His passion has an energy scarcely to be denied : she feels herself carried along on the torrent of his impetuous love, and realises that here is the protective strength, the devotion and the refuge that her heart craves. Yet knowing and feeling this, she masters her inclination and returns to Rome.

The theme of the book is clearly enough the career of an attractive girl who fronts life confidently, gains a few small triumphs, inspires a few loyal affections, yields to the weakness of a momentary infatuation, is miserable, escapes, and returns under compulsion of her sense of duty to the life of torture, for which there seems now no alleviation, and from which only the accident of death may set her free. The one prospect of hope that is given to Caspar Goodwood and the reader is afforded by Henrietta Stackpole : " ' Look here, Mr Goodwood,' she said, ' just you wait.'

" On which he looked up at her—but only to guess from her face, with a revulsion, that she simply meant he was young ! She stood shining at him with that cheap comfort, and it added on the spot thirty years to his life. She walked him away with her, however, as if she had given him the key to patience."

There is not much to be gained by portraying a woman with a mind, if that mind is ultimately to be cramped in its opportunity for growth, nor in emphasising the value of experience, if experience is to lead in the end to a spiritual prison in which the natural impulses of the heart must suffer an inevitable decay. We do not exact from a great artist a comfortable ending. It is not customary to approve Dr Johnson's reproach to Shakespeare for his disregard of poetic justice, and James has high enough sanction for his neglect of that same principle. But the ends of art might have been served, and one's sense of inevitable sequence might have suffered no injury, if some more immediate vista of escape had been granted to Isabel Osmond. This, after all, is not a Hardyesque tragedy, where everything co-operates to precipitate the impending doom, and where the gateless, unscalable wall of circumstance hems us in. It is the story of a girl of quick and eager mind, of affections and impulses equally quick and eager; and if I read the author's intention aright, he desired to illustrate the growth and not the paralysis of all these bounding energies. If there is one lesson that James, ordinarily so little dogmatic, is still inclined to emphasise, it is the value of abundant living. " Live as you like best," Ralph Touchett once told Isabel, " and your character will take care of itself." We know that there is nothing Rabelaisian involved in this prescription of conduct. There is always for James the check of moral decency, and to live abundantly implies with him always to live beautifully as well. But here is a character for whom fullness of life spells disaster, and whose determination to live beautifully seems to lead to no serener fate. Our difficulties in Isabel's case are not to supply explanations for her ultimate decision. These James marks out for us with sufficient clearness. She returns to Osmond not alone, nor chiefly, perhaps, because she had promised Pansy that she would not abandon her. Her main incentive was a kind of spiritual pride that recognised an obligation in her vows of marriage. She had wilfully followed her unsupported judgment in choosing her husband, and she is equally wilful now in her determination to accept the consequences. All this I say is clearly enough expressed, but the flaw in the conclusion still remains. We are cheated of our desire to see an abundant nature expand, and we are not permitted to witness in exchange for this extinguished hope her recovery of strength through suffering. James wrote a later book, *The Golden Bowl*, to prove how a wife, by the exercise of no gross efforts, may redeem a situation that a husband has put in jeopardy. But Amerigo was amenable and affection had not died. Neither condition exists in our present book, where we do not experience the justifiable satisfaction of seeing an impossible situation adjusted, nor entertain even the remote hope of its amelioration. We readily grant the effective manner in which James has represented the actual suffering. The art he displays in the whole second part of the story marks a distinct advance on anything he had hitherto done and points in the direction of his later subtlety and power. With this we must content ourselves and pass to a consideration of the way in which he has organised his fascinating story.

It is organised, as he tells us, after the manner of Turgénief—round a central character. This fact of itself may seem to indicate no departure from the ordinary type of fiction which invariably provides us with a hero or a heroine, and invents incidents that are designed to exhibit their dominant qualities. It is quite possible, therefore, to read *The Portrait of a Lady* with no consciousness of innovation; but we are not doing the book full justice until we realise that the author is tentatively striving after a new method of romantic expression. If, as our self-complacency assures us, we belong to the class of readers who, as James says, insist on shaking his tree for him, and are therefore as much interested in the way situations are presented as in the story itself, *The Portrait* will have merits, and imperfections even, that will reward our closer attention.

I have quarrelled with the book perhaps quite irrationally for what it does not contain, and have recorded a disappointment that is possibly only personal at the abortive ending. Coming to the actual substance of the story, we realise that it has all the elements of a transitional work, and if we rank it only short of James's best efforts in fiction, it is because we feel that the old and the new methods of composition are not perfectly fused. James thought it the most symmetrical of all his productions except *The Ambassadors*, but for many readers the combination of two compositional styles will have the effect of roughening the surface, so to speak, and the book as a result will seem to lack the smoothness of finish and harmony of tone that characterise perhaps even to excess the novels of his full maturity. For example, the long passages of a referential nature that give us Isabel's past in retrospect are inherited from an old tradition that James presently, and I am inclined to think with complete artistic justification, abandoned. Again, he has made in *The Portrait* a great advance towards centralising his interest in one character, yet he has found it necessary to apologise in his preface for so purely intrusive a figure as Henrietta Stackpole, with her still more detached admirer, Mr Bantling. A further development that we will approve is the elimination of the guide-book descriptions of his younger books. His use of local colour is more restrained and apposite, and his power of establishing the physical medium in which his characters move will scarcely admit of further development. But his later books achieve this result by subtler methods and with a surer discrimination of the relation that description should hold to the other elements of the narrative. The descriptions of Osmond's Fiesole house and garden are of this developed type, but more anticipatory still of the later style are the dialogue, the picture and the reflection that build up the scene of Isabel's first meeting with Madame Merle: "The lady played in the same manner as before, softly and solemnly, and while she played the shadows deepened in the room. The autumn twilight gathered in, and from her place Isabel could see the rain, which had now begun in earnest, washing the cold-looking lawn and the wind shaking the great trees."

Coming now to the characters we recognise Lord Warburton and Ralph as fine examples—Ralph, indeed, one of the finest—of the early method. Here, too, belongs the amusing but wholly impertinent

Henrietta Stackpole. Madame Merle and Gilbert
Osmond are children of the newer dispensa-
tion, and Isabel, as I have said, hovers somewhere
in a midway region between the new and old.
What James came to value increasingly in the art
of characterisation was the elimination of the
author's comment in favour of a process of gradual
revelation achieved by the successive notation of
thought and moods and aided by the reflected
perceptions and comments of the various par-
ticipants in the drama. We need only confront
Isabel and Maggie Verver to assure ourselves of
the virtue of a consistent method. Intrinsically
Isabel is the more attractive character and offers a
richer field for exploration, but Maggie is certainly
a greater triumph of art. She is wonderfully
illuminated both from within and without. What
we do not learn of her by the subtle notation of
her own moods and meditations we learn by the
reflected light of the Prince's and Charlotte's
actions, or by the running commentary of Mrs
Assingham's analysis of the situation. We are
free, then, to admire the quiet psychological effec-
tiveness of the chapter where Isabel sits meditating
before the embers of her midnight fire ; but in his
later period he would have launched his character
more promptly. He would not have spent so much
time in the dockyard constructing his craft. We
should have learned of the strength of her structure
by the way she glides over the water and takes the
buffets of the breezes and the waves.

The passage in the book that stands second in
point of significance, and that our memory dwells

on with most affection, is the chapter that gives
us Isabel's final interview with Ralph. I cannot
reconcile myself to a theory of art that would
eliminate a scene so touching and so effective. It
is such a scene that we miss in *The Wings of the
Dove*, where we witness in Merton Densher only
the moral reflection from his interview with the
dying Milly. James by this time had convinced
himself, to the point of infatuation, of the value of
indirect methods. A suggestion was always prefer-
able to a definite statement, the shadow always
more valuable than the substance. The point might
soon have been reached where, in the process of
elimination and rarefaction, incident would be
drained of all its vitality, and where the subtlety
of his analysis would carry us far from the rich,
warm-breathing human scene, which must always
be for the novelist his source of power. In James
the sense of humanity was so constant that for him
we do not seriously dread this threatened divorce
between art and life; but James as an originator
of a new method must be somewhat narrowly
watched. He can always find his moorings in
densest fog or darkest night, but the amateur
sailor navigating by his chart would court disaster
in daylight.

The period between *The Portrait of a Lady* and
The Bostonians (1885) was sufficiently filled with
the writing of short stories and travel sketches to
exempt James's conscience from the reproach of
idleness. These were years of constant peregrina-
tion about his favourite European haunts, and we
have noted two visits to his own country, where, in

255

this interval of time, both his parents died. The
conditions were obviously too disturbed to favour
sustained production, and, furthermore, James had
received no marked encouragement from the public
to devote himself to an extended effort. Such fame
as he enjoyed came to him as the author, not of
The American or *The Portrait*, but as the author of
Daisy Miller. *The Bostonians* is of the year 1885,
and we gather from several references in the letters
that only exigencies of space induced James to
omit it from the New York edition of his works.
He considered the book to possess merely a secondary
value, but he was willing to let it stand for the best
sort of thing he could produce in the old-fashioned
manner. Already he was beginning to weary of
following this much-trodden pathway, and the
almost contemporary *Princess Casamassima* reveals
his intention of striking out in a new direction.
A comparison of these two books, one the best
example of his efforts in the old tradition, the other
by no means the best example of his newer manner,
forces upon us the conclusion that the transition
of method was prompted by a sound artistic instinct.
His choice lay between producing books that a
score of other novelists might have written with
even more entertainment for the reader, and con-
centrating his effort upon a type of work of which
he only possessed the secret. That the second alternative should be adopted seemed to him inevitable, and it is important to note that the choice was
made, not from any desire to shine by singularity
but deliberately in the interests of an art of which
the possibilities had not been thoroughly explored

A more convincing contrast, should we desire to set the relative merits of the two methods in question, might be made between our present book and *The Golden Bowl* or *The Wings of the Dove*. *The Bostonians* we read with effortless ease. The processes of its design are so clear as to seem almost mechanical in their artifice. The author's intention is evident in every line. Everything that has happened is carefully explained, and we are as carefully prepared for everything that is about to happen. When a new character appears he is neatly labelled and docketed. A few pages suffice to put us in complete relation with Olive, with Mrs Luna, Miss Birdseye, the Tarrants, the Burbages and Basil Ransom. Verena is the only character who is not fully revealed to us from the outset, but in her case the mystery is legitimately due to the fact that hers is the only character that has not taken its mould. She is obviously in process of transformation, and we are permitted to gain our estimate of her from a series of anticipatory hints which, but for their inferior subtlety, suggest the art of preparation and gradual revelation that is so signal a virtue in his later work. This obvious transparency of design must not lead us prematurely to conclude the superiority in point of construction of novels like *Roderick Hudson* and *The Bostonians* to the less popular books of the later time. To the merits of a clear structure these early books add the merits of a simple, clear and nervous style, and I am not willing to contest the virtues of either form of clarity. Yet I subscribe to the considered verdict of those judges whose opinion I most value,

and who conclude that this deliberate sacrifice of
easy simplicity is compensated by an inestimable
gain of fullness and beauty and power. James's
new themes measured by incident alone are not
appreciably richer than the old. Perhaps less
indeed, in a journalistic sense may happen, but we
appear to move through a more vibrant atmosphere,
in which moods and actions assume values that
strike us with sharper incidence than reality itself.
The strongest scene in *The Bostonians* is that in
which Ransom invades the dressing-room in the
music-hall and snatches Verena from her impending
triumph. It is well executed, but how incomparably
weaker in its effect upon us than the quiet account
in *The Golden Bowl* of Charlotte's deliberate
approach towards Maggie Verver in the shadows
of the verandah at Fawns. How James secures
this intensification of interest is his own secret. It
is partly, we divine, the result of superior organisa-
tion, but the enhancement of values is due also
to other contributory elements, of which not the
least operative is his developed power of expression.
I have indicated the succinctness and finished
neatness of his earlier style. In its flexibility, its
purity, and in the fine ironic edge to which he can
temper it at will it suggests the classic strain that
Jane Austen inherited from the Addisonian tradition ; but we must recognise that it is a style re-
fractory both to poetry and pathos. Marred though
his later writing is by occasional mannerisms
that irritate when they do not amuse, we feel that
only here do all the elements in James's nature
find their account. He was sensitive as a poet to

the appeal of beauty, and was constrained by the same urgency as the poet to the need of figurative expression. It is this new quality in his style that confers distinction on his later prose, which, without trespassing on its territory, still challenges poetry by the refinement of its expression and the satisfying fullness of its rhythm. A final element of difference between the old and the new might well serve as an introduction to our brief survey of *The Bostonians.* With the growth of his command over his instrument James ventured, so to speak, to play more difficult tunes. Admirable for lightness and wit as are his earlier efforts, he did not venture as yet upon a complicated theme, and the characters of his choice had all their qualities upon the surface. It was not necessary for him, therefore, to set up elaborate mining machinery and strike his shaft into the depths. Such values as existed were to be extracted without undue expenditure of effort. And whereas these earlier personages lend themselves most readily to the method of ironic representation, the later and more complex characters induce in their creator a spirit of sympathy which at once warms and humanises them. Sympathy, it is true, plays through the irony of *Daisy Miller,* but a mere naming of the principal and secondary characters of the novels would establish the general truth of the statement that in the earlier books irony plays over the whole surface, relieved by very occasional touches of sympathy, whereas in the work of his maturity, despite his efforts to be dispassionate and impersonal, it is the sympathy that predominates and the irony that is occasional.

HENRY JAMES : MAN AND AUTHOR

The Bostonians treats of Basil Ransom's curious conquest of Verena Tarrant's affection and of the coincident defeat of Olive Chancellor's hopes for the emancipation of her sex—a triumph in which Verena's genius for oratory was destined to have been a notable factor. Basil is a shrewd young Southerner ruined by the war, who has come to New York to establish himself in the practice of law. Finding himself on business in Boston he calls on his distant cousin, Olive Chancellor, who has so far relaxed her distrust of his sex as to invite him to her house. It was an impulse that she had reason permanently to regret. Basil first encounters her sister, Mrs Luna, who gives him a sufficient hint of Olive's fanatical tendencies. He then suffers a *tête-à-tête* dinner with the young woman, who had invited him to stay from sheer shyness. He makes no concealment of his fixed conservative views on the woman question, but from amused interest he accepts her grudging invitation to accompany her to a female suffrage meeting at Miss Birdseye's house. He judges that this will be a short and ready method of getting to know Boston. His zest for new sensations is amply gratified, and through his eyes we see the whole queer conglomerate set who have gathered to hear Mrs Farrinder voice the wrongs of her downtrodden sex. But the great woman is unwilling to perform, and her place is taken on the spur of the moment by a red-haired girl who had attracted Ransom's attention as she came in with her decidedly queer-looking parents. This is Verena Tarrant, whose mother has proposed that, in default of Mrs Farrinder, her young

daughter should entertain and exalt the guests by
an inspirational speech. Her father, a mesmeric
healer by profession, would soothingly lay his
hands on her, and eloquence would flow effortlessly
from her lips. The fluent speech occurs, and Basil
Ransom, while recognising its flimsiness, is intensely
interested in the young performer. His cousin
Olive, overcome with emotion, urges the girl to
visit her, convinced that in her she has found the
prophetess of the new evangel. Basil pays a very
prompt dinner call next morning, and his hope
of seeing the charming red-haired girl is rewarded.
His attitude towards her opinions is from the
outset contemptuous, but he cannot conceal from
himself, or others, his inexplicable interest in the
girl.

Basil goes back to New York, and for some time
we lose sight of him, while the story develops
Olive's growing infatuation for this predestined
saviour of her sex. She buys her from her parents,
brings her to live with her, and presently takes her
off to Europe to escape the assiduities of a wealthy
Harvard student named Burrage, who has been
persecuting her with his attentions. Olive has
naturally been indoctrinating this girl with the
superior virtues of the virgin state. Meanwhile
Basil has been having a lonely and difficult time in
New York. That worldly, wily woman, Mrs Luna,
has shown him every attention on his return from
Boston, but he seems soon to have wearied of her
assiduities. She knits relations again by a note of
invitation to her house. It opens a comfortable
refuge to the briefless young barrister, and he

almost reaches the point of reconciling himself to the idea of that refuge as a permanency. Their views, at least on the woman question and kindred subjects, are identical, save for the fact that Mrs Luna does not share his admiration for the young girl who had infatuated her sister. Basil learns that they have been to Europe and have returned, and his curiosity to see Verena again is stimulated by Mrs Luna's unflattering report. He finds immediate occasion to return to Boston, and with this visit the story takes its final direction. It now becomes a tug-of-war between Basil and Olive for the possession of the girl. Basil eventually dominates, and demonstrates the truth of his theory that Verena's devotion to the cause of women's rights is the unconsciously insincere aberration of a nature fashioned for love. When she asks him why her gift has been bestowed upon her if only to be wasted, he tells her that her genius can be put to better use in making one man happy than in deluding a gaping multitude. An uncompromising lover this, but that such blunt wooing should break down her defences gives point to his contention. He eventually bears her off from a crowded meeting that had gathered to hear her, and her tears as she drives away from the hall were, as the author admits, not the last that she was destined to shed.

I have said that there is not much poetry or pathos but abundant irony in these early books. There is, however, a decided hint of pathos in the picture of Miss Birdseye, which aroused the protest of some of his friends as a somewhat savage caricature of Miss Peabody, a well-known Boston figure.

Set descriptions of persons and places are to be expected in a writer who has not yet forsaken the old tradition, and I give one of the detailed accounts of Miss Birdseye, in spite of its length, to illustrate how competent our author was in vignette portraiture. The brush-work is perhaps more incisive than gentle, yet there is some degree of tenderness in the way that her almost imbecile goodness is reproduced. Miss Birdseye, it will be remembered, has invited a number of sympathising friends to hear Mrs Farrinder discuss the "Wrongs of Women": "The hall was very narrow; a considerable part of it was occupied by a large hat-tree, from which several coats and shawls already depended; the rest offered space for certain lateral demonstrations on Miss Birdseye's part. She sidled about her visitors, and at last went round to open for them a door of further admission, which happened to be locked inside. She was a little old lady, with an enormous head; that was the first thing Ransom noticed—the vast, fair, protuberant, candid, ungarnished brow, surmounting a pair of weak, kind, tired-looking eyes, and ineffectually balanced in the rear by a cap which had the air of falling backward, and which Miss Birdseye suddenly felt for while she talked, with unsuccessful irrelevant movements. She had a sad, soft, pale face, which (and it was the effect of her whole head) looked as if it had been soaked, blurred, and made vague by exposure to some slow dissolvent. The long practice of philanthropy had not given accent to her features; it had rubbed out their transitions, their meanings. The waves of sympathy, of enthusiasm, had wrought

upon them in the same way in which the waves
of time finally modify the surface of old marble
busts, gradually washing away their sharpness, their
details.   In her large countenance her dim little
smile scarcely showed.   It was a mere sketch of a
smile, a kind of instalment, or payment on account ;
it seemed to say that she would smile more if she
had time, but that you could see, without this, that
she was gentle and easy to beguile.

" She always dressed in the same way : she wore
a loose black jacket, with deep pockets, which were
stuffed with papers, memoranda of a voluminous
correspondence ;   and   from   beneath   her   jacket
depended a short stuff dress.   The brevity of this
simple garment was the one device by which
Miss Birdseye managed to suggest that she was a
woman of business, that she wished to be free for
action.   She belonged to the Short-Skirts League
as a matter of course, for she belonged to any and
every league that had been founded for almost any
purpose whatever.   This did not prevent her being
a confused, entangled, inconsequent, discursive
old woman, whose charity began at home and
ended nowhere, whose credulity kept pace with it,
and who knew less about her fellow-creatures, if
possible, after fifty years of humanitary zeal, than
on the day she had gone into the field to testify
against the iniquity of most arrangements.   Basil
Ransom knew very little about such a life as hers,
but she seemed to him a revelation of a class, and
a multitude of socialistic figures, of names and
episodes that he had heard of grouped themselves
behind her.   She looked as if she had spent her life

on platforms, in audiences, in conventions, in phalansteries, in *séances* ; in her faded face there was a kind of reflection of ugly lecture-lamps ; with its habit of an upward angle it seemed turned toward a public speaker, with an effort of respiration in the thick air in which social reforms are usually discussed. She talked continually, in a voice of which the spring seemed broken, like that of an overworked bell-wire ; and when Miss Chancellor explained that she had brought Mr Ransom because he was so anxious to meet Mrs Farrinder, she gave the young man a delicate, dirty, democratic little hand, looking at him kindly, as she could not help doing, but without the smallest discrimination as against others who might not have the good fortune (which involved, possibly, an injustice) to be present on such an interesting occasion."

Such amplitude of reference James ultimately abandoned, and more particularly did he avoid the multiplication of detail in the background of his picture. In the work of his later prime he was never in doubt as to what his principal theme might be. Here there is some confusion of background and foreground, for even in his own mind he was not clear whether his main purpose was to give a fantastic account of the feminist movement at a time when it was more comical than effective, or to tell the love story of Verena and Basil Ransom. He solved his doubts by blending the two themes, and thus gave himself the licence to wander to the prejudice of unity and concentration. He detects his crime even as he writes, and his confession of error is sufficiently indicated in the lines that I have italicised in the following passage that essays in the spirit of French realism to present us with Basil Ransom's surroundings :

" Basil Ransom lived in New York, rather far to the eastward, and in the upper reaches of the town ; he occupied two small shabby rooms in a somewhat decayed mansion, which stood next to the corner of the Second Avenue. The corner itself was formed by a considerable grocer's shop, the near neighbourhood of which was fatal to any pretensions Ransom and his fellow-lodgers might have had in regard to gentility of situation. The house had a sad, rusty face, and faded green shutters, of which the slats were limp and at variance with each other. In one of the lower windows was suspended a fly-blown card with the words ' Table Board ' affixed in letters cut (not very neatly) out of coloured paper, of graduated tints, and surrounded with a small band of stamped gilt. The two sides of the shop were protected by an immense penthouse shed, which projected over a greasy pavement, and was supported by wooden posts fixed in the curbstone. Beneath it, on the dislocated flags, barrels and baskets were freely and picturesquely grouped ; an open cellar-way yawned beneath the feet of those who might pause to gaze too fondly on the savoury wares displayed in the window ; a strong odour of smoked fish, combined with a fragrance of molasses, hung about the spot ; the pavement, toward the gutters, was fringed with dirty panniers, heaped with potatoes, carrots, and onions ; and a smart, bright waggon, with the horse detached from the shafts, drawn up on the edge of the abominable road (it contained holes and ruts a foot deep, and immemorial accumulations of stagnant mud), imparted an idle, rural, pastoral air to a scene otherwise perhaps expressive of a rank civilisation. The establishment was of the kind known to New Yorkers as a Dutch grocery, and red-faced, yellow-haired, bare-armed venders might have been observed to lounge in the doorway. *I mention it, not on account of any particular influence it may have had on the life or the thoughts of Basil Ransom, but for old acquaintance sake and that of local colour ; besides which, a figure is nothing without a setting, and our young man came and went every day, with rather an indifferent, unperceiving step, it is true, among the objects I have briefly designated.*"

His room is then described, and with some further twinges of conscience the author continues : " If the opportunity were not denied me here I should like to give some account of Basil Ransom's interior, of certain curious persons of both sexes, for the most part not favourites of fortune, who had found an obscure asylum there ; some picture of the crumpled little *table d'hôte*, at two dollars and a half a week, where everything felt sticky, which went forward in the low-ceiled basement, under the conduct of a couple of shuffling negresses, who mingled in the conversation and indulged in low, mysterious chuckles when it took a facetious turn. But we need, in strictness, concern ourselves with it no further than to gather the implication that the young Mississippian, even a year and a half after that momentous visit of his to Boston, had not made his profession very lucrative."

HENRY JAMES : MAN AND AUTHOR

The novel will always be under compulsion to make its characters move in a sensible medium, but the passage I have been at pains to quote indicates some of the dangers to which the incautious writer is exposed, and also how tardy was James's release from the descriptive excesses of Balzacian realism. The age was drenched with local colour, and the appeal to the pictorial sense recognised no limits of measure or proportion. No one has written better on the subject than James himself, and no one in theory or practice has better realised the true function of localisation, which must never detach itself, either on the one hand from the formative influences of environment on character, or on the other from the formative influences operating from character upon environment. By the first law each grim touch of description in *Wuthering Heights* receives its justification ; by the second we reconcile ourselves to every circumstantial detail that Balzac devotes to the miser's house in Saumur. A third prescription, too stringent to impose itself as a law, but still a regulative principle in James's severe practice, subordinates all descriptions, whether of persons or places, to the perceptions of the characters, and serves, when conscientiously applied, the salutary purpose of holding the lyrical expansiveness of the author in check.

Reading this novel, where all the old devices abound, we find it difficult to realise that he was so soon and so radically to change his methods of expression, and even, so it would seem, the very texture of his thought. Between *The Bostonians* and *The Ambassadors* there is a wider gulf than is indicated by the space of years.

The Princess Casamassima (1885), which was concurrently written, is separated by a notably narrower margin. It was an audacious thing for James to attempt a novel treating of social conditions with which he was incompetent to cope, and we are uneasily aware that in *The Princess Casamassima* he is conscious of his difficulties, and is seeking to avoid them by the evasion of the central issues. If this were a book purporting to reveal the acute distress of a great city like London, and the revolutionary activities that misery engenders, it would be a patent and palpable fraud upon our intelligence. If, on the other hand, the amenities of life and the æsthetic conquests of civilisation may be shown to rest inevitably upon a *vague* basis of wretchedness, the author then will be under no constraint to establish a clear case for human misery, and so far as the artistic purposes of his book ar econcerned these evils may remain inferential and undetermined. There are writers of course for whom the social problem imposes more exacting conditions. Mr Galsworthy, for example, would have felt himself compelled to a much more exact notation of the facts, and we should have had a realistic novel in which the artistic and propagandist intention would have striven, perhaps in vain, for reconciliation. James was saved from this dilemma both by the absence in him of all dogmatic tendencies and by his defective knowledge of the actual facts. The reasons, however, that he advances for dodging these latter will not satisfy the most

269

indulgent reader. We might have been contented had he said that he wished to relieve his book as far as possible of controversial matter, or had he confessed frankly his inability to cope with subterranean conditions. It was somewhat disingenuous of him to say : " I felt in full *personal* possession of my matter ; this really seemed the fruit of direct experience. My scheme called for the suggested nearness (to all our apparently ordered life) of some sinister, anarchic underworld, heaving in its pain, its power and its hate ; a presentation, not of sharp particulars, but of loose appearances, vague motions and sounds and symptoms, just perceptible presences and general looming possibilities."

The Lomax Place life is observed and rendered so vividly as to suggest the results of " direct experience," which in the case of an author so fastidious is the equivalent merely of imaginative contact. But in the later foreground of the picture, where we are entitled to expect a definite delineation of revolutionary figures, we are fobbed off with " loose appearances—just perceptible presences and general looming possibilities." We cannot take the fastidious slumming of the Princess very seriously ; Hyacinth recoils from the besotted intelligence of the submerged masses ; and only Lady Aurora would be competent to speak from actual experience of the horrors of the pit, which, for her gentle nature, are an opportunity for hard sacrificial work rather than an occasion for theorising. It is this failure on the author's part to face ultimate facts that accounts for our incomplete sympathy with his hero, and robs his tragedy of its full appeal to our imagination. If a tragedy misses poignancy it misses everything; and when we come to examine into the motives that precipitate Hyacinth into his fatal revolutionary activity, we shall realise why he succeeds in being futile and fails to be impressive. His early history is admirably conveyed, and so successfully is the boy of ten launched that we are keyed up to a high pitch of expectation for the incidents of his subsequent career. The prison scene is one that Dickens or Gissing would have seized upon with avidity, and it is not certain that either of them would have produced a more impressive result. The episode is at least as tender and penetrating as anything that James has given us, and it is a scene that will project its lurid light through all the years of the boy's growing consciousness—the puzzled, shrinking child himself, the timid Pinnie, the inexorable Mrs Bowerbank, and the fevered, yearning mother babbling French phrases. The pity of it is that the author does not carry to its logical conclusion this rankling sense of the world's injustice that had been so powerfully stimulated in the child. Pinnie is for ever there to remind him that he is a little aristocrat; and what ultimately moves him to act is less sympathy for the downtrodden poor than annoyance at being debarred from access to the fuller life to which his father's blood flowing in his veins impelled, if not entitled, him.

Let us consider somewhat attentively the successive contacts to which the impressionable Hyacinth is subjected. An eight years' gap ensues after the prison scene, and during this interval Miss Pynsent has evidently relied greatly on the advice of her opposite neighbour, Mr Vetch, as to how the boy shall be launched on his career. Mr Vetch, whose radicalism grows milder with the years, still numbers some friends of pronounced opinions, among them two communist refugees, the Poupins; and it is through their kind offices that Hyacinth finds employment as a bookbinder's apprentice, and is brought into contact with a group of revolutionary working men, of whom the enigmatic Paul Muniment is the leading figure. His little world is presently enlarged by the reappearance of Millicent Henning, the friend of his childhood, and by the irruption into his life of the infinitely various Princess, who, by virtue of her commanding qualities, gives the book her name.

Millicent Henning, extraordinarily and refreshingly vulgar, is not such a figure as we might be prepared to encounter in a novel of James, and encountering her there we should scarcely expect her to be studied with such discernment and such evident relish. We must admit that she is vulgarity done in the grand manner, but, in spite of the elaborate fineness with which she is presented, we are not aware of any falsification in her attributes. She is a young woman possessed of the highest esteem of her own charms and capabilities, who by unaided efforts has risen wonderfully in the world. She has become a walking model in a fashionable millinery establishment, and her brilliant success reconciles her most absolutely with social conditions that permit her to display herself to such advantage. Having no quarrel with society she feels that she exercises a wholesome, steadying influence on Hyacinth, through whose brain such silly notions scamper. He obviously requires looking after, and her amorous intrigue with Captain Sholto interferes not at all with her maternal solicitude for the pathetic young bookbinder who has been so evidently " sold " by his dazzling, shoddy princess. She inhabits an elemental world that is beyond the range of moral scruples, and Hyacinth's death will move her to a compassion that is singularly free from any twinge of conscience or suspicion of remorse.

For a time Millicent represents to Hyacinth the whole range of feminine possibilities, and the sensitive youngster accommodates himself with a scarcely perceptible condescension to her blatancy of speech and manner and to the multiplied vulgarities which even the suavity of our author's style is powerless to conceal. Before the blunting process is complete the Princess comes into his life and sets the aristocratic and plebeian strains in his nature in violent oscillation.

How such a dazzling personage should establish relations with an obscure bookbinder might seem to constitute a difficulty to be overcome only by recourse to some mechanical expedient, but James deals with the little problem skilfully and solves it in terms of character. Hyacinth has yielded to Millicent's importunities so far as to take her to front balcony seats in a theatre of more pretensions than those they were in the habit of frequenting. The Princess Casamassima is in a box, attended by Madame Grandoni and Captain Sholto. Socialism is her main concern of the moment, and Sholto, as her obedient cavalier, has found his way into many humble political clubs for the purpose of satisfying her curiosity. It is thus that he had recently encountered Hyacinth, and seeing him now in the gallery with a distinctly pretty girl he informs his princess of the fact, and at her bidding effects a change of seats with this interesting specimen of the lower classes.

The Princess Casamassima is the one major character whom James submits to the process of resuscitation. She is Christina Light *rediviva*, and we have known her as the beautiful creature who precipitated the earlier tragedy of Roderick Hudson's career. In that book she is already an enigmatic figure, brilliant, baleful and beautiful, and it is with some diffidence that I attempt an exposition of a character who is bewildering to her friends and inscrutable possibly even to herself.

At the conclusion of the Roderick Hudson episode she had made a marriage of *convenance* with a Neapolitan prince, whom, after some years of loveless splendour, she had abandoned, having apparently exasperated him to an act of physical violence. She still enjoys her husband's wealth, and the latter is apparently anxious to redeem her love, or, failing that, to save his name from disgrace. But her resentment persists, and is reinforced by her capricious disregard of the advantages of her position, which is still sufficiently splendid and still, morally speaking, uncompromised. Madame Grandoni is a standing guarantee of her respectability—that quaint old polyglot bewigged duenna

whom Hyacinth finds with her on entering the box.
The Princess does not delay to exercise her spell
on the sensitive youth. " She was fair, shining,
slender, with an effortless majesty. Her beauty
had an air of perfection; it astonished and lifted
one up; the sight of it seemed a privilege, a reward.
If the first impression it had given Hyacinth was
to make him feel strangely transported, he need
still not have set that down to his simplicity, for
this was the effect the Princess Casamassima produced on persons of a wider experience and greater
pretensions. Her dark eyes, blue or grey, something
that was not brown, were as kind as they were
splendid, and there was an extraordinary light
nobleness in the way she held her head." So the
rhapsody runs on for a page or two. Indeed, for
none of his many beautiful and brilliant women has
James established so carefully itemised and amplified
a register of charms. Nothing false or mean is ever
breathed of her; benignity no less than beauty
breathes from her face; yet the impression she
leaves with us is that she is fundamentally insincere,
or genuine only from moment to moment of her
capricious existence. If she is baleful and malign,
it would seem to be not from any considered intention to multiply wreckage along her path. She is
merely driven by the law of her own nature, which
makes her ravenous for new experience and permits
her to rest tranquilly in none. When Hyacinth
first meets her she has exhausted the possibilities
of social success and has turned from her triumphs
in court and palace to a novel form of excitement,
where she may relish the savour of danger while

comforting her mind with the delusion that she is devoting herself to a sacred cause. I confess that there is something fantastic and ill-grounded in this sudden change of front. Capriciousness and boredom could scarcely breed so holy an enthusiasm. The governors of the underworld are justified in not trusting her, and Paul Muniment foresees her ultimate secession when her husband shall have sufficiently starved her into submission. One may be permitted to refuse an author's suggestion as to events that lie beyond the limits of his book. The Princess is too high-spirited and proud ever to be starved into submission. I can see her rather savouring actual poverty as a further experience, and seeking ultimately some convent sanctuary, where she may pass into another phase, and enjoy the new and final sensation of peace.

Her mechanical function in the book is to open the door for Hyacinth into the world of luxury and refinement. Of course the poor weak boy is dazzled. He follows up the theatre episode with a visit to her wonderful South Street house, arriving there one day when the Prince has come to gain some knowledge of his wife's behaviour and to obtain a clue to her lavish extravagance. The Princess holds aloof until her husband leaves, and then unburdens herself in the frankest way, plying the fascinated youngster with multifarious questions as to the conditions of the poor in London and the extent to which the revolutionary movement has gone. Hyacinth is able to answer only in the vaguest terms, but by the time he sees her next in her country house at Medley he can speak with assurance, for in the interval of time an important thing has happened. He has bound himself by an unconditional oath to commit any action he may be called upon to perform, and he is perfectly aware that this is likely to be an assassination. He gives a hint of his predicament to the Princess without indicating any names. When the Princess connects Diedrich Hoffendahl with the episode and describes her close relations with him, Hyacinth grows more confidential, and in the course of their conversation makes an extraordinary statement :

"'Isn't it enough now to give my life to the beastly cause without giving my sympathy.' 'The beastly cause ? ' the Princess murmured, opening her deep eyes.

"'Of course it's really just as holy as ever ; only the people I find myself pitying now are the rich, the happy.'"

A few days before Hyacinth had bound himself by a solemn oath of consecration to a cause that now moves him to disgust. What has happened in the interval to disillusionise him ? James is perpetually referring to the capriciousness of the Princess, but she is steadfastness itself by comparison with this veering waywardness. The provision he makes for this violent transition is wholly insufficient, and the inadequacy of his explanation diminishes our sympathy with Hyacinth to such a point that his tragic predicament leaves us cold. Much is made of the ascendancy over his mind of the inscrutable Paul Muniment, and much, too, is made of his dual nature, in which centuries of luxury and poverty combine without blending.

The revolutionary pulsing of his mother's blood had prompted him in an hysterical moment to an act of solemn defiance, but this momentary protest produces one heroic gesture and yields without a struggle to the ascendancy of forces that flow in upon him from the paternal side. If the enchantress of Medley had determined to bewitch him with luxury and beauty, we might concede some weight to the hereditary impulse. Her influence, however, is laid wholly in the other scale, and we are forced to the conclusion that Hyacinth had never possessed any genuine sympathy for the cause of the suffering masses. His dedication of his life has been the petulant assertion of his rage at being excluded from privileges that only the wealthy can enjoy, and blended with this petulance was the boyish desire to impress Muniment and the mysterious Hoffendahl with his devotion and courage.

Pinnie dies shortly after Hyacinth's return from Medley, and with her scanty savings, supplemented by a small sum from old Mr Vetch, the youth takes a Continental holiday. This fatal draught of beauty confirms his disrelish of the revolutionary attitude. We are not given the detail of any of his experiences—adventures it would be too much to call his admiration of the polished floors of the Louvre and of the splendours of Tortoni's—but letters to the Princess inform us of his thrilling response to his successive æsthetic contacts. Is it James or the poverty-pinched bookbinder who writes from Venice : " Dear Princess, what an enchanted city, what ineffable impressions, what a revelation of the exquisite!"? He then proceeds to state the new position to which he has been insensibly moving, and here we have the blended accents of Hyacinth and James :

"Nevertheless I'm not wholly pretending it's all your fault if I've lost sight of the sacred cause almost altogether in my recent adventures. It's not that it hasn't been there to see, for that, perhaps, is the clearest result of extending one's horizon— the sense, increasing as we go—that want and toil and suffering are the constant lot of the immense majority of the human race. I've found them everywhere, but haven't minded them. Forgive the cynical confession. What has struck me is the great achievements of which man has been capable in spite of them—the splendid accumulations of the happier few, to which doubtless the miserable many have also in their degree contributed. The face of Europe appears to be covered with them, and they've had much the greater part of my attention. They seem to me inestimably precious and beautiful, and I've become conscious more than ever before of how little I understand what in the great rectification you and Poupin propose to do with them. Dear Princess, there are things I shall be sorry to see you touch, even you with your hands divine ; and—shall I tell you *le fond de ma pensée,* as you used to say ?—I feel myself capable of fighting for them. You can't call me a traitor, for you know the obligation I supremely, I immutably recognise. The monuments and treasures of art, the great palaces and properties, the conquests of learning and taste, the general fabric of civilisation as we know it, based if you will upon all the despotisms, the cruelties, the exclusions, the monopolies and the rapacities of the past, but thanks to which, all the same, the world is less of a bloody sell, and life more of a lark—our friend Hoffendahl seems to me to hold them too cheap and to wish to substitute for them something in which I can't somehow believe as I do in things with which the yearnings and the tears of generations have been mixed."

James has told us that the history of little Hyacinth sprang up for him out of the London pavements. Many and fine though the passages are that render the life of the teeming city, we yet do not obtain from his pages the acrid savour of reality that we taste in Dickens or Wells. He is not willing to sacrifice an orotund fullness for the sake of vividness, and the art of representation is better served—the confession must be made—by their coarser, staccato methods. The passion that actually propelled the story was the sense, so prepotent in our author's mind, of the accumulated values which the past has stored up for our present use, and he merely amused himself with the palpable fiction of an æsthetic anarchist and a revolutionary princess, the one halted on the frontiers of the world of beauty and the other free of that region, yet wantonly forsaking it.

The obligation which Hyacinth "supremely, immutably recognises" is the fulfilment of his oath to shoot some high personage on command. It is with this darkness hanging over him that he resumes his life in London. His dependence on the

Princess grows more extreme, and he is a constant visitor to the mean house in Paddington to which she has migrated. But by gradual degrees he feels himself supplanted, for his radiant patroness has succeeded at last in attracting Paul Muniment into her eccentric orbit, and Hyacinth begins to feel the desolation of disillusionment. The two are probably nothing more than diligent and dangerous plotters, but the Prince, who has followed them into a disreputable quarter, gives Hyacinth ground for graver suspicion, which Madame Grandoni's ultimate desertion of her post does not serve to allay. While he is in this discouraged state the message comes that bids him fulfil his oath. But the bullet that was to have sped the Duke finds its way to his own heart.

The Princess Casamassima (1886) appeared concurrently with *The Bostonians* and five years later than *The Portrait of a Lady*. James's art was obviously in these years in a state of transition, when he was tentatively feeling his way, and was not yet certain which devices of the older method to reject and which to retain. *The Portrait of a Lady* is almost as advanced in its manner as *The Princess*, whereas *The Bostonians* is puzzlingly retrogressive, which means nothing more than to say that it is a plain straightforward romance of the traditional English type, with all the characters honestly labelled and classified on their first appearance. In the comparatively early *Roderick Hudson* James had adopted somewhat cautiously the more artistic device of presenting his personages by a process of gradual revelation. *The Portrait* utilises the same method with greater success, but the book is weighed down with a great amount of preliminary biographical material that his maturer art would have absorbed into the narrative. Then five years later comes *The Bostonians*, with a return to the older treatment, and simultaneously *The Princess Casamassima*, which, though a less attractive book than *The Portrait of a Lady*, for reasons that I have endeavoured to make clear, possesses certain formal advantages. The biographical antecedents of Hyacinth are not more suppressed than they were with Isabel Archer, and if it is a fault to supply such a background, which James asserts and many readers deny it to be, then both books stand upon a level, and from the standpoint of construction are equally defective. But the innovation making for advance in the later book is the Princess herself, whose qualities are never categorically presented to us, and who is studied by the method not only of gradual but also of indirect revelation. A letter to Mrs Humphry Ward, reinforcing various statements in the prefaces, emphasises what our author holds to be of inestimable advantage in the method of indirection —" that magnificent and masterly *indirectness* which means the only dramatic straightness and intensity." He admits that he " goes behind " right and left in *The Princess Casamassima*, but the Princess herself he never goes behind, and what we learn of her is never gained from her own reflections upon her case. The pity of it is that we learn nothing definite of her from any other source, unless to be enigmatic is to be definite, and consequently for this negative result the method is not to be blamed. There would seem to be a certain degree of indecision even with James, who pondered these questions more deeply than other haphazard writers, as to when he shall have recourse to the direct and when to the indirect process. Minor characters of course must not be given the privilege of self-analysis, but with the major ones also there seems to be no settled law. And we must further note that even when James had obtained a greater mastery of the method of indirection than he was possessed of in our present novel, the zest of experimentation was so strong in him that he occasionally flung his system overboard and produced a novel like *The Awkward Age*, in which everybody " goes behind " everybody else and no one behind himself. *The Princess Casamassima*, we conclude, was a sort of *ballon d'essai* to test the upper rarer air in which its author was ambitious to spread his wings. Without denying the validity of his theories one must permit oneself the ironical observation that his successes in this book lie with characters and situations delineated and described after the old fashion, with Miss Pynsent and Mr Vetch rather than with Hyacinth and the Princess; and that even when he was borrowing a leaf from the book of Dickens or Daudet, as witness the descriptions of Mrs Bowerbank and Rose Muniment, his success is not inconsiderable. I am not sure that his most delicate triumph of observation was not achieved in the diffident, dowdy, and wholly delightful Lady Aurora.

HENRY JAMES : MAN AND AUTHOR

It did not require the author's preface to inform us that the theme of *The Tragic Muse* (1889) is a dramatic representation of the æsthetic conscience in difficulties, of the conflict, in short, between art and " the world." This idea immediately assumed concrete form in the writer's mind, and the predicament of the young man, Nick Dormer, who should abandon the most brilliant prospects of worldly advancement for the purely spiritual satisfactions of art, suggested itself as a workable story. But the temptation to enrich his theme at once presented itself, and Miriam Rooth bounced so exuberantly into the book, set her histrionic buskin so emphatically in the scale, that the balance in which Nick's modest interests were laid proved unexpectedly light, and we are not satisfied that the multiplied expedients and proved dexterity of the author have sufficed to preserve the equipoise. She dominates the scene, she usurps the title, and the narrative of Nick's predicament becomes the story of *The Tragic Muse*. The obvious thing to have done to secure a fusion of these scattered interests was to allow the evident inclination of Miriam for Nick to develop into a passion ; but James is always ill at ease amidst the illogicalities of love, and his timidity robs the exuberant girl of the full expression of her nature, and leaves the young man to the end fish-like and cold. A culmination of this sort hovered in the author's mind when Miriam unceremoniously rids herself of her mother in Nick's studio and has the young painter at her mercy. " ' Take your drive and relax your mind,' said the girl, kissing her. ' Come for me in an hour, not later—but not sooner.' She went with her to the door, bundled her out, closed it behind her and came back to the position she had quitted. ' *This* is the peace I want ! ' she gratefully cried as she settled into it.'' A French novelist would not have commenced the following chapter with the words : '' Peter Sherringham said so little during the performance that his companion was struck by his dumbness, especially as Miriam's acting seemed to Nick magnificent.'' Whether it is the New England or merely the artistic conscience that operates I am unable to say, but this is only one of the multiplied instances when James swerves aside on his path to avoid an issue which most modern novelists go out of their way to find. At whatever cost of verisimilitude Nick's austerity is preserved, and his studio remains a joyless place, where he fights his lonely and losing battle against the world.

What keeps this brilliant book out of the front rank of its author's productions is less the disturbance caused by the multiplication of the centres of interest—a difficulty that he measurably overcomes —than the fact that Dormer's particular problem never wholly obtains our sympathy. He begins and ends as a rather brilliant amateur, and a sacrifice by the amateur of substantial, worldly advantage is a theme for compassionate irony at the best. It glances wide of the vital problem that develops when genius fronts its destiny and deliberately makes its choice. But James had Miriam Rooth on his hands, and the exhibition of her prodigiously rapid progress from incompetency to fame forbade him to duplicate the miracle.

Manifold as were her initial obligations to Peter
Sherringham, she is at no pains to refuse his blundering proposal, with its offer of ambassadorial
splendour as a substitute for the glories of the stage
which now seem within her grasp. Her momentary
weakness was on Nick's behalf, born of compassion
for his wan and relegated state. For him she might
conceivably have abandoned her career, but he holds
firm, and Miriam leaves the book in a blaze of
glory with her artistic conscience saved and her
boast of being a " good girl " made secure by the
practically helpful and accommodating husband
whom in the end she finds. The much-enduring
Peter consoles himself with pleasant little Biddy
Dormer, and Nick's boat, after a baffling journey,
rocks safely too in harbour. He has lost Mr Carteret's
fortune for a principle, but Julia in the end commissions him to paint her portrait, and on the basis
of mutual concessions they will undoubtedly face
a happy future together. He will overcome his
distaste for politics now that Gabriel Nash, his
" evil genius," has vanished into thin air, and,
with Miriam Rooth no longer a disturbing element
in the studio, Julia will permit him to flourish his
paint-brush to his heart's desire. Such at least are
the comfortable and old-fashioned inferences we
are permitted to draw from the concluding chapter;
and we are confirmed in our suspicion that James
admitted a partial defeat of his original intention
to present in Nick Dormer a study of genius in
triumphant conflict with the world.

The preparation of the case of Nick Dormer *v.* the
World is ample enough to augur a more auspicious

result. We meet him first in Paris. Lady Agnes and his sister Grace are sitting in bored exhaustion in the gardens of the Palais de l'Industrie, and Nick has detached the amenable and eager Biddy for a further round among the pictures and statues. He has just escaped re-election to Parliament, and in the exhilaration of his liberated state his enthusiasm for art asserts itself and his old ambitions revive. In this excited mood he encounters Gabriel Nash, that brilliant and baffling person whom all the dull, safe people in the book find so disconcerting, and whom as Nick's evil genius they cordially detest and despise. Gabriel is his own sufficient justification, but he has a significance that strikes much deeper than the surface brilliance of his talk. Viewed from one aspect he is less a person than a point of view, a sublimation of all the influences and impulses that went to the shaping of the " æsthetic nineties." Turgénief by an act of divination created a prophetic type in Bazaroff : James had more actual material to draw from (was not Oscar Wilde then on the crest of his notoriety ?), and Gabriel rises to the surface like froth in a pot of bubbling yeast. The ingredients were all in fermentation, the formula of the concoction was known, and the distilled product was a bitter brew for the palate of the *bourgeois*. Like the shades of the poet's imagination he is " a voice and nothing besides," a disembodied presence, an unsubstantial vapour that wreathes itself momentarily into fantastic and beautiful shapes and disappears as mysteriously as it came. We are right in viewing him as the author intended, symbolically, as a projection of Nick Dormer's own mind, for when the gross world reasserts itself he fades away, and even his portrait, with its face against the wall, grows faint and shadowy.

Biddy and Nick and Nash return to the family lunch, which Peter Sherringham had already joined, with the exciting news that Mr Pinks, the member for Harsh, had died, and that Julia was confident that with her influence in the constituency she will get Nick elected. There is much animated conversation on the situation, which admirably adjusts our point of view to the problem that is shaping itself for Nick's solution. Peter says that his sister will, of course, go home at once.

" ' Ah, she won't stay ; she'll go over for her man.'

" ' Her man——? '

" ' The fellow who stands, whoever he is— especially if he's Nick.'

" These last words caused the eyes of Peter Sherringham's companions to meet again, and he went on : ' She'll go straight down to Harsh.'

" ' Wonderful Julia ! ' Lady Agnes panted. ' Of course Nick must go straight there too.'

" ' Well, I suppose he must see first if they'll have him.'

" ' If they'll have him ? Why, how can he tell till he tries ? '

" ' I mean the people at headquarters, the fellows who arrange it.'

" Lady Agnes coloured a little. ' My dear Peter, do you suppose there will be the least doubt of their having the son of his father ? '

" ' Of course it's a good name, Cousin Agnes—a very great name.'

" ' One of the greatest, simply,' Lady Agnes smiled.

" ' It's the best name in the world ! ' said Grace emphatically.

" ' All the same it didn't prevent his losing his seat.'

" ' By half-a-dozen votes : it was too odious ! ' her ladyship cried.

" ' I remember—I remember. And in such a case as that why didn't they immediately put him in somewhere else ? '

" ' How one sees you live abroad, dear Peter. There happens to have been the most extraordinary lack of openings—I never saw anything like it—for a year. They've had their hand on him, keeping him all ready. I dare say they've telegraphed him.'

" ' And he hasn't told you ? '

" Lady Agnes faltered. ' He's so very odd when he's abroad.'

" ' At home he lets things go,' Grace interposed. ' He does so little—takes no trouble.' Her mother suffered this statement to pass unchallenged, and she pursued philosophically :

" ' I suppose it's because he knows he's so clever.'

" ' So he is, dear old man. But what does he do, what has he been doing, in a positive way ? '

" ' He has been painting.'

" ' Ah, not seriously ! ' Lady Agnes protested.

" ' That's the worst way,' said Peter Sherringham. ' Good things ? '

" Neither of the ladies made a direct response to this, but Lady Agnes said : ' He has spoken repeatedly. They're always calling on him.'

" ' He speaks magnificently,' Grace attested.

" ' That's another of the things I lose, living in far countries. And he's doing the Salon now with the great Biddy ? '

" ' Just the things in this part. I can't think what keeps them so long,' Lady Agnes groaned. ' Did you ever see such a dreadful place ? '

" Sherringham stared. ' Aren't the things good ? I had an idea——! '

" ' Good ? ' cried Lady Agnes. ' They're too odious, too wicked.'

" ' Ah,' laughed Peter, ' that's what people fall into if they live abroad. The French oughtn't to live abroad ! '

" ' Here they come,' Grace announced at this point, ' but they've got a strange man with them.'

" ' That's a bore when we want to talk ! ' Lady Agnes sighed."

This passage opens wide the gates into the camp of the Philistines, where Nick could reign a captain in shining armour if he would. All the conditions are propitious, every omen bespeaks a rapid and easy triumph. Nick's brilliant talents, Mr Carteret's benevolent patronage, Julia Dallow's tender interest in him, the prestige that has descended to him from his " famous " father, and the constituency with which Providence at this auspicious moment has provided him — all these things combine to make the only success that is worthy of the name secure. A hint of perversity in Nick furnishes the one element of doubt, but the " Ah, not seriously ! " of Lady Agnes suffices to conjure it away.

There is much irony but no caricature in James's presentation of the world's case through the persons of Lady Agnes, Julia and Mr Carteret. Superficially different by the mere accident of circumstance or sex, in opinion they are fundamentally one, and their opinion is simply that of the great normal majority in any civilised community who are clear-sighted enough for all the practical contingencies of life, but whose minds are sealed to the subtler suggestions of beauty and significance by which the artistic imagination is nourished. Any traffic or commerce with beauty offends their severe sense of duty and rectitude, and is to be condoned only if it is the amiable weakness of leisure hours. As a serious pursuit nothing could be more criminal. " This is dreadful news," the dying Mr Carteret says when Nick comes to announce to him that he has resigned his seat in the House to become a painter. Nick at the moment realises how impossible it will be for him to make his action square with Mr Carteret's notion of sanity. " ' Certainly it must seem so to you, for I've always kept from you—I was ashamed, and my present confusion is a just chastisement—the great interest I have always taken in the——' But Nick broke down with a gasp, to add presently, with an intention of the pleasant and a sense of the foolish : ' In the pencil and the brush.' . . . ' The pencil — the brush ? They're not the weapons of a gentleman,' Mr Carteret pronounced."

Nick's confession to Mr Carteret lost him sixty

thousand pounds, but the ordeal of confession to his mother cost him a severer effort, if not a higher price. He recognised how much his political career had meant to her, whose one idealism had been the sanctification of his father's political memory, and whose every worldly hope—and all her hopes were worldly—had centred in Nick's certain achievement of material success. But now the dream is shattered. The seat is resigned, Julia is estranged, Mr Carteret antagonised, and Nick, under the baleful influence of Gabriel Nash, is proposing to spend his days putting foolish colours on futile strips of canvas. What a pale, meagre substitute for the certain glories of a Parliamentary career! And if rumour speaks truth he will console himself for the loss of Julia by marrying a girl who has won a vulgar fame by posturings on the suburban stage. Lady Agnes has that particular form of patrician pride which permits her with perfect equanimity to be the recipient of Julia Dallow's charitable aid—she accepts the gift of Broadwood with no suspicion that she is a pensioner on her cousin's bounty or that her dignity is in the least compromised—but which passionately resents the betrayal of his class that is involved in Nick's perverse and reckless choice. In her are concentrated all the virtues and the vices of unimaginative respectability.

Julia and Peter represent only slightly differentiated shades of the conventional state. Julia moves on the periphery of the story, but had she been subjected to the most searching analysis, the author could have told us nothing more than that she was a political woman, wealthy, beautiful, and with the circumscribed charm that derives from good looks, wide estates, and a dignity commensurate with these inestimable advantages. Only once is this dignity compromised and the smooth surface of her perfect manners ruffled, and that is when she pays her surprise visit to Nick's studio and finds Miriam in serene possession of the place. Jealousy stings her into life, and she is determined to make Nick pay the price of her discomfiture. The comedy of the situation is admirably sustained. Nick, going by appointment to meet her at her house, is kept waiting an hour. Julia, returning from an otiose drive, takes him into a little business office beside the hall, and there the bewildered if not ardent lover receives her ultimatum : " He put his arm round her, but she detached herself as soon as she felt its pressure. She rose quickly, moving away, while, mystified and chilled, he sat looking up at her as she had looked at himself a few minutes before.

" ' I've thought it all over ; I've been thinking of it all day,' she began. ' That's why I didn't come in.'

" ' Don't think of it too much ; it isn't worth that.'

" ' You like it more than anything else. You do —you can't deny it,' she went on.

" ' My dear child, what are you talking about ? ' Nick asked gently.

" ' That's what you like, doing what you were this morning ; with women lolling—all their things half off—to be painted, and awful people like that man.'

" Nick slowly got up, wondering. ' My dear Julia, apart from the surprise this morning, do you object to the living model ? '

" ' Not a bit, for you.'

" ' What's the inconvenience, then, since in my studio they're only for me ? '

" ' You love it, you revel in it, that's what you want—the only thing you want ! ' Julia broke out.

" ' To have models, lolling undressed women, do you mean ? '

" ' That's what I felt, what I knew,' she went on—' what came over me and haunted me yesterday, so that I couldn't throw it off. It seemed to me that if I could see it with my eyes and have the perfect proof I should feel better, I should be quiet. But now I *am* quiet—after a struggle of some hours, I confess. I *have* seen ; the whole thing's before me and I'm satisfied.'

" ' I'm not ; to me neither the whole thing nor half of it is before me. What exactly are you talking about ? ' Nick demanded.

" ' About what you were doing this morning. That's your innermost preference, that's your secret passion.'

" ' A feeble scratch at something serious ? Yes, it was almost serious,' he said. ' But it was an accident, this morning and yesterday : I got on less wretchedly than I intended.'

" ' I'm sure you've immense talent,' Julia returned with a dreariness that was almost droll.

" ' No, no, I might have had. I've plucked it up ; it's too late for it to flower. My dear Julia, I'm perfectly incompetent and perfectly resigned.'

" ' Yes, you looked so this morning, when you hung over her. Oh, she'll bring back your talent.' " Peter Sherringham is spun out too long and beaten too thin. His main value is that he furnishes Miriam with occasions to reveal her single-minded preoccupation with her career, the engrossing and necessary egoism of genius. Taken for himself he presents us with another aspect of the conventional attitude towards art. Lady Agnes, Mrs Dallow and Mr Carteret are what Arnold would call children of the established fact. Life for them is an affair of tangible assets, and failure is the refusal to reach out after these solid substantialities. But Peter's hold upon the world of fact is compromised by his superficial enthusiasm for art, and Miriam had early divined that his attachment to the imaginative life was prejudiced by his lingering concern for practical things. " ' He's such a curious mixture,' she luxuriously went on ; ' sometimes I quite lose patience with him. It isn't exactly trying to serve both God and Mammon, but it's muddling up the stage and the world. The world be hanged ! The stage, or anything of that sort—I mean one's artistic conscience, one's true faith—comes first.' "

A curious fact to be noted as we come to consider the dominant figure of Miriam Rooth is that James, whose belief in masculine supremacy in the creative sphere is not to be questioned, has produced an extremely long book in which all the triumphs of art go to a woman and all the failures are concentrated in the men. Mr Carteret is not in the reckoning, Peter Sherringham is an amiable mediocrity whose dilettantism recoils from the proof, Gabriel Nash is a mere phantom of the mind, and Nick a failure. Young Dashwood, the only actor introduced, is little better than an errand-boy, and is a most meagre masculine representative to set over against Madame Carré and Miriam— the established reputation and the sudden miracle of fame. James did not advert to this anomaly in his preface, but in the book he seems to be uncomfortably aware of it, and gets out of the difficulty as best he can by the aid of Gabriel Nash, on whose irresponsible tongue he sets various damnatory phrases which dim the glamour of the footlights and challenge even the supremacy of the dramatist's art.

We can lightly dismiss with James the objection of a friend that a novelist is not justified in attaching to an imaginary contemporary figure " a range of interest, of intrinsic distinction, greater than any such display of importance on the part of eminent members of the class as we see them about us." What concerned him more were three difficulties that Miriam's case presented, but which he felt he had successfully overcome. In the first place her problem must not be so particular that it cannot fuse with the large general intention of the book. Then, with so little of the atmosphere of the green room attaching to her, with the suppression of all the scabrous, vivid items that Anatole France so faithfully registers in the *Histoire Comique*, how could the girl be said really to live ? And finally there was the difficulty of rendering her spectacular progress to fame convincing, of taking nothing for granted, but noting within the space of a scant year the stages of her development from her rude beginnings to the finished perfection of her art.

James has overcome with his accustomed skill the merely technical problem of discovering unity in a book whose shifting centres would naturally tend to confusion and dislocation. The various interests are carefully interlocked, each person's story is a part of someone else's story, and from the style itself a tonal harmony is diffused which keeps the narrative consistently in one key. It is the characteristic Jamesian way, and though the reader might yearn for an occasional irruption of the incongruous, our author always works for and attains a smooth continuity of surface. He is the Andrea del Sarto of novelists.

It is always easier for a French writer to sacrifice rather than to preserve the respectability of a character, and only as an exercise in eccentricity would he undertake to delineate a virtuous actress. Now James clings to Miriam's respectability for the value he can derive from it, but the main prompting reason, we are at liberty to suspect, was because he himself was imperfectly acquainted with the geography of Bohemia. He endows his heroine with an exuberant temperament, he permits her to imbibe the easy ethical theories of Madame Carré, for whom the artistic conscience is the all-sufficing moral monitor, he consents to the free circulation of the questionable Miss Rover in her London establishment, but he gives her a mother who cannot divorce herself from the high standard of conduct of the Neville-Nugents of

Castle Nugent, and allows Miriam to reiterate to Peter with almost nauseating frequency the fact that she is a " good girl." The logic of her character nearly fulfils itself when she is prepared to sacrifice everything—even her career—to the unheeding Nick, but the logic of the book, as James viewed it, preserved her intact from all amatory complications, and in the end she marries for mere convenience, with an unencumbered conscience, but, above all, with her pathway clear to the goal of her ambition.

He might conceivably have improved the story if he had followed another logic. Vulgar intrigues might have yielded a more lively reality had Anatole France contrived them, yet James was certainly well advised to refrain from rivalry in a form so ill adapted to his leisurely and dignified method. But to have let Miriam's nature run free in a generous passion, which whether it kindled her or devastated her would still have searched her heart to the depths,—this surely would have been within his competence; and it is just such an experience that would have prepared us for the miraculous ripening of her art and would have solved the other teasing difficulty of harmonising the scattered interests of the story. As matters now stand, Miriam's genius is developed only by the severest discipline of labour; and as for the fusion of the scattered elements in the story, the most we can admit is that the seams in the canvas are dexterously painted over.

The longest interval from novel to novel is that between *The Tragic Muse* and *The Wings of the*

Dove (1902). The gap of time was thirteen years, and we may remind ourselves that this period of abstinence explains itself by his preoccupation with short fiction and dramatic production. His period of greatest achievement in the short story begins with his establishment at Rye in 1896, the immediately preceding years having been filled with his disconcerting dramatic experiences. He wrote some eight pieces at that time for the stage, of which only two were produced, the adapted *American* and *Guy Domville*, whose ill-success cured him momentarily of his infatuation.

A popular novelist is the victim of his facility and the creature of his success; but James, with no public to disappoint, could indulge in these recreative pauses and find his profit in them. And so it came to pass, for the three masterpieces which three successive years produced owe something of their virtue in a negative way to his long abstention from the novel, and something in a positive sense to the constructive theories he arrived at in the practice of allied forms of expression.

In the case of no other novel of Henry James has the inspiring motive been so long cherished or so tenderly displayed as in *The Wings of the Dove*. " I can scarce remember the time," he writes in his prefatory note, " when the situation on which this long-drawn fiction mainly rests was not vividly present to me."

With the death at twenty-four of his cousin, Minnie (Mary) Temple, James felt that his own youth had closed. Her cheerfulness, her courage, the clear light of her imagination, and her zest for life, which

grew intenser with the approach of death, made an
ineffaceable impression upon him, and no figure of
the early days is touched with the tenderness that
in his autobiographical record he bestows on the
memory of this brilliant girl. " If I have spoken
of the elements and presences round about us that
' counted,' Mary Temple was to count, and in more
lives than can now be named, to an extraordinary
degree; count as a young and shining apparition,
a creature who owed to the charm of her every
aspect (her aspects were so many !) and the originality, vivacity, audacity, generosity of her spirit
an indescribable grace and weight—if one might
impute weight to a being so imponderable in
common scales." If she was the heroine of her
scene it was " wholly without effort or desire on
her part, for never was a girl less consciously or
consentingly or vulgarly dominant; everything that
took place around her took place as if primarily
in relation to her and in her interest : that is, in
the interest of drawing her out and displaying her
the more. . . . She had, beyond any equally young
creature I have known, a sense for verity of character and play of life in others, for their acting out
of their force or their weakness, whatever either
might be, at no matter what cost to herself; and
it was this instinct that made her care so for life
in general, just as it was her being thereby so
engaged in that tangle that made her, as I have
expressed it, ever the heroine of the scene. Life
claimed her and used her and beset her—made her
range in her groping, her naturally immature and
unlighted way from end to end of the scale. . . .

She was absolutely afraid of nothing she might come to by living with enough sincerity and enough wonder; and I think it is because one was to see her launched on that adventure in such bedimmed, such almost tragically compromised conditions, that one is caught by her title to the heroic and pathetic mark. . . . One may have wondered rather doubtingly what life would have had for her and how her exquisite faculty of challenge could have ' worked in ' with what she was likely otherwise to have encountered or been confined to. None the less did she in fact cling to consciousness; death, at the last, was dreadful to her; she would have given anything to live—and the image of this, which was long to remain with me, appeared so of the essence of tragedy that I was in the far-off aftertime to seek to lay the ghost by wrapping it, a particular occasion aiding, in the beauty and dignity of art."

We stand then on the sure ground of fact in identifying Mary Temple with the Milly Theale of *The Wings of the Dove*; but this is only one of the multiplied instances in the work of James where life has given the suggestion and art has manipulated the result. The personalities of these two figures from the living and the fictional world have differences as marked as the qualities they share in common, and their fates, save that each dies when her capacity for joy is keenest, are singularly diverse. In Milly there is a certain innocence of mind that is incapable of ironic detachment, with a consequent deficiency in her of critical discernment—of ability to estimate the motives and intentions that focus upon her as a centre. Mary Temple is not to the same extent the dupe of her enthusiasms, and she seems altogether a less defenceless figure, set too in a world that demanded less wary walking than the labyrinth in which Milly's helpless feet were enmeshed. For as soon as a novelist has appropriated a situation or a character from the world of actuality his imagination forthwith complicates the issues and subjects them to a rigorous logic that we do nôt discover in the less compactly regulated affairs of life. The day-by-day existence of Mary Temple will furnish, then, no material for shaping our heroine's career. But while the incidents of the real life will count as nothing, the idea suggested by her frustrate destiny appeals irresistibly to the creative sense, and this idea, "reduced to its essence, is that of a young person conscious of a great capacity for life, but early stricken and doomed, condemned to die under short respite, while also enamoured of the world ; aware, moreover, of the condemnation, and passionately desiring to 'put in' before extinction as many of the finer vibrations as possible, and so achieve, however briefly and brokenly, the sense of having lived."

The unprepared reader will begin this novel under the impression that its dominant theme is the love affair of Kate Croy and Merton Densher, for it is not until the third book that we are made aware of Milly Theale's existence. Every novel as James conceived it is governed by its own law, and he felt his present circuitous exposition justified by the necessity of establishing the human relations, in the midst of which the unpractised

Milly is to play her part. Kate is only gradually revealed to us, and her creator in stating her case has presented with masterly impartiality the motives that explain, though they cannot justify, her course. Her family life of poverty and parental disgrace had embittered her childhood. Shortly before her mother's death she had encountered Merton Densher, a journalist whose scanty income was not the measure, if it was the natural reward, of his intellectual power, and this acquaintance-ship had ripened into love. When her mother died her rich aunt, Mrs Lowder, adopted her, less from affection or compassion than because she recognised her brilliance and her social charm. Such a com-bination of beauty and brains would make the fortune of any London drawing-room, and Mrs Lowder soon found her reward in Kate's easy mastery of the social occasion. At the moment Lord Mark seems the best available conquest, and Mrs Lowder is determined to press the spring of luxury to its fullest recoil, that she may induce her headstrong yet coolly calculating niece to the proper course.

The first book, which we might name the book of Kate, deals exhaustively with this situation; but since its slow progress keeps Milly so long wait-ing on the threshold, we feel that less amplitude of reference should have sufficed to establish the register of Kate's subsequent actions. Too leisurely a beginning begets a hurried and unduly fore-shortened conclusion, and it is precisely the pro-portion of the parts that has suffered in the result. Our satisfaction is that when Milly finally appears we are in full possession of the arbiter of her fate, and can recognise how dangerous an instrument of destiny a girl may be who fights with her back against the wall without counting the odds. Kate's love for Densher, though mainly so, is not entirely an affair of intellectual affinity; yet while a passional basis exists it is not sufficiently strong to obliterate the mercenary risks of a precipitate marriage. Densher is anxious enough at any moment to cut the knot of their difficulties in that way, but like many another infatuated man he still makes it an affair of conscience to offer a luxurious girl a cottage and a crust. It is in this honourable if ineffective fashion that he drifts into his manipulated state, for he is never in any doubt as to Kate's high competence to deal with their mutual difficulties. Their hugger-mugger meetings are a constant exasperation, and Densher is readily enough induced to see how Milly's hotel may offer itself as a luxurious alternative for park or pavement. The nefarious plot that soon develops is wholly of Kate's contriving, who, like some passion-ridden women of whom history holds the record, has lost in her extremity the moral appreciation that would reveal to her the enormity of her offence. A man is not exculpated at such easy cost, and James labours heroically but without complete success to maintain Densher's integrity unimpaired.

He gives us, at an early stage, an extenuating hint of his youth: "He suggested above all, however, that wondrous state of youth in which the elements, the metals more or less precious, are so in fusion and fermentation that the question of the final stamp, the pressure that fixes the values, must wait for comparative coolness." He gives us also the full measure of his amiability ; but excessive amiability is a species of weakness, and Densher's anxiety to please all round commits him to a course on which difficulties and evasions multiply. He accepts Kate's lead at the outset, and acquiesces in her view of the necessity for marking time, and above all for conciliating Mrs Lowder. It is not long before Kate's views and Mrs Lowder's coincide as to the consideration which Densher must show to Milly, and these pressures are presently reinforced by Mrs Stringham, who has learned from Sir Luke Strett what Milly's best restorative might be. It is a pretty case of petticoat government, but Densher's resentment is not severe so long as it is a mere case of innocent philandering under orders with a thoroughly attractive girl. Nor does his exasperation, when it develops, bear the colour of self-castigation for moral slackness. It is a lover's revolt, prompted by Kate's systematic aloofness and studied coldness. Their passages of passion were already of the distant past, and he feels himself cheated of his lover's due. " There glowed for him in fact a kind of rage at what he wasn't having; an exasperation, a resentment, begotten truly by the very impatience of desire, in respect to his postponed and relegated, his so extremely manipulated state. It was beautifully done of her, but what was the real meaning of it unless that he was perpetually bent to her will ? . . . His question, as we have called it, was the interesting question of whether he had really no will left. How could he know — that was the point — without putting the matter to the test ? " These reflections pass through his mind on the *traghetto* in Venice, and his moral solution of the problem is to re-engage his old suite of rooms, that he may learn, " by putting the matter to the test," how genuine Kate's love for him may be. The Lowder party are to leave Venice, and it is arranged that Densher shall stay for Milly's consolation. His consent is purchased by Kate's sacrifice of herself. She comes to his rooms and the bargain is closed between them. Densher will show daily devotion to the dying girl, and on a hint from her of marriage, as princesses are wont to signify their wishes, he will not resist the command.

There is no gainsaying the fact that *The Wings of the Dove*, for all its beauty, is an uncomfortable story. We breathe a miasmatic air, and the grossness is barely purged at the end by Densher's regeneration under stress of Milly's brave innocence. We cannot reconcile ourselves to finding ostensibly decent people engaged in a nefarious insurance plot, though of the taint of mercenariness Densher at least remains free. Lord Mark thinks him as tarnished as Kate, but Mark looks at things through the jaundiced eyes of a rejected suitor. The clearsighted Mrs Stringham sees his predicament early in the day, but the reader cannot be expected to give him the full measure of charity that she accords him. Milly, too, in her dying interview gives him unstinted absolution, but even this does not suffice to remove the taint. Stories of course, and necessarily tragedies, are concocted of human weaknesses.

Had Densher asserted himself with emphasis when
Kate's full purpose had first dawned upon him,
we should have missed our tragic complications,
and the tale would not have been written. After
all, Lord Mark, who is made to bear the burden of
Milly's death, is the one person in the book who
tells the truth.

We are not permitted to forget, amidst all this
coil of circumstances, that Mildred Theale is our
author's chief concern. It was his hope that this
studiously elaborated drama of Kate and Merton
should ultimately be seen in true perspective and
merge in proper subordination with the more vital
drama of Milly's career. But it is only on attentive
reperusal of *The Wings of the Dove* that the perspective adjusts itself, and, as I have pointed out,
not without some sacrifice of ease in the later
phases of the story. When Milly lifts the latch of
Mrs Lowder's door she comes into a world of which
we know, to the advantage of our subsequent discernment, all the contours and contingencies, but
we are disconcerted by the long delay of her appearance, and we experience a jarring sense of dislocation
when a new system of machinery has to be installed
and set in motion.

It is in the third book, then, that we first
encounter Milly and her friend Mrs Stringham on
their high perch among the Alps. All the essential
antecedents of the younger woman's life and the
preliminary indications of her character are conveyed to us through Mrs Stringham's reflections
and by that process of " indirection " which James
conceived to be at once the subtlest and most

dramatic method of presentation—" that magnificent and masterly *indirectness*," he once wrote
to Mrs Humphry Ward, " which means the *only*
dramatic straightness and intensity." Only twice
in the book—namely, at Mrs Lowder's first dinner-
party and after the second visit to Sir Luke Strett
—are we permitted to participate at any length
in the operations of Milly's own consciousness,
and our participations even in her conversations
are but sparsely multiplied throughout the story.
" I note how again and again I go but a little way
with the direct—that is, with the straight—exhibition of Milly ; it resorts for relief, this process,
wherever it can, to some kinder, some merciful
indirection ; all as if to approach her circuitously,
deal with her at second hand, as an unspotted
princess is ever dealt with ; the pressure all round
her kept easy for her, the sounds, the movements
regulated, the forms and ambiguities made charming. All of which proceeds, obviously, from her
painter's tenderness of imagination about her,
which reduces him to watching her, as it were,
through the successive windows of other people's
interest in her." If we had not James's own assurance of the superior virtue that resides in this
indirect method of presentation, we should have
suspected that his cherished memory of Minnie
Temple had made him forbear, as from some
threatened profanation of delicacy, from a more
intimate approach to the heart and mind of his
heroine. Realising, perhaps, our foiled expectations
of coming to close quarters with Mildred Theale,
he permits himself for once the unusual licence of

the author's comment to justify his indirectness : " She worked—and seemingly quite without design —upon the sympathy, the curiosity, the fancy of her associates, and we shall really ourselves scarce otherwise come closer to her than by feeling their impression and sharing, if need be, their confusion."

The superstition of the *scène à faire* and the climax-compelling exigencies of serial publication had established the " great situation " as a settled convention of our English fiction, and it was perhaps his aristocratic disdain of vulgar custom that induced James to seek out a quieter and subtler method for securing his results. In *The Portrait of a Lady* we are accorded the old-fashioned pleasure of participating in the last interview between Isabel and Ralph Touchett. In *The Wings of the Dove*, when the dying Milly, aware of the stratagems practised upon her, has summoned Densher to her *palazzo*, a situation fraught with definitely greater dramatic possibilities presents itself, but the occasion is refused, and we must perforce content ourselves with the pallid after-report. It is a severe method indeed that sacrifices opportunities which the novelist is so amply capable of exploiting, and it is for the reader to decide whether this cheating of his natural human curiosity is fully compensated by the appeal to his imagination, which in the developed art of James is the substitute offered for the cruder vibrations of immediate sensation. We are flattered, but are we satisfied ? Is the shadow more significant than the substance that throws the shadow, and are the reverberations of events in the human consciousness more vital than the events themselves ?

In Henry James, and I would speak of both the novelist and the man, there is a curious blending of opposed elements. He would be the most sophisticated of men and writers if he were not so ingenuously naïve, and it may well be this unwonted union of *naïveté* and sophistication that establishes his identity, that gives his character its mould and his work its distinguishing quality. No writer, however stubbornly objective he may strive to be, can avoid the personal confession. When we have divined the master passion from which a creative energy reacts, the autobiographic portents multiply. A complicated nature is not necessarily reduced to one master passion, but while this fact may render difficult the access to the inner mind of our innumerous Shakespeares and Dantes, it does not constitute a prohibitive barrier to the understanding of our present author. His pre-eminent interests are clearly enough to be found in the refinements of a developed civilisation, and the two most authentic witnesses of this master passion, the very voices through which it speaks, are the Passionate Pilgrim and Lambert Strether, the central figure of *The Ambassadors* (1903). The experiences through which the latter passes are richer, and the art that presents them is more secure, but they are both the same person, and they are both Henry James. If they differ, it is only in the degree of their initiation. We are permitted to think of James as a highly civilised person. He has had the freedom of Europe conferred upon him, but he has forfeited none of

THE AMBASSADORS

his alien rights, and of these the principal is the
privilege of looking upon the customs and institutions of the Old World with a fresh and wondering eye. It would never occur to an Englishman to
celebrate the romantic charm of a breakfast muffin,
yet so simple a delight was capable of moving our
author almost to tears in a Liverpool restaurant;
and no native writer could estimate like James
the successive assaults upon the senses of Strether
in the quiet of sleepy Chester, in the comforting
gloom of London, or in the vibrating air of Paris.
This is because he remembers so well the progressive
stages of his own emancipation, which is never so
developed that vestiges of his former *naïveté* do
not cling to it. Strether, in a dingy London theatre,
is acquainting Maria Gostrey and the reader with
the circumstances of his European quest. He feels
some diffidence in mentioning the source of Mrs
Newsome's fortune. We never discover whether
it is wash-tubs or shoe-laces. In Woollett, Massachusetts, it was easy and natural to discuss it.
" 'Unmentionable? Oh, no, we constantly talk of
it; we are quite familiar and brazen about it.
Only, as a small, trivial, rather ridiculous object
of the commonest domestic use, it's just wanting
in—what shall I say? Well, dignity, or the least
approach to distinction. Right here, therefore,
with everything about us so grand!' In short,
he shrank.
    " 'It's a false note?'
    " 'Sadly. It's vulgar.'
    " 'But surely not vulgarer than this!' Then
on his wondering, as she herself had done: 'Than

311

everything about us.' She seemed a trifle irritated.
' What do you take this for ? '
" ' Why, for—comparatively—divine ! '
" ' This dreadful London theatre ? It's impossible,
if you really want to know.'
" ' Oh, then,' laughed Strether, ' I *don't* really
want to know ! ' "

At the close of the book the education of
Lambert Strether, which is largely an affair of imaginative adaptations to sense impressions, has so
far advanced that his standard of values at least is
secure; but though his judgment ripens, it is never
at the expense of his appreciation. Both bud and
blossom hang upon the same tree; and it is because
James also had never lost this primitive freshness of
admiration that he is so admirably equipped to present the case for Europe. Woollett, Massachusetts,
will think him a biased observer, and Woollett will
be enraged at preferences in which it divines not only
obliquity of vision but a lurking immorality. The
least that Europe can do in return is to appreciate
the fineness of the tribute which is paid to her.
Her own novelists are zealous to prove her civilisation a sham, her institutions decadent, her customs
hollow and insincere. But a transatlantic writer
tells her that the labour of centuries has not been
in vain. and that the long experiment in living has
accumulated forms and traditions from which the
vital energy has not yet departed.

It required not only much courage but intense
conviction to flout one's fellow-countrymen, as
James has essayed to do in *The Ambassadors*. He
assails Puritanism in its entrenched stronghold,

the New England conscience, and before his task is
ended he has been logically forced into the position
of an apologist for licence. And we, his readers, if
we appreciate the steps of his argument, are somewhat uncomfortably coerced into a position where
we must accommodate ourselves to the anomalous
conclusion that these time-honoured forms of the
European world are capable of convenient adjustments to suit the individual case. Nothing is,
after all, fixed but the *convenances*, and if these
are safeguarded, the European scheme of morals is
flexible to every demand that enlightened hedonism
can make upon it.

Strether's confession of faith to little Bilham in
Gloriani's garden is emphasised for us by James
as both the starting-point and central motive of
his story. Praise of the joy of living from the lips
of an ageing man made a pathetic appeal to his
imagination, and he could not rest satisfied until he
had accounted for his hero's spiritual predicament.
Both the logic and the art which present us with
the brief for Strether are unimpeachable, and
demand from us only the preliminary admission
that life as Woollett conceives it is barren of joy
and censorious in the measure of its narrowness.
The Waymarshes, the Mrs Newsomes and the Mrs
Pococks who essay to read the book will deny the
premise. The world, as they have made it for
themselves, is the best of possible worlds, and
Chad and Strether have betrayed its purest traditions. But, while they will resent the evident bias
of the author and will charge him with special
pleading on behalf of his own subversive views of

decency and morality, they can have no justification
for accusing him of not stating their case fairly.
His intention may have been, indeed most probably was, to represent their collective attitude as
ridiculous; but from the facts as presented they
will feel their actions and their inferences confirmed,
and Waymarsh's " sacred rage " and Mrs Newsome's
moral grimness must seem to these estimable people
the natural and necessary protest against outraged
decency.

Let us turn now with more particular attention
to the story itself, and note the tap of the hammer
as each little golden nail is driven in. We might
improve on the novelist's metaphor, which suggests,
though the nails are golden, a piece of rough joinery
work, and prefer to think of this novel, its author's
chosen production for fineness and finish, as a specimen of exquisite marqueterie, in which design and
craftsmanship co-operate in effortless perfection.
Or abandoning metaphor altogether, one might
describe the book in plain terms as a wonderfully
finished example of the novelist's art, and in like
plain fashion proceed to its examination.

In the interests of unity of design James felt
himself compelled to focus his whole picture in the
mind of Strether. He gains certain advantages in
consequence, but only at the expense of forgoing
valuable privileges. The author's summary of the
various situations as they arise is denied him, and
Strether's reflections, supplemented by the comments of the other characters in conversation with
him alone, are the necessitated substitute. They
never converse with one another, and we are not

allowed the entertainment of a heart-to-heart talk
between Waymarsh, for example, and Sarah Pocock.
That would have been capital fun, but James was
unable to convince himself that their blunt vision
could penetrate beneath the surface of the subtle
problem, all compact of fine nuances and delicate
discriminations, with which he had to deal.

The people of awakened consciousness in the
book, apart from Strether, are Chad Newsome,
Madame de Vionnet, little Bilham, Miss Barrace
and Maria Gostrey. The same rigorous law of
concentrated interest has denied him access to
their private reflections. In other novels, even of
the later time, he allows himself the privilege of
" going behind " a chosen few of the characters
whose mental processes merit exploration. It
was obvious to him, and should be obvious to
the careful reader, that this admirable expedient
for obtaining both verity and illumination was not
available on the terms of his chosen theme. The
love affair of Chad Newsome and Madame de
Vionnet is merely incidental to the emancipation of
Strether from the limiting prejudices of Woollett,
Massachusetts; and if either of these self-centred
lovers had been permitted to converse apart, or had
the author undertaken independently to explore
their minds, their own private passion, and not the
predicament in which Strether stood, must inevitably have been their prime concern. The pressure
that rests upon Strether is therefore extremely
heavy : it is no less than the whole weight of a
large two-volume novel ; and if he comes out of
the ordeal successfully, if this sad man of fifty-five

can provide us, thus unaided, with interest, entertainment and variety, we must admit the result to be a triumph over difficulties which no novelist has yet had the courage to face.

In his preface James anticipates and answers another not unimportant critical question: Why, when he is so anxious to attain variety with unity, and when he has already concentrated his interest so exclusively in one person, does he not take the further step and make his novel frankly autobiographical—an account in the first person of the experiences through which the hero is now conducted by a dispassionate outsider? " It may be asked why, if one so keeps to one's hero, one shouldn't make a single mouthful of ' method,' shouldn't throw the reins on his neck and, letting them flap there as free as in *Gil Blas* or in *David Copperfield*, equip him with the double privilege of subject and object—a course that has at least the merit of brushing away questions at a sweep. The answer to which is, I think, that one makes the surrender only if one is prepared *not* to make certain precious discriminations." And then he tells us presently that what he dreads above all is " the terrible fluidity of self-revelation." Measure and proportion are the qualities in which he finds most English and much Continental fiction deficient, and recognising his own inordinate habit of amplification he sought to save himself by erecting barriers to his expansiveness. This explains his positive delight in structural difficulties, and why, having multiplied them even beyond his wont in *The Ambassadors*, he should have contemplated the result with more

than his usual complacency. He certainly has produced for his readers a most satisfying smoothness
of surface. He gives the sensation of travelling
de luxe over a perfect road-bed. The officials are
all polite, the service is exquisite, and the time-
schedule is scrupulously observed. But we pass
all sorts of jolly little way-stations at full speed,
and we sometimes feel that the traveller in the
third-class carriage, uncomfortably jostled though
he be, has more contact with the realities of life.

Now that we are in a position to estimate the
virtue of the story itself, an amusing doubt confronts us. What story, we ask ourselves, can
emanate from the belated enlargement of experience of an ageing man ? Our author's fastidiousness prohibits him from leading Strether through
the ordinary devastating adventures that pass for
experience in the case of the average middle-aged
American on a holiday. Strether is compelled to
enjoy, to suffer, and to grow through the mind
alone, and we are not predisposed to admit that a
series of internal adjustments can furnish material
for a full-statured romance. But our actual difficulty
is quite of a contrary order, for so closely woven is
the mesh of the intricate pattern he executes, that
we can follow the course only of a few of the more
highly coloured threads.

Maria Gostrey takes Strether in hand as soon
as he arrives in Chester for his rendezvous with
his fellow-countryman, Waymarsh. She makes no
ceremonial scruples in her determined pounce upon
him in the hall of the hotel. His age was safe, his
appearance evidently distinguished, and he seemed

for the moment in need of information that she could supply. Miss Gostrey's value was thus early determined for the author. He calls her whimsically the most abandoned of *ficelles*, but he justifies her at every turn by the uses he puts her to as initiator, counsellor and friend. Her easy familiarity with the European scene makes her most acceptable to Strether in the first, as in the last, stages of his enlightenment; and to the reader she is invaluable for her skill in eliciting Strether's past and for her discernment in divining his future. An American herself, she knows her country's type, and how few of her compatriots are capable of catching the tone of Europe. She cannot prevent them from coming in always increasing numbers, but she confesses to Strether that she sends them back as fast as she can.

" ' Oh, I know—you take them to Liverpool.'

" ' Any port will serve in a storm. I'm—with all my other functions—an agent for repatriation. I want to repeople our stricken country. What will become of it else ? I want to discourage others.'

" The ordered English garden, in the freshness of the day, was delightful to Strether, who liked the sound, under his feet, of the tight fine gravel, packed with the chronic damp, and who had the idlest eye for the deep smoothness of turf and clean curves of paths. ' Other people ? '

" ' Other countries. Other people—yes. I want to encourage our own.'

" Strether wondered. ' Not to come ? Why, then, do you meet them—since it doesn't appear to stop them ? '

"'Oh, that they shouldn't come is as yet too much to ask. What I attend to is that they come quickly and return still more so. I meet them to help it to be over as soon as possible, and though I don't stop them, I've my way of putting them through. That's my little system ; and, if you want to know,' said Maria Gostrey, ' it's my real secret, my innermost mission and use. I only seem, you see, to beguile and approve ; but I've thought it all out and I'm working all the while underground. I can't perhaps quite give you my formula, but I think that practically I succeed. I send you back spent. So you stay back. Passed through my hands——'

"'We don't turn up again?' The farther she went the farther he always saw himself able to follow. 'I don't want your formula—I feel quite enough, as I hinted yesterday, your abysses. Spent!' he echoed. ' If that's how you're arranging so subtly to send me, I thank you for the warning.'

"For a minute, amid the pleasantness—poetry in tariffed items, but all the more, for guests already convicted, a challenge to consumption—they smiled at each other in confirmed fellowship. 'Do you call it subtly? It's a plain, poor tale. Besides, you're a special case.'"

When Strether arrives in Paris Maria Gostrey lets the spell of the wonderful city operate for a few days before her reappearance. We are in possession by now of the circumscribed range of his Woollett interests. He is Mrs Newsome's ambassador to Paris to reclaim Chad from the influence of some designing woman who is detaining

HENRY JAMES : MAN AND AUTHOR

him year by year from his business interests at home, and the success of his venture is evidently to be rewarded with the bribe of the wealthy widow's hand. Already Miss Gostrey has injected into his mind a doubt as to Chad's actual wickedness, and with his own buried memories of the past stirred to life in the reviving air he reconciles himself in advance to Chad's choice of a dwelling-place and a career. On his way to the young man's apartment in the Boulevard Malesherbes Strether loiters for sheer enjoyment among the Odéon stalls. The faint memories of twenty-five years ago stir into life. " He found the effect of tone and tint, in the long charged tables and shelves, delicate and appetising; the impression—substituting one kind of low-priced *consommation* for another—might have been that of one of the pleasant cafés that overlapped, under an awning, to the pavement; but he edged along, grazing the tables, with his hands firmly behind him. He wasn't there to dip, to consume—he was there to reconstruct. He wasn't there for his own profit—not, that is, the direct; he was there on some chance of feeling the brush of the wing of the stray spirit of youth. He felt it in fact; he had it beside him; the old arcade indeed, as his inner sense listened, gave out the faint sound, as from far off, of the wild waving of wings. They were folded now over the breasts of buried generations; but a flutter or two lived again in the turned page of shock-headed, slouch-hatted loiterers, whose young intensity of type, in the direction of pale acuteness, deepened his vision, and even his appreciation, of racial differences. . . ."

320

THE AMBASSADORS

Little Bilham, a Continentalised young American, is in occupation of Chad's flat. Strether receives a most friendly welcome, and a *déjeuner* is arranged for him and the gloomy Waymarsh, with Miss Barrace, one of Chad's set, as the fourth guest. Another stage in Strether's readjustment to the new code of conduct is reached. " It was the way the irregular life sat upon Bilham and Miss Barrace that was the insidious, the delicate marvel. He was eager to concede that their relation to it was all indirect, for anything else in him would have shown the grossness of bad manners ; but the indirectness was none the less consonant—that was striking—with a grateful enjoyment of everything that was Chad's. They spoke of him repeatedly, invoking his good name and good nature, and the worst confusion of mind for Strether was that all their mention of him was of a kind to do him honour. They commended his munificence and approved his taste, and in doing so sat down, as it seemed to Strether, in the very soil out of which these things flowered. Our friend's final predicament was that he himself was sitting down, for the time, *with* them, and there was a supreme moment at which, compared with his collapse, Waymarsh's erectness affected him as really high. One thing was certain —he saw he must make up his mind. He must approach Chad, must wait for him, deal with him, master him, but he mustn't dispossess himself of the faculty of seeing things as they were."

Chad presently enters upon the scene, and the manner of his appearance impresses Strether in a degree that the reader, in spite of so much elaborate

321

preparation, will hardly appreciate. One defect of James's indirect method is that we are never allowed to see very far into Chad, and such conclusions as we arrive at with reference to his character are not favourable. He strikes us, I fear, as rather a fatuous young man, with excellent manners. But Strether's first glance at Chad as he arrives late but with the utmost composure in the theatre box convinces him that he is a very different person from the raw youth of the Woollett time, and he can never divest himself in the future of this impression. If Chad has so visibly improved, Paris is in part responsible, but he must also reckon with the influence of this still unnamed and undiscovered woman.

The interest of the novel deepens from the moment of Madame de Vionnet's appearance, for James has used all his skill within the severe limits he has imposed upon himself to convey to us a sense of her charm, and to exhibit the operation of this charm on Strether's plastic mind. The whole Parisian scene, little Bilham, Miss Gostrey and Chad have had their share in his transformation, but it is she who makes the complete conquest of his sympathies and refashions his moral code. Deluding himself at first with belief in the innocence of her friendship with Chad, he accommodates himself in the end to the fullest knowledge of the actual facts, and finds beauty in a relationship that would formerly have appalled his moral sense. He had come to Paris, as James tells us, " primed with a moral scheme of the most approved pattern which was yet framed to break down on any approach to vivid facts—that is, to any at all liberal appreciation of them. There would of course have been the case of the Strether prepared, wherever presenting himself, only to judge and to feel meanly ; but he would have moved for me, I confess, enveloped in no legend whatever. The actual man's note, from the first of our seeing it struck, is the note of discrimination. It would have been his blest imagination, we have seen, that had already helped him to discriminate ; the element that was for so much of the pleasure of my cutting thick, as I have intimated, into his intellectual, into his moral substance.''

We can find modified entertainment in this book even should we disregard its fine intricacy of design. We have the usual contrast of two civilisations— the hedonistic and the Puritanic—the chief distinguishing feature of the book being the unwonted acerbity in the delineation of the latter, as if James were determined to settle once for all a long outstanding score. The contrast is effected by three groups of characters revolving round Strether. There is the pure European strain represented in Madame de Vionnet, the transformed American type exhibited in Chad, and more successfully in Maria Gostrey, and lastly, the immutable, unadulterated American species embodied in Waymarsh, Sarah Pocock and the invisible but omnipresent and once omnipotent Mrs Newsome. These latter three take their pleasures very simply and very sadly. Sarah's husband, Jim, who is loosely attached to the group, is faintly indicated to us as the middle-aged family man, vulgar and unperceptive like his associates, but dangerously attracted by the grosser allurements of the wicked city, to which the fine-grained Strether never devotes a thought. Possessed of a more vivid imagination, he has merely passed through the transformation stages more rapidly than Chad or Maria Gostrey, and has compressed the experience of years into a few summer months. He returns to Woollett a sadder and a wiser man, with only dreams for his comfort, with no regrets for the striking of his name from the pale green covers of *The Woollett Review*, nor greatly lamenting, perhaps, his loss of Mrs Newsome's esteem, her fortune, and her hand. What most perturbs him is that circumstances have robbed him of the fuller life for which he discovered in himself such belated aptitudes, and also the haunting fear, almost indeed the ironic certainty, that Chad, to whom that life lies open, will abjure it.

The Golden Bowl (1904), James's last complete novel, is a work of so curious and difficult a beauty that of all our author's major novels it most profits by renewed contact with its pages. It is an attractive book therefore to explore attentively, and its interpreter may have the serene assurance that his analysis will be only for the limited public which looks for values where the author seeks to place them.

The story in its bare elements is simple enough— its complexity is wholly an affair of treatment. The situation is not tediously triangular, but more amply quadrilateral. The play of contacts is not merely between Maggie, the Prince, and Charlotte, for we have not gone far before we learn the preponderating rôle that Maggie's so simple-seeming father is destined to play. James could not afford to make him at any moment ridiculous, but it would seem as if, for the high amusement's sake, he assented to his apparent insignificance. Maggie loves him with admiration throughout—her love for him being indeed a controlling element in the issue of events —but then again we are slow to learn the full measure of Maggie's value or recognise a rightness in her judgments, and we incline too readily to place the ingenuous pair in the category of unprotesting sacrificial victims. One of the irritant causes that projected the Prince upon his dangerous course was his sense of their unsuspecting candour —such trustfulness existed only to be beguiled—and he owed his redemption from folly to his enforced recognition of the actual strength their high moral decency concealed.

James has so often been called to account for his alleged misrepresentation of American conditions and his travesty of American types that one welcomes the easy occasion of indicating his actual fairness. His preference for the old-world civilisation, when it was a question of personal choice, is evident enough from the circumstances of his life, but this should not blind us to the fact that among the characters in his fiction who are most endeared to us, and to whom his own sympathies were most graciously extended, Americans largely predominate. I do not suppose that James ever beguiled the social hour with the searching question: "Who is your favourite character in fiction?" and he would have

considered such a query addressed to him on the
basis of his own creations as in an ultimate degree
indelicate and indiscreet. Yet it is not wholly at
random that one avers that Milly Theale stands first
in the order of his preferences, with Maggie Verver
and Isabel Archer in close sequence behind her. The
man of his choice quite as unquestionably would
be the somewhat blighted Strether, with Ralph
Touchett nonchalantly strolling not so far in his
rear, and Abraham Verver within hailing distance.
The mark that denotes them all is their capacity
for emancipation, their lively impressionability to
environments not natively their own. In their
estimates of moral values there is some flexibility
of range to be noted. Ralph and Strether have
accommodating consciences. Rightness for them,
as for Mrs Assingham of our present book, resides
in the forms, in the sanctions that is to say of a
befitting decency from which—and in Strether's case
not without a struggle of conscience—the grosser
elements of Puritanic constraint have been expelled.
In Maggie and her fat'ier the Puritanic strain is
present, shorn of all its obnoxious rigours, yet of prevailing power in a situation of exceptional difficulty.
The defect of Puritanism is a lack of charity; its
merit is that it has a standard of discrimination
between right and wrong that resists the easy ebb
and flow of occasion and arbitrates between our
duties and our desires. Formidable and even repellent in its worst victims of the Waymarsh and
Mrs Newsome order, it can assert itself at times—
as in the Ververs—with definite beauty, and it is
quite evident that James deliberately permitted it

in the end to dominate the somewhat atrophied organ of conduct by which Amerigo contrived to regulate his actions. Mrs Assingham tells the Prince in their earliest London interview that she would like to see some sense he did not possess. "He produced one on the spot: 'The moral, dear Mrs Assingham, I mean always as you others consider it. I've of course something that in our poor dear backward old Rome sufficiently passes for it. But it's no more like yours than the tortuous stone staircase—half ruined into the bargain!—in some castle of our *quattrocento* is like the lightning elevator in one of Mr Verver's fifteen-storey buildings. Your moral sense works by steam—it sends you up like a rocket. Ours is slow and steep and unlighted, with so many of the steps missing that—well, that it's as short in almost any case to turn round and come down again!'"

It is obvious that the Prince's morality has hitherto sat lightly upon him. Recognising nothing esoteric or rigidly absolute in the term, his easy sense of definition would not have strained beyond the limits of decent behaviour with its implied regard for the traditional usages of a polite though corrupt society. He would have counted himself on just such facile grounds religious—religion being on a somewhat sumptuous scale an observation of the forms, grandiose and splendid, but exempt from all suspicion of reverence and devoutness, and the more inspiring for these exemptions. Now a great number of Jamesian people, whom their creator evidently approves, subscribe to this pleasant worldly code of ethics. It is indeed Strether's high virtue in *The*

Ambassadors that he achieves the flexible view and
mentally embraces a mode of life that fate and the
passing years deny him ; and Miss Gostrey is another
example, among many, of a woman in whom personal
decency and virtue are compatible with the most
accommodating charity of opinion.   It is by her
aid that Strether, the emancipated Puritan, comes
to see in the end a positive beauty in Chad's relation with Madame de Vionnet.   Mrs Assingham in
our present book is a matured Miss Gostrey, whose
function it is to enlighten the reader rather than
initiate or direct any of the actors in the drama—
except of course for the part she plays in engineering
the marriages.   A colloquy with her husband, when
they are discussing the dangerous intimacy between
the Prince and Charlotte, might have served Cardinal
Newman for a text in that chapter of the *Idea of a
University* where he exhibits the natural affinities between vice and politeness.   In the grave priest this
relationship inspires horror.   To Mrs Assingham, who
feels herself so deeply committed to the fortunes
of the involved four, the only consolation in distress
is the irreproachable surface which the guilty two
present to the world, and their exquisite solicitude
for the two who suffer.

"' I'm down, down, down,' she declared.   ' Yet '—
she as quickly added—' there's just one little thing
that helps to save my life.'   And she kept him waiting
but an instant.   ' They might easily—they would
perhaps even certainly—have done something worse.'

" He thought.   ' Worse than that Charlotte——?'

"' Ah, don't tell me,' she cried, ' that there *could*
have been nothing worse.   There might, as they were,

have been many things. Charlotte, in her way, is
extraordinary ! '
  " He was almost simultaneous. ' Extraordinary ! '
  " ' She observes the forms,' said Fanny Assingham.
  " ' With the Prince——? '
  " ' *For* the Prince. And with the others,' she went
on. ' With Mr Verver—wonderfully. But above all
with Maggie. And the forms '—she had to do them
justice—' are two-thirds of conduct. Say he had
married a woman who would have made a hash of
them ! ' "
  I recognise the idleness of arguing upon abstract
grounds the never too thrilling question of the morality
of art, yet there is, after all, a way in which the subject
may be profitably approached. I am not certain, for
example, whether the ethical standards of each succeed-
ing generation are not constituted, in large measure,
by the fiction and the drama of the period, with greater
importance attaching to the former inasmuch as fiction
usually bears the closer relation to normal experience.
The risk we run of contamination is therefore not
inconsiderable, and the responsibilities of authorship
evidently transcend the mere fashioning of a work of
art. A writer's value may be gauged in many ways,
but the ultimate test of his greatness is, after all, the
extent of his wisdom and the security of his judgment. Temperamental eccentricities may suffice to
conquer a sudden popularity as skill of execution may
justify a temporary fame, but permanency of reputation in fiction or drama belongs only to the man
who can move securely through the complexities of
life, and whose report of human experience bears the
stamp of authority and authenticity. The novelist,

whose main concern lies in these varied human relationships, has to tell us how people behave and think and feel under conditions that are devised to elicit their characteristic qualities. The more competent and conscientious he is as an artist the less will he incline to promulgate his own opinions; therefore, in dealing with such a consummate artist as James it may seem hazardous to ascribe to him any dogmatic intentions of a moral kind. But glancing at large over the whole range of his work we see that his faculty of discrimination is never idle, and more particularly does he compel us to feel in *The Wings of the Dove* and our present book that behind and beneath the artistic purpose there lies a moral intention at once distinct and measurable. His intense interest in how people behave implies necessarily a standard of values for human conduct, and when we have ascertained what this standard of values is we are in full possession of his ethical system, which, to save him from any dogmatic imputation, we might name in all simplicity his art of living. In the books I have associated together James has used all the resources of his art to represent two characters of singular beauty, and he would have counted his labour wasted if he had not succeeded in exhibiting the moral ascendency that two such women as Milly Theale and Maggie Verver must inevitably exercise. In each case let us note that their conquest is of people who, to borrow Mrs Assingham's phrase, have lived scrupulously "in the forms." This perhaps is the full extent of James's ethical claim, but it is sufficient. In his estimate of conduct the emphasis is always rightly placed.

The episodes through which Maggie serenely and securely moves would have carried most novelists into the sexual abyss. Irregular relationships are the pivotal element in the plot and the dominant ethical motive of the ordinary modern novel, in which passion is usually deemed competent to absolve all casual bonds from the taint of immorality. It is not from squeamishness but from a considered purpose that James minimises the sensual appeal in his books. Again and again he passes by an opportunity to develop a physical situation from the desire to gain the reader's attention on more reasoned grounds. His views on the question are admirably stated in his essays on D'Annunzio and Mathilde Serao, two novelists who have made the psychology of passion their peculiar concern. James felt that if one should begin to make concessions to such an appeal it would obliterate too many other considerations, and he consequently refused to be dominated by this tyranny. In *The Golden Bowl* he had multiplied opportunities for this form of allurement, by yielding to which he might certainly have made his story more exciting. Such an occasion occurs in the third book when Charlotte comes in a four-wheeler to Portland Place knowing that she would find the Prince alone. They talk with much tenderness of the father and daughter —their respective husband and wife—they pity their unprotected innocence, and kiss one another passionately on the lips on the strength of their sacred duty to preserve that innocence inviolate. The chapter that follows has no dialogue and no action. What it gives us are the ruminations of the Prince, and I feel that here for once James's habit of evasiveness when a physical situation has begun to develop has led him astray. Even on his own terms he should have illustrated the Prince's mental reaction from this new lively posture of affairs; but the chapter is really dull and does not strike home to the main issue on which the Prince's reflections, if we must have them, should have centred. The other physical crisis of the book is later at Matcham, but here the Jamesian way justifies itself. A situation is artfully led up to, is developed, and then suddenly suspended. But as the whole sequel hinges upon it we are contented to have a substitution of consequences for incident, and we cannot fail to see that a more detailed treatment of the intrigue would have greatly compromised the central theme of the story.

Let us examine now somewhat more attentively how James has secured his effects in this closely calculated narrative. In so doing I would claim the collateral privilege of indicating certain places where the treatment seems, by reference to his own exacting standards, inferior. We know his method well enough by now to realise his engrossing thoroughness. He will leave nothing to chance, and it is a matter of conscience with him to account for everything, confident as he is in his ability to evade the obvious.

We meet the Prince strolling through the streets of London, whither he has come from Rome on the eve of his marriage with the many-millioned Maggie Verver. The details of a recent conversation with her pass through his mind, and we recognise in him a certain uneasiness at the incongruousness of their proposed union. He feels himself so sophisticated, and Maggie and her father so eagerly romantic and idealistic. He had asked for and received her confidence: " You do believe I'm not a hypocrite. You recognise that I don't lie nor dissemble nor deceive ? " Her assurance had not entirely satisfied him, and, as he thus reminiscently strolls, his steps instinctively lead him to Mrs Assingham's house. She is an old friend of the Roman time to whom he owed his intimacy with the Ververs, and she is moreover a woman who combines their idealising tendency— a last remnant of her fading Americanism—with a generous dash of the ironic spirit, the fruit of many Continental years. He is really anxious to steer a straight course, but is momentarily confused in his bearings. Maggie's point of view seems so oddly different from his, which he attributes somewhat whimsically to their different scale of moral values —his so rickety and Roman, hers so unswervingly direct. Mrs Assingham promises him her constant support; but an unwonted uneasiness in her manner makes Amerigo suspect that she is holding something back. He taxes her with this concealment, whereupon she admits that she is much worried by the sudden arrival from America of Charlotte Stant, whom she was momentarily expecting at the house.

James has a wonderful knack of getting people in and out of a room (Mrs Rance's case notwithstanding), and Charlotte's entrance is so well managed that we can take in the situation at a glance—her attractiveness and, if not her beauty, at least her perfect style and admirable self-command — what her despised and rejected countrymen would call her "perfect poise." Mrs Assingham leaves them alone,

and the Prince has a thrill of doubt whether she
will throw herself into his arms or be "otherwise
wonderful. She would see what he would do—so
their queer minute without words told him; and
she would act accordingly. But what could he do
but just let her see that he would make anything,
everything for her, as honourably easy as possible?
Even if she should throw herself into his arms he
would make that easy—easy, that is, to overlook,
to ignore, not to remember, and not, by the same
token, either, to regret. This was not what in fact
happened, though it was also not at a single touch,
but by the finest gradations, that his tensions subsided.
'It's too delightful to be back!' she said at last;
and it was all she definitely gave him—being moreover nothing but what anyone else might have said.
Yet with two or three other things that, on his
response, followed it, it quite pointed the path, while
the tone of it, and her whole attitude, were as far
removed as need have been from the truth of her
situation."

It does not require Mrs Assingham's subsequent
midnight talks with her quizzing but unanalytic
husband to inform the reader that Amerigo and
Charlotte have had a past, and that Charlotte is still
desperately in love with the Prince. They would
have married in the older time, but for their combined
lack of means, and we have only Mrs Assingham's
assurance that they had managed to hold their passion
in check. The situation seemed more dangerous
now with the new element of jealousy introduced,
and not its least dramatic feature is the fact that
Maggie is Charlotte's closest friend, and is in entire

ignorance of this passionate chapter in her past history. Charlotte binds Amerigo to promise her his help in secretly choosing a wedding present for Maggie, and this leads us on to the discovery and rejection of the Golden Bowl in a little Bloomsbury shop. They are both saying good-bye to their past, and slipping into their old habit of Italian speech they have no care to mitigate the tenderness of their expressions. The shopkeeper, an Italianate Jew, has the more reason to remember the affectionate tone of their conversation because Amerigo, divining by a queer intuition a flaw in the crystal, rejects the bowl, and the distinguished pair go away empty-handed.

Two years pass, and Maggie and her husband, with a Principino now added to the family circle, are at Fawns, Mr Verver's magnificent country house in Kent. The establishment impresses us as grand in the *bourgeois* way, and we are allowed to suspect that the Prince despite all the splendour feels his surroundings uncongenial. He has no reason to doubt his wife's devotion, but he has to reckon with the fact that she seems much more in love with her father than with him, and that for both of them he seems to bear the character of a fine antique—a museum piece of rare distinction which Mr Verver, the sumptuous collector, does not fail to appreciate at its full market value. And then the strange western people who come to the house are beyond his power to fathom. Maggie, who eagerly appreciates his vogue with women, does not fail to perceive his inability to cope with Mrs Rance and the Misses Lutch. To this is added the fear that one or other of them will discover her father's reluctance to utter an emphatic " No "; and to make this more clear an unpardonably long chapter is devoted to Mrs Rance's efforts to stalk her prey in the billiard-room when the rest of the party are at church. She opens the door at page 129, and comes into the room at page 152. The interim is occupied with an exploration of Mr Verver's reflections, and Mrs Rance's arrival in the room is merely an arrival.

Mrs Assingham also is depressed by the lack of style in the midst of so much magnificence, and is constantly telling Maggie and her father that they should live in a grander way. Her suggested corrective is that they should ask Charlotte Stant to pay them a long visit. The Lutches and the Rances would disappear like mists before the morning sun.

So it happens, and in her dread of a worse fate Maggie plots and plans for her father's marriage with her friend. This achieved, the book moves on with its own momentum, for the author has elaborated a situation that necessitates a climax. But his originality in organising this climax has never been more abundantly evident. Each situation as it develops is squeezed of its last drops of significance. He has arranged his searchlights so cunningly that every nook and cranny yields up its lurking shadows. Mrs Assingham, who is so deeply committed to the fortunes of the involved four, is for ever pondering a condition of affairs for whose growing complexity she feels herself not irresponsible. She can vent herself at first only with her husband, who, luckily for the reader, has, or affects to have, perceptions too

dense to cope with the multiplying difficulties. For
him, therefore, and for the enlightenment also of our
plodding wits, she has to dot her *i's* and cross her *t's*.
In the later stage of the crisis Maggie invokes her
aid, but by this time we have come to realise the
unsuspected resources of Maggie's nature, so that it
is not as a helpless weakling that she makes her
appeal for sympathy.

It was one of the difficult necessities of James's
problem so far to retain our regard for Amerigo
that we should recognise him as worth saving.
James does not attempt to gloss over the fact that
he has acted despicably, but he does concern himself with extraordinary care to exhibit the grounds of
his dereliction. Like everyone but Maggie's father,
Amerigo was unaware of the strength of his wife's
character and of her unerring intelligence. A woman
who seemed, and perhaps was, in every worldly way
superior to her is brought by chance into the intimacy
of his life. This woman is passionately in love with
him, and the home-keeping devotion of the other two
throws upon Amerigo and Charlotte the whole onus
of their now extensive social life. "Nothing stranger
surely," so ran their exculpating thought, "had ever
happened to a conscientious, a well-meaning, a perfectly passive pair: no more extraordinary decree
had ever been launched against such victims than
this of forcing them against their will into a relation of mutual close contact that they had done
everything to avoid."

It is after the Matcham episode that Maggie begins
her campaign. She has as yet no founded suspicions
of her husband's misconduct, and she realises to the

full that her father and herself are responsible for throwing the two so intimately together. Charlotte and the Prince had given the Assinghams the slip at Matcham, and had gone off for the day to Gloucester. Mrs Assingham spent the afternoon with Maggie at Eaton Square and came home to soliloquise at length with her puzzled husband. Maggie on her part does a very simple thing. Instead of staying on to dinner with her father she goes home to dine at whatever late hour her husband may come back, and awaits his return dressed with unwonted splendour for such an otherwise simple occasion. But all these so casual-seeming scenes are charged with the fullest significance, and we are intensely interested to note the dawning suspicions in her mind. When the belated husband returns he is charming and affectionate, and she is unreproachful, but she was later to remember his puzzled look as he stood hesitating on the threshold. For the first time she has proved an enigma to him, and the Prince now realises that he has to deal with a fully alert intelligence. In the morning Maggie seeks out Charlotte at her father's house, and from her manner she divines that some secret code of action has been arranged between her stepmother and her husband. Their solicitude for Maggie and her father grows more extreme, and a shifting of relations is established by which Maggie and Charlotte, and the Prince and Verver, are thrown together. What Maggie cannot discover is whether her father shares her suspicions, but the reader is allowed gradually to divine that the father is equally anxious on his side to shield Maggie from any knowledge of the guilt of which he is now shrewdly confident. Full knowledge comes to Maggie by her accidental discovery of the Golden Bowl. Prowling in the Bloomsbury region in search of some slight birthday gift for her father she enters the fatal shop and buys the bowl that the Prince and Charlotte had rejected years before. The shopkeeper, visited by a twinge of conscience at the excessive price he had charged, goes to Portland Place to tell Maggie that the crystal had a flaw. He sees the photographs of Charlotte and the Prince, and innocently narrates the old episode, not omitting the endearing terms that the brilliant couple had used. Maggie therefore learns the hateful truth that her husband and Charlotte had been lovers before her marriage and were obviously lovers still.

It is not necessary to pursue the story in further detail. Suffice it to say that the evolution of the crisis is one of the most masterly things in fiction. Neither Maggie nor her father takes the way of vulgar recrimination. Each desires passionately to shelter the other from knowledge of the guilt, and each works independently to redeem the situation from its grosser consequences. From the moment of the Golden Bowl discovery Maggie gains the completest ascendency over her husband, who leaves the baffled Charlotte entirely in the dark as to the extent of Maggie's knowledge. There is a remarkable scene in the closing days at Fawns, beyond the competence of any novelist of our day, where Charlotte seeks to wring the truth or the denial of the truth from Maggie. The latter, overcome by her sense of the hidden drama their calm exterior conceals, has passed out to the terrace from the room where her father, Mrs Assingham, Charlotte, and the Prince are playing bridge. "She walked to the end far out of the light; she returned and saw the others still where she had left them; she passed round the house and looked into the drawing - room, lighted also, but empty now, and seeming to speak the more in its own voice of all the possibilities she controlled. Spacious and splendid, like a stage again awaiting a drama, it was a scene she might people, by the press of her spring, either with serenities and dignities and decencies, or with terrors and shames and ruins, things as ugly as those formless fragments of her golden bowl she was trying so hard to pick up.

"She continued to walk and continued to pause; she stopped afresh for the look into the smoking-room, and by this time—it was as if the recognition had of itself arrested her—she saw as in a picture, with the temptation she had fled from quite extinct, why it was she had been able to give herself from the first so little to the vulgar heat of her wrong. She might fairly, as she watched them, have missed it as a lost thing; have yearned for it, for the straight vindictive view, the rights of resentment, the rages of jealousy, the protests of passion, as for something she had been cheated of not least: a range of feelings which for many women would have meant so much, but which for *her* husband's wife, for her father's daughter, figured nothing nearer to experience than a wild eastern caravan, looming into view with crude colours in the sun, fierce pipes in the air, high spears against the sky, all a thrill, a natural joy to mingle with, but turning off short before it reached her and plunging into other defiles."

Charlotte presently follows her out into the dark night, stalking her, as one might say, in the gloom of the terrace. By a curious reversal of conditions it is Charlotte who is resolute and Maggie who is alarmed. Her terror is for her father's sake lest the impending scene will involve him publicly in the horrors she has so long subdued in her own private breast. She knows the suppressed tortures that Charlotte has been enduring, but now she seemed to have broken the bars: " The splendid shining supple creature was out of the cage, was at large. . . . Charlotte, extending her search, appeared now to define herself vaguely in the distance; of this after an instant the princess was sure, though the darkness was thick, for the projected clearness of the smoking-room windows had presently contributed its help. Her friend came slowly into that circle—having also, for herself, by this time, not indistinguishably discovered that Maggie was on the terrace. Maggie, from the end, saw her stop before one of the windows to look at the group within, and then saw her come nearer and pause again, still with a considerable length of the place between them.

" Yes, Charlotte had seen she was watching her from afar, and had stopped now to put her further attention to the test. Her face was fixed on her through the night; she was the creature who had escaped from her cage, yet there was in her whole motion assuredly, even as so dimly discerned, a kind of portentous intelligent stillness. She had escaped with an intention, but with an intention the more definite that it could so accord with quiet measures. The two women at all events only hovered there, for these first minutes, face to face over their interval and exchanging no sign. . . ."

So the scene is launched and the sequel is as admirably wrought with that quiet intensity which the admirers of James are satisfied to prefer to the sharp snipsnap of angry repartee whereby the ordinary novelist secures his more cheaply acquired dramatic effects. A few chapters further on, when a new phase has come over the situation, this scene is reinforced by a parallel one where Maggie, her heart burning with pity, seeks out her friend and stepmother in the garden house to which she had retreated in her distress, and it is interesting to note how constant are these echoes and parallelisms in the compositional scheme of this subtly contrived book.

I forbear to name it the finest of his novels, yet in many ways *The Golden Bowl* seems to me most effectively to combine all the resources of James's developed art. We shall find some of his conversations unnatural, some of his subtleties teasing to the attention, and some of his scenes overlaboured, and, may we hint it, dull. Yet none of his books more abounds in admirable writing, and none, as I have said, more satisfactorily combines the results of his repeated experimentation in method. He has abandoned the excessive centrality of *The Ambassadors*, and allows us here three reflecting minds through which we may read the significance of the developing action. In *The Wings of the Dove* he would seem to have moved too far away from the direct transcription of dramatic contacts, but here he gives us repeatedly the scenes in which we wish to participate with no prejudice, as it seems to me, to our appreciation of the moral reactions which these human contacts engender. What endears the story to most readers is the exquisite way in which Maggie's character is presented. James painted for us in the older time the attractive portrait of Isabel Archer, but it was after all largely an author's portrait, and we see him plying his brush assiduously to get the desired effects. Maggie is not so obviously in the author's debt, but her image is more vividly stamped upon our minds by this abnegation. She reveals herself, Mrs Assingham, her father and her husband reveal her, but her actual creator is only too content to give them all credit for the triumph of the result.

CONCLUSION

THE important problems presented by Henry James's literary effort have at least emerged in the preceding analysis, and lie open to the reader's judgment. My own inferences from the evidence are necessarily personal, and I have not the presumption to suppose that I can sway opinions that are legitimately, if obstinately, bent in a contrary direction. I am doubtful therefore of my ability to influence those who subscribe to the dual thesis so brilliantly defended by Mr Van Wyck Brooks to the effect that there is a notable declension of value in the whole range of our author's later work, and that this declension derives from his failure after half a life-time of effort to accommodate himself to English conditions. I am quite content to differ without argument from those who after fair trial given to the studious complexities of these later books prefer the earlier ones by virtue of their more apparent ease and spontaneity, and though again I do not agree I have no quarrel with those who affirm that James would have been well advised to stay at home. But a thesis such as that maintained by Mr Brooks demands special pleading, and special pleading leads too frequently to deficiency of statement on the one side and extravagance on the other. I affirm, there-fore, most inflexibly, that he has never divined either the early or the late James who consents to the spirit of the following sentence: "Magnificent

344

pretensions, petty performances! the fruits of an irresponsible imagination, of a deranged sense of values, of a mind working in the void, uncorrected by any clear consciousness of human cause and effect." There is surely a milder and a truer way of affirming one's preferences, and any effective comparison of the earlier with the later James must proceed by confronting one great achievement with another.

Henry James's generation were slaves of the note-book and the document. Though never constrained in like degree with his fellow-realists by the superstition of facts, and preferring always an imaginative actuality to the causal sequences of "stupid life," James still refused to minimise the indebtedness of the author to his material. It is by his admission only the fullest "saturation" in his subject that permits him the ideal adaptations which constitute the virtue of any art. If therefore it could be proved that James, by his self-imposed expatriation, lost all contact with his original world and gained no compensating access into his new environment, his contribution to fiction would bear a diminished value. Candour compels the admission that in the creations of Balzac, Dickens and Dostoiefsky there is a more diversified and an intenser play of life. The difficulty lies in determining whether native strength of genius had not more part in the result than the mere fortune of birth that gave these others an environment so congenial to the liberation of their powers.

The successful literature of exile is written by poets like Shelley, who inhabit an ideal world, by

novelists like Turgénief, who renovate themselves
yearly by reviving contacts, or dramatists like Ibsen,
whose hatreds grow more rancorous with absence.
James could claim no poetic exemptions; he was
severed from his native land for the quarter of a
century in which his creative powers were at their
height; and his æsthetic distress at certain remembered aspects of American life could not be
designated as hatred of the country or the race.
The conditions of exile by these tests would not
seem to have been propitious to James. We cannot
reject the contention so amply confirmed in the
letters that his American memories were becoming
pallid and sapless. The recurring nostalgic stabs
are genuine expressions of a mood that grew more
frequent with the years, and I would not obscure
the fact that he had occasional fears that his art
had suffered in the process of transplantation. Thus
far our concessions may freely run, and we may yield
a further point by admitting that James, who was
made so free of the English social world, remained
something of an alien to the end. But in their
eagerness to make out a case the extremists now
put James in the witness-box to testify against
himself. They have asked selected questions, and
have stultified their argument by the merest forensic
cleverness. They have allowed a passing mood of
doubt and disappointment to go down on the records
as symptomatic of the whole man's spiritual outlook,
and have ignored the deep-seated and abiding contentment which was his habitual response to his new
environment.

It is obvious that the predicament of James

constitutes a very special case. Dissociation from one's country is sometimes regrettable, but is not always so disastrous as the special pleader would incline us to believe. It would be a rash departure, and prejudicial to their art, if Mr Carl Sandburg, or Mr Sherwood Anderson, or Mr Sinclair Lewis sailed for ever from their native shores. They are singularly adaptable Americans and, whether for sympathy or irony, their material lies abundantly at their doors. But James, at the age of thirty, had absorbed all the American impressions that his nature was capable of receiving, and when he consulted his own convenience and peace of mind by his quiet exit he was consulting also, whether consciously or unconsciously, the highest interest of his art.

347

INDEX

349

INDEX

INDEX